PRAISE FOR BROKEN PROMISES

'The history of modern Bihar has, indeed, been one of broken promises. Mrityunjay Sharma's compelling and meticulously researched magnum opus is the best work I have read on chronicling this betrayal.'

—Pavan K. Varma, former Indian diplomat, former Member of Parliament and author

'This work by Sharma is undoubtedly an important addition to the writings on political tumult in India's heartland. It's a gripping narration of the way the politics of OBC assertion, Hindu identity, left-wing extremism and the unique crime industry played out in the state of Bihar with profound consequences for the political discourse in entire the country.'

—Parakala Prabhakar, political economist and author

'A very fluid and interesting read. Mrityunjay Sharma's riveting storytelling style explains the electoral equations in one of the most complicated states of India.'

—Yashwant Deshmukh, founder, CVoter

'A fascinating account of one of India's most important and populous states. If UP and Bihar fail, India fails, and what comes through in the book is how history and politics have played havoc with the long-suffering people of Bihar. Our caste system and the moral neutrality to inequality by birth has been the greatest obstacle in our democratic evolution, and Bihar represents the most extreme example of the caste-politics-crime-corruption nexus that plagues our polity and society. Sharma has illustrated how horribly things can go wrong in a flawed democracy, and how much vision and leadership matter.'

—Dr Jayaprakash Narayan, founder, Lok Satta Party

'This gripping narrative weaves a tale of resilience and rebellion, capturing the raw essence of a state grappling with political upheaval and social change. Detailed, eye-opening and eminently readable.'

—Abhayanand, former DGP, Bihar and educationist

'Giving a good rear view of Bihar's past and an overview of its present, this book evocatively encapsulates its crucial landmarks as if giving a crash course in politics. One can see the author's disappointment at the promises that were made to Bihar and broken but also the hope that returning on its feet, the state will cover the ground fast.'

—Santosh Singh, senior assistant editor, *The Indian Express*

BROKEN PROMISES

CASTE, CRIME AND POLITICS IN

BIHAR

Best wishes!
Mrityunjay Sharma

MRITYUNJAY SHARMA

WESTLAND
NON·FICTION

WESTLAND
NON-FICTION

First published by Westland Non-Fiction, an imprint of Westland Books, a division of Nasadiya Technologies Private Limited, in 2024

No. 269/2B, First Floor, 'Irai Arul', Vimalraj Street, Nethaji Nagar, Alapakkam Main Road, Maduravoyal, Chennai 600095

Westland, the Westland logo, Westland Non-Fiction and the Westland Non-Fiction logo are the trademarks of Nasadiya Technologies Private Limited, or its affiliates.

ISBN: 9789360455224

10 9 8 7 6 5 4 3 2 1

Typeset by Jojy Philip, New Delhi
Printed at Manipal Technologies Limited, Manipal

CONTENTS

IN THE NAME OF REVOLUTION

NITISH: THE ENIGMA

To my parents,

Jalsa Devi and
Satyendra N. Sharma,

who weathered the greatest of hardships so
I could thrive

PREFACE

I was barely six when on a typical winter morning, the newspapers reported the tragic news of a massacre at Barra village in Gaya, claiming the lives of thirty-five individuals. One among the names listed was 'Sanjay', coincidentally also the name of my cousin residing in the same village. This news threw us into a state of panic, prompting my parents to hastily arrange for a trekker (a commercial vehicle for passengers) to transport us to Barra. Upon arrival, we discovered that it was a different Sanjay who had been a victim of the tragedy, not my cousin. In fact, my aunt's house was one of the few the Naxalites hadn't been able to barge into, and so they survived.

I was born in the undivided state of Bihar. I spent my childhood in Rajrappa, a small township sixty kilometres from Ranchi. My father's job in the coalfields there provided us with an ordinary and peaceful life in this self-sustained township, detached from the dynamism of Bihar. The state's reality dawned on me only during summer vacations when I visited my father's village, Guljana, in the notorious Tekari block of Gaya.

Throughout the '90s, Guljana remained tense and ready for combat, its villagers armed and vigilant for imminent Naxal attacks. Every house invariably had some members sleeping on the terrace of the house. Anybody who saw or sensed danger was supposed to shout an alarm and wake up everyone. I vividly remember waking up one night amidst commotion when somebody mistook an approaching Jeep for an attack by Naxalites. I recall casually asking my uncle that if they attacked, which side of the village would they be coming from. I guess he didn't have an answer, but just to satiate my curiosity, he pointed towards the road as an obvious choice.

Other villages, like my maternal grandfather's in Aurangabad, were not as fortunate, experiencing four Naxal attacks in six years. Bandeya, a small village cut off from all avenues of commuting and communication became so sensitive in the 2000s that a dedicated police picket was established in the village with ten policemen to guard it. The last attack that happened on the village was during Dussehra when some of the policemen had been moved for other duties. My maternal uncle, who barely stayed in the village, was caught on the wrong day. He held a rifle for the first time, firing in the dark from his terrace, to stop the Naxalites from entering the village. His own house at the outer edge of the village was one of the most vulnerable.

My knowledge of the realities of Bihar widened when I went to attend high school at DPS, Bokaro. It is here that I made friends from all corners of Bihar, who told me the horrifying tales of their places. Details about Siwan's dreaded gangster Shahabuddin, Munger's gun factories, Bihar's electricity woes, annual north Bihar floods, and rampant lawlessness left me stunned.

The revelation continued upon my move to Delhi in 2004, where derogatory comments like 'Oye, Bihari hai kya' from DTC (Delhi Transport Corporation) bus drivers were commonplace. I recall one of my classmates hemming and hawing when asked where he was from, before reluctantly and remorsefully announcing, 'Chhapra, Bihar se hain, madam'. This stuck and stayed with me for years. What could be so wrong about a place that a teenager felt ashamed and apologetic about being from there? Some of my friends from other states would sympathetically tell me, 'You don't look like a Bihari'. They, of course, expected me to take it as a compliment. How could I?

It wasn't until much later that I connected the dots and comprehended the tumultuous phase Bihar underwent between 1990 and 2005. This period, widely discussed by economists, sociologists, political scientists, and the public, stands out as one of the most controversial in the history of any state in independent India.

The story of *Broken Promises* revolves around that period and begins with Lalu Prasad Yadav taking the oath as the chief minister of Bihar in 1990. At the historic Gandhi Maidan, an exuberant Lalu declared, *'Ab koi atyachaar nahi hoga, ab koi zulm nahi hoga, ab koi bhrashtachar nahi hoga, ab koi bayimaani nahi hogi, ye kasam hum khaaye hain. Ab asal loktantra banana hai, logon ka loktantra'* (There shall be no atrocities, no excesses, no corruption and no dishonesty henceforth. This is a pledge I have taken. We will build a true democracy, the democracy of people).

It felt like a natural culmination of the decades-long struggle of the backward castes against upper caste hegemony and oppression in Bihar. Lalu's oath brought hope to millions of marginalised Biharis in the state plagued by poverty, caste atrocities and profound social and economic inequalities.

Lalu, a prodigy of the JP Movement, seemed like the perfect leader to carry forward the baton of socialism and the changes that had been ushered in by the zamindari abolition, the subsequent land reforms, leftist movements and the brief tenures of chief ministers from backward and Dalit communities such as Karpoori Thakur and Bhola Paswan Shastri.

Ironically, over the next fifteen years, Bihar came eerily close to becoming a failed state with a floundering economy, widespread corruption, lawlessness, bloody wars between private caste armies, ingenious crimes across every corner of the state, the exodus of businessmen and students, and an apathetic political leadership. Bihar, once the cradle of modern civilisation and birthplace of the JP movement, plummeted in every socio-economic parameter to become the worst-performing state in the country. The administrative structures collapsed courtesy a corrupt and resigned bureaucracy, widespread government vacancies, unpaid salaries to government employees, blatant casteism in appointments and the dictatorial decision-making based on the whims of one man, Lalu Prasad Yadav. '*Vikas nahi, sammaan chahiye*' (Respect over Development)—Lalu had a quick retort for anyone probing him on development.

Lalu's ascent was accompanied by the rise of some of the most dreaded bahubalis, who went on to carve out fiefdoms in various parts of the lawless state. Often when their paths crossed, the tales of their rivalries and the resulting bloodshed became part of folklore. Concurrently, the caste wars between Ranvir Sena, a private army of landlords, and the Naxalites in Central Bihar saw some of the bloodiest massacres in independent India, wiping out entire villages. The situation deteriorated to the point that Bihar began to be referred as a mini-Somalia in the heart of India.

Throughout this tumultuous period, Lalu, the champion of Mandal Politics, maintained a firm grip on his carefully crafted vote bank. His efforts to dismantle elitist power structures, combat corruption, control communal riots and implement social justice measures such as increasing OBC reservation quotas won him adulation from a significant section of the populace, particularly the backward communities. Lalu kept fanning caste divisions through his contempt for and open challenge to upper-caste dominance, thus consolidating his own constituency. He had, in a matter of few years, become the unchallenged ruler of Bihar and a prominent figure in national politics. However, his infallibility suffered a major setback with his conviction and arrest in the 900-crore fodder scam. This marked the beginning of the end for Lalu's empire, but not before Bihar hit rock bottom in every conceivable development parameter.

The only areas where Bihar excelled were in ignominious aspects such as an exploding population, audacious crimes (such as the lynching of a district magistrate) and competitive examination rackets (such as the leak of CAT exam papers). It came to be highlighted in national politics for unique, unprecedented scenarios such as that of a sitting chief minister being arrested for corruption and installing his unlettered wife as the next chief minister. It gained shameful notoriety for creating an industry out of kidnapping and extortion. Many of these things sound like tales from a distant land in a barbarian era. Therefore, when Nitish Kumar, Lalu Prasad Yadav's old ally-turned-ardent critic, finally took over Bihar's reins in 2005 as the new chief minister, his position was hardly envied by any.

The period from 1990-2005 was a long and tragic period in the recent history of Bihar. Ironically, tragedies often make for the most compelling stories. My book is a humble attempt to give the unfamiliar reader a chance to understand what it actually meant to live through the 'Jungle Raj' years of Bihar and how it pushed Bihar forever into the realm of irredeemable ignominy. For those who have lived through the tumultuous period, this provides a way to make sense of the chaos they once grappled with.

Mrityunjay Sharma
1 February 2024

THE RISE OF A STAR

Kshama shobhti uss bhujang ko jiske paas garal ho,
Usko kya jo dantheen, vishrahit, vineet, saral ho

Forgiveness befits the serpent, which possesses venom
Not the one that lacks fangs, is non-poisonous, humble, and simple

—Ramdhari Singh 'Dinkar'

WHIFF OF CHANGE

March 1990

Gopalganj, Bihar

A forty-two-year-old kurta-clad man, donning a Sadhana-cut hairstyle,[1] reaches Phulwaria, a nondescript village in the district of Gopalganj in northern Bihar, walks to his mother, touches her feet and announces ebulliently:[2]

> '*Mayee hum mukhyamantri ban gaynee* (Mother, I have become the chief minister).'
>
> '*Ee ka ho la* (What is that?)'
>
> '*Ee jo Hathua Maharaj baadan, unko se bad* (It is a position bigger than even Hathua Maharaj's, head of a zamindari estate in Gopalganj).'
>
> '*Achcha thik ba, jaaye de, lekin tohra sarkaari naukri naa nu milal* (That's fine, but you still couldn't secure a government job).'

Lalu would chuckle and tell this story over and over again in the years to come.

Lalu Prasad Yadav, the new chief minister of Bihar, was born in 1948 in the same nondescript village. Born as the sixth of the seven children of Kundan Rai and Marachhiya Devi, he was brought up in a family with barely one bigha of land and modest means. Lalu recalls that no one in his family knew his precise date of birth. Once, when Lalu coaxed his mother beyond her comfort, she retorted vexingly, '*Hamra naikhe yaad, tu anhariya me janamla ki injoriya me*' (I don't recall if you were born in the bright fortnight or the dark fortnight). Like almost all other mothers in Bihar, she was referring to the two halves of each month, the Krishna Paksh and Shukl Paksh, based on lunar movements. The statement put an end to the birthday debate, and the date on Lalu's school certificate became final.

With the exception of its roads, a police station and a power substation, which were all acquired after Lalu's ascendancy to chief ministership, Phulwaria was and still represents a typical concoction of Bihar's societal complexities. The village has around thirty households belonging to the upper castes of Bhumihars and Brahmins; sixty houses of Yadavs; fifty of Baniyas and Telis; ten of Gonds; five each of Kushwahas, Dhobis and Muslims; and ten of Dalits.[3] To someone who has never visited Bihar, such a diversity of castes living in the same village may give the impression of cosmopolitanism. However, these household groups of different castes are well demarcated from one another—as they are in other villages of Bihar—and reside in their own little caste-based tolas or colonies. The colonies are accordingly called the Yadav Tola, Harijan Tola, Muslim Tola, and so on.

Upper caste households, which account for barely 10 per cent of the village, have historically held almost 80 per cent of the land in Phulwaria. Unfortunately, this skewed landholding pattern is not an anomaly but rather a reflection of the real economic patterns in most parts of Bihar. The massive inequalities caused by this landholding pattern had resulted in a power structure dominated by the upper castes over the years, exacerbating the economic miseries of the landless lower castes by depriving them of even basic human dignity.

The boy from Phulwaria was soon to challenge this social and economic disparity. He would question every tenet of caste and social structure prescribed in the Manusmriti. He would demand that the privileged upper castes be held accountable for years of injustice and oppression. As a show of defiance, he would ask the oppressed castes to build houses that were taller than those of the upper castes. And, like any true master, Lalu and his family put this into practice before preaching. The size and grandeur of his and his family's buildings, farm houses and malls challenge the wealthiest of upper caste landlords, as if Lalu is mocking them, having already outrun them in a metaphorical hundred-metre sprint.

Nothing remarkable or documented about Lalu's childhood existed until, of course, he became the chief minister of Bihar. Only later did embellished versions of his antics and romanticised depictions of his family's poverty make their way through his biographies and autobiographies, establishing Lalu as the underdog hero who triumphed against all odds.

In his autobiography *Gopalganj to Raisina*, Lalu recalls how he was the most sought-after kid in his village because of his mimicry and showmanship. He paints a vivid picture of himself—a young Lalu singing songs while riding his buffalo, surrounded by other village kids. Lalu had often performed during festival celebrations in his village, and this love for the stage and the desire for adoration continued to be an integral part of his life even long after his foray into politics.

Lalu left for Patna as a six-year-old boy with his maternal uncle, Yadunand Rai, who had a *doodhwala's* (milkman) job at Patna Veterinary College. Lalu would never look back to Phulwaria again. He began his education at the nearby Bihar

Military Police (BMP) camp school before being transferred to Miller High School. For a family that was not particularly academically inclined, the fact that Lalu passed high school with a third division was no small feat.

Tryst with Destiny

Shortly after, Lalu enrolled at Bihar National (B.N.) College in Patna, which had become a hotbed of university politics by the 1960s. At this time, not only B.N. College but also Patna, and indeed the entire state of Bihar, was politically charged. The socialists, led by Ram Manohar Lohia, were banding together and challenging existing social structures to overthrow the hegemony of the upper castes. Politics had become deeply polarised and aligned to caste lines. The Congress party had the support of the upper castes, Dalits and Muslims, which helped it form a winning coalition. The Jan Sangh wielded power in a few urban enclaves and among trading communities, whereas the socialists were largely backed by backward castes.[4]

Lalu chose to go with the Socialist Party not because he was inclined to their ideology or because he was enamoured with Lohia but because it was the natural home for Bihar's backward castes. With his histrionics and penchant for all things dramatic, Lalu quickly rose to prominence in university politics. Politics provided him with everything he desired: the opportunity to meet influential people, the means to attract and address large crowds and a way to unleash his youthful energy. However, when it came to discussions on ideology, societal issues and the like, Lalu was barely interested. He avoided anything deliberative or serious. He didn't care to read about socialism or Lohia, but when he needed to sway a crowd, he would use the subject with such unapologetic conviction that he could pass himself off as an expert.

Life would take numerous twists and turns, most of them in no particular pattern, making it impossible to predict that 'Lalua'—as he was fondly addressed in his childhood—would go on to become the premier of one of India's largest states. To an outsider, the odds looked stacked against Lalu for he had no political lineage, he belonged to the Yadavs, an Other Backward Class (OBC) that was not as politically influential as the upper castes; and even when it came to choosing a chief minister in 1990, he wasn't the then prime minister V.P. Singh's preferred candidate.

While Lalu's ascendancy to the top post is as fascinating as his subsequent life, the phalgun of 1990—as March is known in the panchang or the Hindu calendar—when Lalu took oath, suddenly brought a sense of hope and expectation to millions of Biharis reeling under the worst of poverty, caste atrocities and lawlessness for decades. The twinkling eyes of Dalits and hitherto oppressed castes glistened with anticipation as Lalu roared from the dais in Gandhi Maidan.

> *Ab koi atyachaar nahi hoga, ab koi zulm nahi hoga, ab koi bhrashtachar nahi hoga, ab koi bayimaani nahi hogi, ye kasam hum khaaye hain. Ab asal loktantra banana hai, logon ka loktantra.*
>
> There shall be no atrocities, no excesses, no corruption and no dishonesty henceforth. This is a pledge I have taken. We will build a real democracy, a democracy of the people.

For his oath-taking, Lalu picked the historic Gandhi Maidan instead of Raj Bhavan. This was just the first of a string of unusual and unconventional decisions that would characterise his tenure as chief minister. Even after taking oath as chief minister, Lalu continued to stay in his uncle's servant quarters in the Patna Veterinary College campus, which had been his home for the last two decades. Resembling more a cattle shed than a college, this dingy housing amidst heaps of cow-dung would hardly have seemed to anyone the breeding ground for a young man's lofty ambitions. However, the veterinary college would continue to hold a special place in Lalu's life because it was here that he began student politics, rose to become the leader of the opposition in the Bihar Assembly and later the chief minister. It is also the same place that would later engulf him in one of India's largest-ever scams, leading to his incarceration as India's first sitting chief minister to be jailed on corruption charges.

The Unconventional Politician

Upon taking charge, Lalu began to ride a bicycle from his servant quarters at the veterinary college to the secretariat, and so did his entourage. The public would be pleasantly amused with such simplicity shown by a chief minister. His predecessors, particularly Congress party chief ministers such as Jagannath Mishra, were stalwarts and larger-than-life politicians who were often too distant and unapproachable to the common people. When asked about the difference between his government and the previous one, Lalu once said, '*Jagannath Mishra ki sarkar ko to bas swarg me seedhi lagana baaki tha*' (The only thing left out by the Jagannath Mishra government was to place a ladder to heaven).[5] During the late 1980s, Lalu often attacked Mishra's government, which had come to be known as one of the most corrupt governments ever, in his inimitable style. Lalu once stood up from the opposition benches in the assembly and claimed that Mishra was having trouble walking because he had grafted into his stomach kilos of gold and diamonds obtained through corrupt means. He demanded that the matter be thoroughly investigated and that the riches be recovered by cutting open the chief minister's stomach! Lalu then declared that if he were wrong, he would resign from the assembly or else Mishra should quit. No one, of course, believed him. But even as everyone in the assembly erupted in laughter, Lalu had made his point.[6]

Lalu was a refreshing change from the elitist and distant politics of the Congress party. He was approachable. He projected himself as one among the masses, and he enjoyed being among them, joking with them and sharing their joys and sorrows. This image and demeanour would also pervade his style of administration and other aspects of his political life.

The month of March, when Lalu took oath, is also the season of Holi in Bihar. This festival of colours also marks the beginning of the Hindu new year. In Bihar, Holi is celebrated quite fondly and in a peculiarly boisterous way. In fact, over the years, it has come to be associated with raunchy Bhojpuri songs, boozing and debauchery. Yet, it is one of the most popular festivals in Bihar. Not surprisingly, Lalu loved Holi. He made sure to organise a Holi milan or gathering, every year playing dhol and singing faguwa (traditional Holi songs), with the who's who of Bihar in attendance and bhang in abundance. This would fit in nicely with Lalu's carefully cultivated image of being a 'son of the soil'.

With his oratorical skills, Lalu could immediately connect with the most marginalised. He switched between Hindi and Bhojpuri, using the tone and dialect that best fit the situation. Lalu's speeches and interviews were frequently peppered with a peculiar Bihari tone of Hindi, intended to appeal to his overwhelmingly rural voter base. He would often use witty Bhojpuri idioms before abruptly switching to a broken line of English to add some extra spice. Lalu was never afraid of making fun of himself; in fact, he revelled in it. Never before or since has a politician used vernacularisation so extensively and effectively to his advantage. All of Lalu's competitors, including his closest rival and fellow Janata Dal (JD) compatriot Mulayam Singh Yadav, were far behind. For outsiders, Lalu's style of speaking and mannerisms became the defining feature of Bihar over time. The initial fascination with his peculiar personality quickly turned into a major source of entertainment, with every other mimicry artiste attempting to imitate Lalu. Lalu's accent became the quintessential Bihari accent in Bollywood films, while his flippant demeanour became synonymous with the typical Bihari character.

Soon after he became chief minister, Lalu made his intentions clear. He was going to challenge every existing social structure, order and norm. He was going to challenge the hegemony of the upper castes. In fact, he would match, if not outdo, the militancy of the upper castes in order to retain their territories. Almost all of Lalu Yadav's actions and decisions had some caste and social order bearing. No decision, not even one concerning development, was exempt from this.

Lalu's demeanour and decision-making style were unlike anything else seen before, not just among bureaucrats in official circles but also among the common Biharis in the farthest corners of the state. People had never before seen a chief minister holding an open court under a tree by the roadside. Cabinet meetings were suddenly being held in the style of a village panchayat on a concrete platform under open skies. Lalu was breaking rules at a speed never seen or imagined before. He simply did not agree with bureaucrats' versions of what could and couldn't be done. He would often make new rules on the spot whenever the existing rules didn't fit his idea of justice. Rarely would anybody around have the gumption to question or give a second thought to Lalu's orders. He had a typical reply to any objections raised against his ideas: '*Hum chief minister hain, hum sab jaante hain.*

Jaisa hum kehte hain, waisa kijiye' (I am the chief minister; I know best. Do as I say).

When asked by a journalist how he planned to rule after taking the oath, Lalu replied, '*Hum dictator ki tarah kaam karenge.*' He essentially meant that he wanted to run the state efficiently but chose the wrong words to express it. Ironically, he lived up to those words.[7]

Often in a dystopian society, people fancy a dictatorial leader to rise up to solve their problems. As if dictatorship could be a panacea to all of the system's corruption and inefficiency. Lalu's dictatorial style appealed to the same disenfranchised, oppressed and despondent masses. Biharis had long known governments to be nothing but a close cabal of corrupt, immoral and inefficient politicians and bureaucrats. Lalu was a fresh change from all that. He was trying to change the system for these people, who had lost hope. However, in the minds of Biharis, including Lalu's own people, this assessment of his personality would soon change. In the moment, however, he was their saviour, a godsend.

Beginner's Luck?

Lalu suddenly became the most talked about politician, not just in Bihar but across the country. It wasn't just his politics, but more his style and mannerisms. Lalu would often enter the settlements of the poor with water tankers and make the unkempt kids bathe in the spray from tankers. They were offered new clothes and their hair was combed. He often sat in the middle of a busy road in Patna with a stick in hand, passing instructions to an administration in a tizzy. He often publicly chastised senior officers, drawing cheers and applause from the public, who saw babus as the biggest perpetrators of corruption and injustice. Lalu didn't hesitate to order the dismissals of delinquent officers, making a public spectacle of the process. He also went around raiding liquor shops and revoking their licences on the spot. In fact, if you have ever seen the Bollywood movie *Nayak*, Lalu was a living example of that, long before the movie was even conceived. Lalu loved such theatrics; he saw them as a visible challenge to the hegemony of the upper castes and the privileged class. The newly emerging electronic media loved Lalu, and he reciprocated.

Lalu's 'Janta Darbar', a weekly open session for public grievances at the chief minister's residence, was equally colourful. He barely accepted any papers and preferred to sort issues in the style of a village sarpanch. The decisions were quick and often quirky. Once, a handicapped man in his early twenties came to see Lalu. The man was in tattered clothes, stinking, and could barely walk even with the support of an attendant. Lalu went into his house, brought him soap, pumped water for him to bathe and offered him food. The onlooking crowd of Lalu's protégés and press went gaga over the scene. Lalu definitely had a knack for hogging the limelight.

But he was quick to pick up the tricks of administration too and had his priorities clear. Whether those priorities augured well for the future of Bihar, we will see later in the book. The bureaucrats from Lalu's early days would comment that Lalu was good at grasping subjects quickly but he rarely went into details or read through thick files. '*File sign karte karte kareja dukhta hai (I get chest pains signing so many files)*' he would say.[8]

Lalu needed a bureaucrat he could trust in order to carry out the mundane tasks of administration while he reached out to his people. He chose Mukund Prasad, a 1966 batch Indian Administrative Services (IAS) officer, as his principal secretary. Prasad, being an OBC and from Lalu's home district of Chhapra, gave Lalu additional confidence. Prasad would go on to serve in the same position till his retirement in 2002, including under Rabri Devi, and even thereafter as a contractual employee till 2005.

If the first few months were any indication, Lalu ran an administration that was high on rhetoric but not bad on the ground. The first applause for the chief minister came from none other than the Union Home Minister, Mufti Mohammad Sayeed, who spoke about the improved law and order situation in Bihar on the floor of the Lok Sabha. However, what earned Lalu the highest praise was the way he handled communal tensions in Bihar. The memories of the 1989 Bhagalpur riots, in which over a thousand people were killed, were fresh in the minds of the people of Bihar. The Ayodhya movement, alongside the Mandal debates, had created a deep schism in society, with people strongly divided on either side. Lalu held the district magistrates and the superintendent of police accountable for any communal flare-up in their areas. Some incidents that occurred in Nawada, Jamshedpur and Bhagalpur and which had the potential to escalate into bloody riots were suppressed with a heavy hand.

Ram Navami, which had earned the moniker 'Danga Navmi' as a result of frequent disputes over procession routes, was also purged of the bad name. Lalu took a strong stance, disallowing Ram Navami processions to pass through sensitive areas.[9] While this infuriated many Hindus and religious groups, it also ensured that communal incidents rarely occurred.

Lalu also earned accolades for his crusade against corruption, or what seemed like it in the initial months. Whether to call it beginner's luck or a new and young chief minister's initial enthusiasm is a tough call. Lalu's fifteen-year tenure as chief minister, or as a proxy chief minister, shows that he was hardly concerned about corruption. In numerous instances, he and his closest family members and colleagues were neck-deep in it.

However, immediately after taking oath, Lalu declared that he would take the toughest measures possible to curb corruption and break the deeply entrenched contractor–engineer nexus in the state. An interesting thing about bureaucracy in general is that it quickly adapts to the incumbent government and conveniently realigns its loyalties. In this case, Lalu's verbal crusade against corruption sounded sincere, and officials not wanting to be on the wrong side of things cruised along. The Vigilance Department, which had been given stern warnings of being wound up if pending corruption cases weren't resolved, acted immediately. The houses of 35 senior officials were raided and huge proportions of unaccounted wealth was seized. Even senior officials weren't spared. The chairman of the Bihar School Examination Board was arrested after hundreds of illegal appointments were detected. Similarly, an inquiry was instituted against the chairman of the State Intermediate Council for 700 illegal appointments. Certain Indian Police Service (IPS) officers also fell victim to the overenthusiastic prosecution spree.

Voices were raised about the selective prosecution of Lalu's adversaries or those not known to be close to him. The majority of the offices raided had incumbents who were appointees of the previous government. Thus, while some of the correlations of ulterior motives made sense, the general public, regardless of their political leanings, was pleased and enthusiastic about action against powerful corrupt elements.

Newspapers often reported on how government babus were arriving on time due to surprise inspections conducted by ministers, including the chief minister himself. According to one report, the chief minister had already suspended 400 officials in the first three months of his tenure on discovering they were absent or sleeping during working hours. The power sector improved significantly, with power generation more than doubling from a dismal 250 MW out of a total installed capacity of 1,310 MW.[10]

A Taste of Social Justice

Some of the first decisions taken by the Janata Dal government also reflected its commitment to social justice. For example, the government increased old-age pension from 30 rupees to 100 rupees. Similarly, it announced an allowance for pregnant women for a nutritious diet during their pregnancy. Women and the elderly were not the only ones who had their hopes raised. The youth were given free travel on state road transport buses if they were unemployed. Travelling for examinations or government interviews was also made free. Lalu promised jobs for one lakh educated youth by the end of the first year of his rule, including filling up more than 60,000 posts lying vacant in government departments.

In all his speeches and interviews, Lalu also showed a strong resolve to fight the state's education mafia. Vice chancellors of universities were told to improve the functioning of their universities or resign. Technical institutions, run by the powerful education mafia who were mostly Congress(I) heavyweights, were quickly banned.[11]

The quick actions and bold steps taken by the government earned it widespread praise and popular support from almost all segments of society. Lalu was a breath of fresh air with his ebullient nature and optimism for an egalitarian society free from vices. The most deprived of the lot became the most optimistic. The poorest, the Dalits and the landless began to look up to Lalu as a figure who would not only restore their long-lost dignity but also provide them with a way out of their miserable lives.

A sudden and significant shift started to be seen in the police's response to complaints from Dalits and OBCs. In an upper caste-dominated Congress regime, police stations that would rarely listen to or act on complaints from the poor and Dalits began to pay attention to them. Yadavs now became the first to be offered chairs at police stations. Just a few months after Lalu had taken over, a Scheduled Caste (SC) person was murdered in Begusarai. No arrests had been made despite the accused, who belonged to an upper caste, being known to most. When Lalu arrived at the site accompanied by his officers, he firmly planted himself on a chair, declaring that he wouldn't budge until the culprits were arrested. The culprits, though influential in the region, were arrested within the next five hours. Lalu made several such visits, making sure that the perpetrators of such crimes were not spared. Such signals were enough for the police to take their cues from. First Information Reports (FIRs) from OBCs and Dalits began to be registered. Caste atrocities started receiving intervention from the highest levels of the police hierarchy.

Caste and discrimination based on it had long been entrenched in Bihar's psyche. Even after chief ministers such as Daroga Rai, Karpoori Thakur and Bhola Paswan or Ram Sunder Das from the OBC, EBC and SC sections, respectively, had ruled the state, the common upper caste public wouldn't offer their chair or cot to a lower caste man. Lalu was visibly rankled by this lack of dignity. He wanted to change it and change it fast. The modality didn't matter to him.

Lalu backed up his ideas of social justice with a slew of schemes, many of which appeared bizarre at first. While it is debatable whether it made much of a difference on the ground because powerful social groups would still find ways to circumvent such laws, it did win Lalu a devoted following among those oppressed castes and groups.

Toddy, a drink extracted from palm trees, is traditionally extracted by Pasis, a Scheduled Caste in Bihar. Previous governments auctioned the palm trees from which toddy was extracted and made about Rs 2.5 crore in income annually. Lalu abolished the auction system and allotted the palm trees to Pasis directly.

His popularity among the caste group skyrocketed as a result of this. Fishing ponds, likewise, were previously auctioned and largely controlled by upper caste groups. Lalu abolished auctions here as well, allocating the ponds to private societies formed by Mallahs, a fishermen caste. The Mallahs, who were previously paid a pittance to collect fish, were now the owners of these ponds. Lalu often addressed these caste men with catchy names such as *macchli-pakadne-walon* for fisherman and *ghongha-pakadne-walon* for snail catchers.

Lalu wanted these and other marginalised castes to be empowered, through any and every means possible. He urged them to come together and fight for their rights, and even invited himself to some of their social functions. Lalu would openly discuss caste at public rallies and in his speeches.

Lalu also established Charwaha Vidyalaya to help cattle grazers attend school alongside their daily routines. It was aimed at children in the age group of five to fifteen who were generally cattle rearers. The children could bring their cattle and attend classes while their cattle grazed in the same campus.[12] However, what could have been a game-changing initiative in adult literacy failed miserably. It was attributed to the chief minister's habit of launching initiatives with fanfare but never bothering to follow up to ensure proper execution. A large section of the cattle rearing community also saw the Charwaha Vidyalaya to be a caste-specific scheme for Yadavs and felt alienated.

Lalu's brief fascination with governance and novel initiatives, however, dissipated after his first few months in office. He may have realised that governance moved too slowly, the results were erratic at best and too far in the future. He also noticed reluctance among a section of bureaucrats to support him. The upper castes, too, were still unwilling to accept him as chief minister. In private conversations, even within government offices, Lalu was still referred to as 'Lalua'.

Lalu soon realised that there was an easier way to hold on to power—through caste consolidation rather than governance initiatives. He witnessed a much faster and more enthusiastic response to his call for the restoration of pride and respect for backward castes and Dalits. He had started enjoying the adulation of large sections of backward and Dalit communities, as well as the raw political power that came with it. He knew that these enthusiastic crowds would always rally behind him.

The attempts at caste consolidation and shunning of the development imperative appeared more pronounced after the results of the 1991 parliamentary elections. Lalu now openly declared, '*Vikas nahi, sammaan chahiye*' (Need respect, not development). To anybody asking for roads in their village, he would chuckle and say that if roads were built, the upper castes would benefit because they were the ones with vehicles, not the poor. The gullible poor would shout praise to Lalu's witticism in return.

Lalu didn't apply the same principle to Phulwaria, his native village. His village soon got an electric sub-station, a railway station, a hospital, a police station and a block status with all block-level offices. A new concrete road now connects Phulwaria and Mirganj, the nearest town. The town also boasts of a Marachhiya Devi Chowk, named after Lalu's mother.

At an election rally in Dhanbad in 1991, Lalu marched from his chopper to the stage wearing a khadi vest over his kurta. Lalu announced to the chuckling audience, 'We have long played vest to the upper castes. It's time to swap roles now. It's time to get the vest over the shirt now.'[13] Lalu had cleverly framed the entire conflict as a battle between the privileged and the oppressed. While it appeared to be purely a class struggle, the way it was carried out and projected frequently caused the classes to coincide with caste groups.

At the height of his arrogance, Lalu's paan-chewing habit necessitated the use of a spittoon, which had to be carried to his mouth by anyone sitting closest to him. It didn't matter if the person was a senior bureaucrat or a minister on his cabinet. Sometime in 1991, Lalu had just entered a wedding function at the Patna Club. Chandrika Rai, a cabinet minister and son of former chief minister Daroga Rai, snuck away from his chair to avoid Lalu's gaze. When asked later by a senior journalist about why he was fleeing his own chief minister, he confided that if he had sat next to Lalu, the arrogant chief minister might have asked Rai to pick up the spittoon to his mouth.[14] Ironically, Chandrika Rai would later become Lalu's samdhi, with his daughter Aishwarya Rai getting married to Lalu's elder son, Tej Pratap Yadav. But the marriage would soon fall apart, resulting in an episode full of family drama.

On other occasions, Lalu would discreetly indicate his need for khaini—by pressing his thumb to his palm. A man dedicated to the cause would promptly offer his palm, concealing the prepared khaini within. These were Lalu's own crude methods to derive a sense of power.

However, Lalu's run was not without its set of challenges. His government, which was running with the support of both the Left and the BJP, was already shaky. When combined with internal Janata Dal dissension, the situation would occasionally necessitate frequent political manoeuvring from Lalu, a skill he had recently mastered. News of the growing differences between Lalu and Ram Sundar Das, the state Janata Dal president whom Lalu had defeated to win the chief ministerial seat, would often circulate.

Lalu's first year was tumultuous due to three major events: the implementation of the Mandal Commission recommendations, L.K. Advani's Rath Yatra and the fall of the National Front government at the Centre. The trifecta of these events would see Lalu seasoning into a politician far beyond the buffoonery by which he was often characterised.

THE THREE ACES

In September 2015, just weeks before Bihar was to go to polls, Mohan Bhagwat, the Rashtriya Swayamsevak Sangh (RSS) chief—referred to as Sarsanghchalak—spoke in an interview of the need for a debate on reservations. The JD(U)-Rashtriya Janata Dal (RJD)-Congress alliance, which was pitted against the BJP's mammoth election machinery, couldn't have asked for better electoral fodder. While election debates up to that point had been centred around Nitish Kumar's track record of development and social justice, it was quickly overtaken by the discussions and speeches around reservations. Lalu, a legatee of Mandal politics, wouldn't let such a golden chance slip. He dared the Narendra Modi government to scrap reservations, saying, 'If you have had your mother's milk—*mai ka doodh*—then have it scrapped. Each would know his strength.'

The BJP received a huge blow when the results were declared on 8 November 2015. It bagged only 53 seats in a house of 243. A post-poll analysis showed Bhagwat's reservation remarks as having done major damage to BJP's prospects. However, it wasn't the first time that debates over reservation and Mandalisation had influenced Bihar's politics or its election results.

The debates on reservations can be traced all the way back to the initial constituent assembly debates on affirmative action for historically underrepresented groups. The constituent assembly had decided on a 22.5 per cent reservation—15 per cent for the SCs and 7.5 per cent for Scheduled Tribes (STs)—for all vacancies in the central government. Reservation for OBCs, on the other hand, has its origins in the post-Emergency days of the Janata Party government at the Centre, led by Morarji Desai. On 1 January 1979, the government named Bindeshwari Prasad Mandal, a former chief minister of Bihar, to lead the second Backward Class Commission. Mandal submitted his report exactly two years later, on 31 December 1980. The commission concluded that caste was the main indicator of backwardness. It used the 1931 census data to determine the combined population of such 'socially and educationally backward classes' to be 52 per cent.[15] These castes, known as OBCs, occupied the hierarchy between the upper castes and SCs, and came primarily from the Shudras of the ancient four-varna system. The majority of the castes in the group are 'occupation' castes, such as Dhobi, Teli, Lohar, Sunar and Halwai. Despite their size, the commission concluded that they were underrepresented in the administration, particularly at the top levels.[16]

The commission, among several other measures to redress this anomaly, recommended a 27 per cent reservation for OBCs in central government jobs. However, Morarji Desai's government had lost power by then, and elections ushered in Indira Gandhi as the new prime minister. The report never saw any action during Indira and Rajiv Gandhi's tenures. One probable reason for the inaction is that both tenures had strong support from upper caste groups, who may have reacted adversely to OBC reservations.

Genie of Mandal

The Mandal Commission's report appeared destined to be shelved like numerous other government reports, but only until V.P. Singh assumed office as prime minister on 2 December 1989.

Singh had been mulling for some time over the way forward to consolidate backward caste votes and thus strengthen the Janata Dal's presence in the Hindi heartland. The OBCs, while lagging behind in administrative positions, had over the last few decades gained economically through land reforms and politically through the ballot box. Some of these castes, such as the Jats in Punjab and Haryana, the Marathas in Maharashtra, the Vokkaligas in Karnataka and the Yadavs in UP and Bihar, had become dominant castes—numerically significant, well organised and exercising economic and social power.[17] The Mandal Commission's recommendations seemed to be the right tool for their consolidation. On 7 August 1990, Singh announced in Parliament that his government would implement the 27 per cent reservation for OBC candidates in government jobs, as recommended by the Mandal Commission.

The sudden announcement caught everyone by surprise and created a quick polarisation between the supporters and opponents of the idea. The opposition came largely from the upper castes. Even among those who supported it, a significant number of people, including Singh's own party members and allies, were unhappy with the manner of its implementation. The recommendations were implemented hastily, without due consultation with its allies, the BJP and the Left. The two parties, as well as Lalu's friend Nitish Kumar, wanted it to be based on Karpoori Thakur's 'Bihar formula'. The formula essentially divided the entire OBC quota into two categories: backward castes and Extremely Backward Castes (EBCs). The EBCs were created to provide a separate quota for the group's more vulnerable castes so that the upper backwards didn't appropriate all the quota benefits. The formula also excluded income tax-paying citizens from availing quota benefits and included a separate 3 per cent reservation for the economically vulnerable among the upper castes.[18]

However, Singh had his own compulsions in expediting the process, which had been sent into political exile for over ten years. First, his fallout with Jat leader Devi Lal had caused the alliance of Ahir, Jat, Gujar and Rajput (AJGAR) to slip away from Janata Dal's captive vote bank. This had also made the coalition governments in the states of Bihar and UP uneasy. Second, Singh required a dedicated caste grouping to take on the role of committed party cadre at various levels of the party, particularly in the states of north India. The third and most immediate goal was to blunt the BJP's Hindu vote consolidation on the back of a rising Ayodhya movement. With the new caste realignment, Singh became the undisputed champion of 'social justice'. He won the support of a large number of OBCs who would benefit from the implementation of Mandal Commission's recommendations.

The announcement sparked fierce debates between supporters and opponents of the idea and was soon followed by scattered student protests in Delhi and across the Hindi heartland. On 19 September 1990, Rajeev Goswami, a University of Delhi student, set himself on fire to protest the new reservation policies. Rajeev survived with 50 per cent burn injuries, but his act set off a spark to the movement. This was followed by larger protests and several self-immolation bids across the country. A total of 62 people died as a result of nearly 200 suicide attempts.[19] Rajeev later went on to be elected as Delhi University Students' Union (DUSU) president.

The protests, however, were largely concentrated in the north Indian states, with the protesting forces scattered and their agitations sporadic. In his book *India After Gandhi*, Ramchandra Guha identifies three reasons for the movement's failure to gain traction in the southern states. The first being the difference in the numerical strength of upper castes in north Indian states vis-à-vis the southern states. While in north India, it stood at over 20 per cent in most states, the same barely touched 10 per cent in south Indian states. The south also had a long history of affirmative action programmes aimed at the upliftment of backward communities. Guha also says that because the south had a thriving industrial sector, the educated youth's reliance on government jobs was lower.[20]

P.S. Krishnan, an Andhra cadre IAS officer who was then Secretary, Ministry of Welfare, and had to sign the 7 August 1990 Mandal notification, recalls the stormy run-up to that signature. Krishnan recalls having to do a lot of firefighting, even within the system. As the immolations and protests began, he recalls having a meeting with then attorney general Soli Sorabjee, who asked him, 'Bhai, what is this *caste-shaste*?' Krishnan recounts, 'When I explained how fortunate he was to have been born a Parsi and not have to deal with the full force of the caste system, he immediately came to my side.'[21]

In Bihar, the Janata Dal and Lalu stood to gain the most from the implementation of the Mandal recommendations. Lalu was also opposed to Karpoori Thakur's 'Bihar formula', which included a separate quota for EBCs. He believed that it would splinter and weaken the backward caste movement against the hegemony of the upper castes. Most Janata Dal leaders were also opposed to any exclusion of higher-income earners among the OBCs as well as any reservation for the economically disadvantaged among the upper castes. Lalu was the most prominent of them. In fact, he claims in his autobiography that it was he who urged V.P. Singh to put the Commission's recommendations into action. Nitish, who supported Karpoori Thakur's Bihar formula, commented much later in an interview:

> When I look back, I wonder how inexperienced and immature I was. I couldn't see what Karpoori Ji could see through his vast experience and knowledge: that the Extremely Backward castes wouldn't benefit positively in the absence of a separate sub-quota for them. They are way behind the upper backwards in terms of education and resources and will never be able to compete with them.

However, Nitish also realised that the backward castes had to be organised together to tackle the massive backlash expected from the upper castes. He, therefore, decided to put this concern on hold for the greater good.

As anti-reservation protests spread across the other parts of the Hindi heartland, Bihar appeared to have receded to the chaotic anti-reservation days of 1978. The divide this time was much deeper; the protests were more vigorous. The anti-reservation upper castes took to the streets, rampaging through government property, attacking the shops and properties owned by backward castes and setting them on fire in several places. The pro-reservationists quickly followed suit with equal if not greater vigour, with implicit support from Lalu. With a long and deep history of caste divisions, the state witnessed some of the bloodiest anti-Mandal protests.

The difference between Lalu and Karpoori Thakur's styles, the two leaders at the helm of state during these anti-reservation protests, was a major reason for increased hostility this time compared to the 1978 protests. Karpoori had a conciliatory approach and worked to assuage the fears of the upper castes. Lalu, instead of mediating between the two warring groups, gave speeches that widened the chasm.[22] He used the situation to rant vituperatively against the upper castes, fuelling the rage of backward castes against them. He wanted to instil fear among the upper castes. The more they despised him, the bigger and more powerful a hero he became for the backward castes. The state police were instructed to tackle the anti-Mandal protests with a heavy hand. Almost a dozen upper-caste youth were killed by police repression in different parts of the state.[23]

Despite his reservations about Lalu's divisive tactics, Nitish chose to stand side by side with him. He declared at a pro-reservation rally in Gandhi Maidan. 'There is no way anyone can turn back the clock of social justice.'

The movement in Bihar, as elsewhere, was led by students trained in university politics. In the midst of widespread unemployment, upper-caste youth made Mandal implementation a matter of life and death. To the youth of backward castes, this looked like a pivotal moment to reclaim the opportunities they had long been denied. Invoking reservations in government jobs was one of the simplest ways for politicians to connect with OBC voters. Even with the reservation benefits, Lalu knew he would be able to create only a few thousand jobs every year for lakhs of unemployed OBC youths. The new liberalisation policies had shifted the balance even further away from government jobs and towards the private sector.

Lalu was well aware of the limitations of Mandal implementation in making a significant difference in the lives of millions of OBC citizens. He, therefore, used Mandal as a tool of political messaging rather than being concerned about its actual capacity for empowering backward castes. This is also evident in his indifferent approach to implementing central and state schemes related to education and economic uplift of marginalised castes.

The Mandal agitation sparked several conflicts in urban centres, and it didn't take long for them to spread to rural areas as well. The warring groups heard of most often were the Rajputs and Bhumihars against the Yadavs. The Rajputs and Bhumihars, who had historically held dominant positions, found themselves in opposition to the Yadavs, who became the primary beneficiary of the implementation. The Yadavs further gained a more assertive voice with Lalu's ascension to power. The backlash to anti-reservation protests was often led by people close to Lalu, such as Pappu Yadav, a first-time but powerful MLA. It was reported that a backward caste group going to the 8 October 1990 rally in Patna to be addressed by the then prime minister V.P. Singh was attacked by Bhumihars.[24] The backward castes retaliated by smashing buses belonging to the forward castes and even ordering them off the roads in some cases.[25]

The Rashtriya Sawarna Mukti Morcha (National Upper Caste Liberation Front) was one of the many fronts formed to oppose the reservations. Set up in the Bhumihar-dominated belt of Muzaffarpur, it demanded a separate 'Sawarna Rajya' for the upper castes, comprising areas of Bihar, West Bengal, Uttar Pradesh, Madhya Pradesh and Haryana.[26] However, serious divisions within the movement arose over the issue of leadership, and the movement never grew into a mass movement. Notably, student leaders from Patna University formed the Mandal Commission Virodhi Morcha. However, a tussle over the leadership question resulted in a split in the 1,001-member group, resulting in two parallel organisations with the same name.

By the time the protests cooled down, the social relations among the castes in Bihar were no longer the same. The brief period saw the upper OBCs assuming a leading role rather than remaining on the periphery, as had often been the case. It appeared to be the culmination of a shift that began in the 1960s and was bolstered by the election of Karpoori Thakur as Bihar's chief minister in 1977. Lalu had built a shining kingdom on the foundation laid by Karpoori. While the latter had encouraged backward castes to assert equality with upper castes, Lalu had taken it a step further. He wouldn't accept anything less than complete dominance over the upper castes.

The Mandal implementation also split political parties in Bihar along caste lines. Former chief minister Jagannath Mishra came out openly against the implementation of the Mandal Commission report. He remarked, 'As the Muslim League introduced communalism in the country before Independence, V.P. Singh has introduced the politics of castes.' Both are equally lethal to society.[27] However, his party, the Congress (I), remained non-committed to either side. Sharad Yadav, a leader of one of the beneficiary castes, led pro-reservation rallies in Delhi. He continued exhorting students from the backward communities to come out and match the huge numbers at anti-reservation rallies.

The BJP, however, was caught in a classical dilemma amidst the Mandal episode. Its support for Mandal legislation would cost it urban supporters, while its opposition would cost it the support of backward Hindus in rural areas. The dilemma made the party equivocal, taking a measured approach to the issue. When the BJP suggested inviting the protesting students to a dialogue, then welfare minister Ram Vilas Paswan retorted angrily: 'This only shows how upper castes still resist any change in the system. Every political party promised the Mandal Commission implementation in its manifesto, but now they want us to drag our feet.'[28]

The BJP's uncommitted stance aided the Janata Dal in monopolising the OBC vote, while Congress (I)'s opposition in some areas put it in competition with the BJP for urban votes. Mandal had thus posed a serious threat to the BJP's carefully crafted vote bank based on Hindu unity. This became evident when angry students gheraoed L.K. Advani and Madan Lal Khurana in Delhi, demanding that they protest the Mandal implementation unequivocally. This was an ultimatum from the upper caste and urban voters to the BJP. The gherao may have been the turning point at which Advani decided to wield the Ayodhya sword with unwavering determination.

The BJP, led by its chief Lal Krishna Advani, thus decided to shift the debate from the Mandal Report to Ram Mandir, and Advani embarked on his Rath Yatra with the slogan that made his intent apparent. *'Hinduon ko todo mat, Ramchandra ko chhodo mat'* (Do not foment splits among the Hindus, do not forget Lord Rama).

Mandal versus Kamandal

Amidst the cacophony of reservation debates, Advani decided to tour India to educate people about the Ayodhya movement. The movement aimed to reclaim 'Ram Janmabhoomi', which the Hindus believe is the birthplace of their deity, Lord Ram. It is believed that the Babri Masjid was built in 1528 by Mughal General Mir Baqi after destroying a pre-existing Ram temple on the site. The mosque was named after the first Mughal emperor, Babur. Though disputable, the claims had become a point of contention between the Hindus and Muslims since 1853, when Nirmohi Akhara, a Hindu sect, laid claim to the mosque.[29] The unresolved issue was reignited in 1949 when some Hindus placed the idols of Ram and Sita in the mosque, sparking Muslim protests and prompting the government to declare the mosque a disputed site and close its gates.

In the 1980s, the Vishwa Hindu Parishad (VHP) took up the cause, advocating for the demolition of the mosque and the construction of a grand Ram temple in its place. The BJP also shifted strongly towards a hardline Hindu nationalism with the Ram Mandir as a central issue, after a poor showing in the 1984 parliamentary elections. It was the strong support for this movement by Atal Bihari Vajpayee and the Advani-led BJP that catapulted it to 85 seats in the 1989 general elections, up from just two seats five years ago. V.P. Singh became prime minister in 1989 with the support of the BJP. As Singh was attempting to consolidate his vote base among the backward castes by implementing the Mandal Commission's recommendations, the BJP saw this as a division in its carefully consolidated Hindu vote base. It was in the backdrop of this tussle between Singh's Mandalisation and the BJP's Hinduism that Advani decided to launch his Rath Yatra.

Interestingly, the yatra was originally intended to be a padyatra. However, it was turned into a Rath Yatra when Pramod Mahajan, a late BJP leader from Maharashtra, pointed out the slow progress that could be made on foot.[30] A Toyota minibus was converted into a rath that would take Advani from Somnath in Gujarat through central India's numerous towns and villages before finally arriving in Ayodhya on 30 October 1990. Both Somnath and Ayodhya were significant to the yatra given their historical association with Muslim invaders and as a symbol of Hindu pride. While Somnath was reclaimed with the construction of Somnath temple in the 1950s, Ayodhya remained a reminder of Hindu subjugation at the hands of foreign invaders.

The yatra began in the holy city of Somnath on 25 September 1990, seeking to capitalise on the recent anti-Mandal protests that had gained momentum across north and central India. Advani was greeted with rapturous applause in each town he passed through, with VHP volunteers striving to make each stop grander than the last. Advani was presented with saffron flags, swords and bow-arrows by a huge crowd of supporters who chanted praises to Lord Ram and raised war cries to build a grand new Ram temple at Ayodhya. People would often smear the rath with tilak and shower Advani with flowers. Some believers would go so far as to smear the dust on the rath's wheel on their foreheads. Advani travelled an average of 300 kilometres per day addressing about six public rallies a day to roaring crowds. Flanked by party leaders such as Pramod Mahajan, Narendra Modi and others in different legs of the journey, Advani addressed the themes of Hindu awakening and nationalism. He portrayed the battle for the Ram temple as a battle between Lord Ram and Babur, the Mughal emperor. Shiv Sena leader Bal Thackeray, who accompanied Advani during his tour through Maharashtra, threatened to wipe out the 'unholy green'—the colour usually associated with Islam—if the Ram temple construction was obstructed.[31]

V.P. Singh, who was confident initially that his Mandal card would trounce the BJP's Kamandal, began to feel the heat as the yatra progressed. Advani halted in Delhi for several days in the midst of his yatra, practically challenging the government to arrest him, which it didn't.[32]

While Advani was attempting to consolidate the Hindu vote bank through his yatra, V.P. Singh was attempting to drive a wedge between the forward and backward caste Hindus in order to consolidate the latter. Advani and Singh both hoped that their consolidation bid would drown out the other's. While Advani was touring the country on his Rath, Singh was addressing rallies and educating people about the historic decision he had made by granting reservation to the OBCs.

A massive rally was organised in Patna's Gandhi Maidan on 8 October, with over two lakh people attending to hear V.P. Singh and his cabinet colleagues. A reporter wrote that the 'Sadbhavna Yatra', as it was dubbed, was anything but that. Singh was greeted with thunderous applause when he said, 'I agree I can be removed as prime minister. That my government can be removed. They can remove me from Delhi, but they cannot remove me from the doorsteps of the poor.'[33] It sounded so apt for the race that Singh was running between being pushed out of office and attempting to build a bankable cult among the backwards, as their messiah. He just hoped that the second came before the inevitable first.

At the same rally, Lalu roared, '*Chahe zameen aasman mein latak jaye, chahe aasman zameen par gir jaye, magar Mandal Commission lagoo ho ke rahega. Is par koi samjhauta nahin hoga*' (Even if heaven and earth clash, there will be no compromise on the implementation of the Mandal report). More than the spoken words, it was the mood at the rally and in Patna on that day that was unprecedented. People from backward castes had poured into Patna from all corners of the state, in spite of the 'Janata curfew', a bandh called by anti-Mandal forces. The slogans they raised reflected their newfound assertiveness: '*Brahmin saala desh chhodo*' (Brahmins, leave the country) and '*Ranganath hoshiyar, Nagnath hoshiyar*' (Ranganath beware, the cobra king is ready). The Ranganath reference was to Ranganath Misra, chief justice of the Supreme Court, who was to make a decision about the constitutional validity of the OBC reservations. While Singh and his colleagues were speaking at the Sadbhavna rally, Pappu Yadav, one of Lalu's MLAs with a long criminal record, opened fire on anti-reservationists at several places, killing a constable and a Bhumihar youth.[34]

Advani's yatra was scheduled to begin in Bihar just two weeks later, on 20 October 1990. In an unsuccessful attempt to persuade him to cancel the yatra, Lalu met Advani in Delhi. Lalu colourfully recounted his conversation with Advani in the following words:

> Lalu: '*Aap ye danga phailane wala yatra rok dijiye. Bahut parishram se humne Bihar me bhaichara kayam kiya hai. Agar aap danga yatra nikalenge to hum chhodenge nahin.*'
>
> You stop this riot-triggering yatra. It has taken us a lot of work to establish peace in Bihar. If you proceed with this riot march, we won't spare you.
>
> Advani: '*Dekhta hoon, kaun mayee ka doodh piya hai jo mera rath yatra rokega.*'
>
> Let me see, who has had his mother's milk, who has the guts to stop my Rath Yatra.
>
> Lalu: '*Maine maa aur bhains dono ka doodh piya hai. Aayiye Bihar me batata hun.*'[35]
>
> I have had the milk of my mother as well as buffaloes. I will show you when you are in Bihar.

Like his speeches, Lalu's autobiography is accentuated by rhetoric and can't be relied on for word-for-word accuracy. However, it does give an idea of how swords were drawn even before Advani arrived in Bihar with his yatra.

The second phase of Advani's yatra was scheduled to begin from Dhanbad in Bihar on 20 October 1990. He would cross through and address crowds in Ranchi, Ramgarh and Gaya before arriving in Samastipur on 23 October 1990.

S.D. Narayan, a veteran journalist who was heading the Press Trust of India's (PTI) Patna Bureau at the time, was asked to follow the Rath Yatra from Hajipur to Samastipur. He recalls the rapturous welcome that Advani received in Hajipur, but what struck him as odd was the presence of helicopters hovering in the sky. Narayan then recalls receiving a call from Lalu early in the morning on 23 October 1990:

> It was early in the morning when my telephone rang. I was surprised to find the chief minister on the other side. He was his usual chatty self. He asked me *kitna sote hain* (How do you sleep so long?) Knowing that Lalu Prasad himself was a late riser, I enquired what made him wake up so early. *Baba ko pakad liya* (we have caught Advani) was his terse response.

Lalu had directed two of his most trusted lieutenants, IAS officer R.K. Singh[36] and IPS officer Rameshwar Oraon, to execute the covert operation. Advani was arrested in the early hours of 23 October at the guest house in Samastipur. He was immediately flown to a government guest house in Massanjore, now in Jharkhand's Dumka district.

In his memoir, *Gopalganj to Raisina*, Lalu writes:

> To be honest, nobody had asked me to stop the procession or arrest Advani. The prime minister had said nothing. Mufti Mohammad Sayeed, who was the union minister for home affairs [...] said, 'Why are you taking it upon yourself?'[37]

In Uttar Pradesh, the then chief minister and, incidentally, another Yadav, Mulayam Singh Yadav, backed up his rhetoric with state force. As the rath began approaching UP, a list of RSS and BJP workers compiled by the Congress (I) during the Emergency was dug up in order to arrest them. Almost 275 arrests were made under the National Security Act. Twenty BJP MLAs, including the party's leader, Kalyan Singh, were arrested. Almost 2,00,000 people were arrested in Bihar and UP combined, far more than the 1,65,000 arrested during the Emergency and the 60,000 arrested during the Quit India Movement.[38]

However, in his letter to Lalu in 1992, Nitish Kumar reveals some different details, paving the way for his split with Lalu and Janata Dal. He writes:

> It was two–three of us who had collectively laid the outline of the programme of Advani's arrest and were awake all night to formulate a strategy to successfully execute it. However, we never tried to take credit for it. It was you [Lalu] alone who kept taking the credit for it, in rallies and through media, in Bihar and even in other states, in your typical way. You never cared to clarify that it was the result of teamwork and the credit for it goes to the entire team and not an individual.

The news of Advani's arrest quickly spread through the print media and radio broadcasts. Despite the fact that his arrest brought the Rath Yatra to an abrupt end, it sparked massive protests and communal riots across north India. The arrest further enraged the karsevaks, or volunteers, who continued to march towards Ayodhya from all over the country. The congregation of karsevaks tried to march to the site of Babri Masjid on 30 October, where the police tried to stop them and eventually opened fire. Twenty-eight karsevaks were killed in the firing. Mulayam Singh, the then chief minister of UP, justified the police action as a means of preserving the country's unity and integrity.

Advani's arrest eventually led to V.P. Singh's worst nightmare coming true. The BJP withdrew support from the National Front government, leading to its fall. Just a week before his arrest, Advani had attended a three-day party conclave in Bhopal, which was attended by over 700 of his party's MPs and MLAs.

In a scathing attack, Advani had described the nine-month rule of the V.P. Singh government as dismal. 'This government has failed on all four major issues on which it was elected—Kashmir, Punjab, Bofors and prices,' he said. However, it was Uma Bharti, the young firebrand MP from Chhatarpur, whose statement was premonitory of what lay ahead. 'The construction of the temple is so important to me that I don't care whether the government remains or goes.'[39]

Interestingly, the two clear beneficiaries of the movement were the BJP and Lalu. The BJP nearly doubled its vote share in the 1991 general elections. With his deft handling of Advani's arrest, Lalu was catapulted to the status of a messiah for the minority community. He was now at the forefront of the anti-saffron camp.

Fall of the National Front Government: Close Save for Lalu

With constant pressure from groups such as Chandra Shekhar's and Devi Lal's, V.P. Singh's race to ensure the longevity of his government hit many roadblocks. However, the last nail in its coffin came in the form of Advani's arrest in Bihar. The BJP, which had been supporting the National Front government, pulled the plug immediately after Advani's arrest.

V.P. Singh resigned on 7 November 1990, after delivering a passionate speech in Parliament, projecting himself as the crusader of secular democracy: 'What kind of country do you want? You have to decide this once and for all.' However, it was not enough to save his government, which could garner only 142 votes against the 346 MPs who voted against it.

Singh's eleven months in power were far from a golden period, despite being jam-packed with intense action on a variety of important and contentious issues like the Mandal Commission report and the Mandir Andolan. Singh went through phases in his own image before and during his prime ministerial stint. Prior to the formation of the government, he was regarded as someone who was far removed from the allure of office and power. Singh had also suggested on several occasions that he wouldn't take the prime ministerial post even if it came to him. His rejection of alluring political positions, as well as his tenacious opposition to the previous government's corruption, had earned him the reputation of a crusader. If Singh's public image had a high point, it was at the Janata Dal's meeting to elect him as the party's leader. Everything thereafter went downhill for him.

Chandra Shekhar, who had been waiting for Singh to step down as prime minister, seized the opportunity. He led a faction of Janata Dal MPs, which included the disgruntled Devi Lal, Deve Gowda, Maneka Gandhi, Om Prakash Chautala, Mulayam Singh Yadav, Yashwant Sinha and others to form a new party, the Janata Dal (Socialist). Despite having only 60 MPs, he staked claim to forming the government at the Centre with the support of Rajiv Gandhi's Congress.[40] However, his government would also last only a few months before his resignation and the calling of fresh elections.

Chandra Shekhar's government's first target was Lalu's regime in Bihar. Lalu had multiple adversaries in the new government at the Centre, including Prime Minister Chandra Shekhar and Deputy Prime Minister Devi Lal. Lalu had a sour relationship with Chandra Shekhar, whose advice he had disregarded on previous occasions, including during Chadra Shekhar's own attempt to become prime minister.

During the 1990 Haryana crisis, when Devi Lal's son Om Prakash Chautala was installed as chief minister following the worst political malpractices, Lalu, taking a tough stand, said that Chautala must go. But Devi Lal was now the deputy prime minister. His son, Chautala, was the new JD(S) secretary. It was only natural that they trained their guns at Lalu.

Lalu was already running a minority government with the loss of support from 39 BJP MLAs. With the new unfavourable political alliance in Delhi, BJP campmen, such as Raghunath Jha, Anand Mohan, Prabhunath Singh and Suryadeo Singh, began demanding Lalu's resignation. Lalu didn't waste any time in expelling ten MLAs from the party, including Raghunath Jha and Suryadeo Singh, for anti-party activities. The dissidents, backed by Congress(I) and ambiguous support from the BJP, began plotting to topple the government. However, they lacked the numbers, as was proven when Lalu called a Vidhan Sabha session to prove his majority. A parallel attempt was also made by Jagannath Mishra and Congress(I) to persuade the Centre to impose President's rule in Bihar, owing to the poor law and order situation.

On the other hand, when the issue was put to a vote on 22 November 1990, the incumbent government received 202 votes to the opposition's 108.[41] The BJP abstained from the vote. The dissidents had failed to secure the necessary support and alliances. Chandra Shekhar's hasty constitution of a committee to look into the demand for a separate state of Jharkhand failed to win over Jharkhand Mukti Morcha, which had 19 MLAs. Similarly, Raghunath Jha couldn't win over the state party chief, Ram Sunder Das, who sided with his old rival, Lalu. On the other hand, Lalu was backed strongly by the Left parties and a majority of the thirty independents in the house.

While Lalu managed to survive the assault, he was well aware that he was treading on thin ice in the face of hostile opposition and dissidents within his own party. He thus decided to undergo a massive expansion of his eleven-member cabinet by adding 58 more MLAs to his council of ministers. The government now had 69 ministers, one for every three MLAs supporting it. Everything was fair for Lalu in his love of power and war against upper-caste hegemony.

THE RUN-UP TO JUNGLE RAJ

Sadiyon ki thandhi-bujhi raakh sugbuga uthi,
Mitti sone ka taaj pahan ithalaati hai;
Do raah, samay ke rath ka gharghar-naad suno,
Singhasan khaali karo ki janata aati hai.

The cold-extinguished ashes of centuries rose flagrantly,
The soil flaunts wearing a crown of gold;
Make way, listen to the rumbling of the chariot of time,
Vacate the throne for the people are coming.

—Ramdhari Singh 'Dinkar'

FROM GLORY TO IGNOMINY

The glint of hope with Lalu's ascendancy and gradual coming to terms with reality wasn't a new phenomenon being witnessed by Biharis. They had seen too much and for far too long to be easily excited or disillusioned.

Bihar, once the cradle of culture, knowledge and excellence, has always been an enigma for historians. The impoverished state had seen flourishing cities and civilisations five centuries before the Christian era. It was once the epicentre of the Mauryan Empire, and the glorious role it played in every possible field of art and science is well documented. The state, currently divided deeply along caste lines, once played the most significant role in uniting India. The first all-India Mauryan Empire, established by Chandragupta Maurya, was headquartered in Patliputra, the present-day Patna. This established the first unified command over the land of Aryavarta and a uniformity of law and order, the defining characteristic of a nation state.

However, to summarise Bihar's role as just the administrative torchbearer of the nation would be belittling its huge contributions in the fields of education, health, spirituality, religion and science. Nalanda, believed to be the oldest university in the world, flourished along with a number of equally illustrious universities such as Vikramshila between the fifth century BC and the twelfth century AD. The great mathematician Aryabhatta, whose prowess in the diverse fields of mathematics and astronomy is still looked upon with deep reverence, chose Patna as his place of work. Faxian, the Chinese monk traveller, was deeply impressed by the tradition of free medical service for all in Patliputra in the early fifth century. In comparison, even the most developed nations today struggle to provide affordable medical care, and free medical care is still a distant dream.

Bihar also became the seat of two of the major world religions, Buddhism and Jainism. Both religions originated here and then spread to the rest of India and the world. Both religions can also be seen as the first visible strike on the vices that had crept into Hinduism, such as caste hierarchy and the exclusion of women. The Buddhist global councils, first held at Rajagriha (present-day Rajgir), just after Buddha's death, promoted the tradition of social decisions through public discourse. Religious and social matters were widely discussed before making any final decisions, with a free-flowing exchange of ideas and information. The practice can be held as one of the inspirations for 'government by discussion'. Bihar also contributed directly to the theories of governance, particularly through Kautilya's *Arthashastra*, composed in the third and second centuries BC.

Bihar's accomplishments continued through medieval history too, which gives us a glimpse into the infrastructural focus and expertise of Sher Shah Suri's administration. Suri, a sixteenth-century king, was a visionary in constructing roads, bridges and the like, and is hailed for the present-day Grand Trunk Road, cutting across a major length and breadth of the country. Suri is also credited with the introduction of a coin named 'Rupia', to which the modern rupee can be traced. He also introduced levying customs duties.

The Decline of an Erstwhile Star

There's a stark similarity between how India went on to become a Third World country from being one of the world's wealthiest nations till the eighteenth century and Bihar's fall from the seat of power and influence. Indians and Biharis can often be seen reminiscing alike about how their country and state, respectively, were once the greatest and most prosperous places on the globe. However, it is not a result of the usual romanticisation of the past that is common in human behaviour, but rather of an era that was genuinely experienced and recounted by their forefathers.

Bihar's fall from a position of prosperity can be attributed to multiple factors spread over the last two centuries. However, the three most important factors for Bihar's economic decline in the period of modern history have been listed by Arnab Mukherji and Anjan Mukherji in a 2012 paper titled 'Bihar: What Went Wrong? And What Changed?'[42]

The Permanent Settlement

Under the subjugation of British rule, different land revenue systems were implemented across different parts of the country. The three most important land revenue systems were the Permanent Settlement, the Ryotwari system and the Mahalwari system. Bihar, which was a part of the larger Bengal state at the time, came under the Permanent Settlement, brought into effect by Lord Cornwallis in 1793.

Under the policy of Permanent Settlement, tax revenues were fixed for each zamindar, and the revenue was delinked from agricultural output. This limited any incentive or efforts on the part of the government to improve agricultural productivity through investment in infrastructure or public goods. The Permanent Settlement land revenue policy was in sharp contrast to the Ryotwari system introduced by Thomas Munro in the Madras and Bombay Provinces, which determined tax revenue in relation to agricultural output. The Ryotwari system created incentives for improving the productivity of farms, and so, invariably led to better investments in public health, education and infrastructure. The long-term result of Permanent Settlement was an ailing agricultural sector and associated agrarian sectors with minimal public investment. Its impact also spilled over to the quality of public services such as health and education in Bengal, Bihar and Orissa.

The Freight Equalisation Policy

The Freight Equalisation policy was one of the first industrial policies applied immediately post Independence. It formed the bedrock of Jawaharlal Nehru's vision of heavy industry-led development of the nation. The policy was adopted in 1948 with the intention that industry could develop all over the country without undue disadvantage to areas with minimal mineral deposits. This ensured that basic raw materials like coal and iron ore were available at the same price throughout the country. Experts argue that this policy led to an erosion of what could have been a comparative advantage for Bihar in developing value-added activities and mineral-based industries. Industries such as automobiles, which require steel as a major input, based themselves in western and southern states rather than Bihar since they could purchase inputs at the same price anywhere. This had a serious long-term impact on the composition of Bihar's GDP, which remained heavily dependent on agriculture.

The Period of 1990–2005

The most recent and the larger reason for Bihar's fall from grace is what this book is about. The period from 1990 to 2005, often dubbed as 'Jungle Raj', was a controversial period in which the government de-emphasised the state's urgent development issues in order to pursue the ostensibly higher goal of social empowerment. Recruitments to public posts and development expenditure were highly curtailed in the belief that it would primarily benefit the upper castes. During these fifteen years, the state experienced an average annual growth rate of less than 1 per cent, while real per capita income nearly stagnated.[43]

Some of the other factors attributed to Bihar's backwardness are arguably a lack of focus by the central government, as also seen in the skewed allocation of revenue and resources away from states such as Bihar and Orissa. As a result, infrastructure and public goods such as health and education were underfunded.

It is ironic how Bihar, the pioneer of education, free public health and movements against caste and social inequality, is today plagued by the same problems that it once presented solutions to, for the entire country and world. While Bihar in modern history has never been a poster boy of economic or social development, it certainly wasn't as bad when it entered the twentieth century. In fact, when Bishop Hebber was sailing up the river from Kolkata in the early nineteenth century, he thought Patna was much like St Petersburg. Bihar, post its formation as a separate state from Bengal in 1912, provided outstanding leadership during the freedom struggle, in the form of Dr Rajendra Prasad, Jayaprakash Narayan and Jagjivan Ram, among others. Even after Independence they went on to play major roles: Dr Rajendra Prasad was the first president of India from 1950 to 1962, Jayaprakash Narayan was hailed as the architect of 'total revolution' and the principal leader of opposition against the Emergency in the 1970s, and Jagjivan Ram was one of the tallest Dalit leaders and deputy prime minister of India from 1977 to 1979.

From Independence until 1990, Congress dominated Bihar with the exception of brief periods under the rule of socialist parties and then the Janata Party in 1977–80. The Congress leadership, largely upper caste-dominated, enjoyed the unconditional support of upper castes, Dalits and Muslims over the years to form a deep seat of power. In 1990–91, Bihar was already lagging with a per capita income that was 49 per cent of the national per capita income. However, this fell further to 33 per cent of the national average by 2004–05.[44]

Social Churn in Twentieth-century Bihar

Bihar had always been one of those states where the privileges and social status enjoyed by the upper castes had been disproportionate to their numerical strength. Their low numerical strength had always been compensated by their ritual status, economic prowess and accumulated social prestige. Within the upper castes, the highest ritualistic status has always been enjoyed by the Brahmins. The Kayastha, with their miniscule numerical strength, historically rivalled the others in everything connected with the pen. The dominance of the Bhumihars and Rajputs can be attributed to their significant landownership, which consequently contributed to their economic prowess.[45] However, these factors are not independent of each other, and more often than not, the economic status of a particular caste is highly correlated with their ritual status in the caste hierarchy. This is evident as we move across the caste spectrum to see the low extent of land holdings among the backward and Scheduled

Castes. Low land holdings further increased their dependence on farm wages provided by the landed upper castes. However, the inequality didn't start or end with land but was further manifested in other fields. When new opportunities were created post the carving out of Bihar as a separate state from Bengal in 1912 and then after India's independence in 1947, they were mostly appropriated by the more literate and aware upper castes. This further widened the inequality.

The birth of Bihar itself was a manifestation of discontent because of the appropriation of opportunities by Bengalis in undivided Bengal. The government services, as well as professions like law and teaching, were dominated by Bengalis.[46] The Bengali domination was a major obstacle for educationally advanced castes, mainly the Kayasthas. It was frequently claimed that the Bengalis would push their relatives to various vacancies and opportunities as they arose. This particularly hurt the Kayasthas, who were especially dependent on government jobs and such professions for their economic well-being and social advancement. It is not surprising, therefore, that the movement for separation from Bengal was led by a Kayastha, Sachchidananda Sinha. The creation of Bihar thus greatly helped the aspiring sections of Bihar to wrest control of government jobs and opportunities such as contracts and favours. However, as educational opportunities grew and information asymmetry was reduced, more and more castes and social groups began competing for the limited pie. This began to create hostilities between different competing groups, which soon transferred from just jobs to other planes of the social realm.

The first caste group to seriously challenge and dent the hegemony of the Kayasthas was the numerically more significant and economically entrenched Bhumihars. This led to the Kayasthas aligning with the Rajputs to safeguard their privileged position.[47] However, they couldn't protect their turf for long as they were outnumbered by other social groups. A simple analysis of the members of the Congress Executive Committee shows that while Kayasthas occupied 54 per cent of the Congress Executive Committee seats in 1934, it was reduced to a mere 5 per cent in 1960.

The first attempts at challenging the upper caste-dominated Congress were made by an organisation called Triveni Sangh formed in the 1930s. Named after the confluence of three mighty rivers—the Ganga, Yamuna and mythical Saraswati at Allahabad (now Prayagraj)—the Triveni Sangh was a coalition of the three upper backward castes of Bihar, namely the Yadavs, Koeris and Kurmis. Though it couldn't achieve much success because of intra-group rivalry between Yadavs and Kurmis, it paved the way for political alliances and associations to serve caste group interests.

The preference of political leaders for their own caste men wasn't a new phenomenon and can be seen to be ingrained even in pre-Independence India, as illustrated by a letter sent in 1945 by a Congressman to Dr Rajendra Prasad.

> In all its forms and deeds, the Indian National Congress is essentially a national organisation. But I am pained to say that the composition of the higher ranks of the Congress in this province of Bihar is predominantly sectional. Among the Congress members of the provincial assembly, just dissolved, the Bhumihars, the Rajputs, the Kayasthas and the Harijans together comprised almost two-thirds of the actual members of the Congress MLAs. But actually speaking, it was, and it is to this day, that the ruling trio of Bhumihars, Kayasthas and Rajputs lay down the policy and fill most of the executive posts of the district and provincial committees.[48]

Alliances led to counter-alliances, and the sphere of competing groups began expanding, with more and more castes coming to the fore. Lower castes, unable to articulate their demands and rights, sided with one of the more politically aware castes. However, the leaders from these lower castes, who started as second-rung leaders in the alliance, soon emerged as leaders in their own right and charted their own independent paths. After the depressed classes and social groups began realising the importance of politics as the singular tool with which they could wrench power and prestige, the sphere of political competition kept expanding. The political scene, which was once dominated by one or two of the most powerful castes, soon saw the inclusion of a broader base of middle and submerged caste groups.

The precarious yet long-sustaining social equilibrium in Bihar, as in every other stratified society, was balanced not only by the acquiescence of marginalised groups but also by the feeling of their right to rule amongst the privileged castes. The feeling has long been manifested by the Hindu religious beliefs and philosophical doctrines of dharma and karma. The varna system justified the existence of upper castes and gave legitimacy to their superior position. The doctrine of karma instilled in the lower castes the belief that their lower status was simply a result of their actions in previous lives.

It is unnatural, though, to expect any society to remain in perpetual equilibrium and be unaffected by external influences. Even with a society deeply influenced by and conforming to the Hindu societal structure, Bihar began experiencing change with contact—first in British India and then through social reformist movements in general. The subsequent changes in society, such as industrialisation and urbanisation, enhanced connectivity, information flow, technological advancement and increased educational facilities, increased the avenues of social mobility. An important factor was the introduction and subsequent strengthening of democratic institutions in independent India. So was the introduction of the Universal Adult Franchise[49] in 1950 and its subsequent adoption by the remotest of villages. These factors, combined with conscious state efforts, made the first strike at challenging the established caste structure.

Abolition of the Zamindari System

Bihar became the first state in independent India to abolish the zamindari system in 1950. The urgency of such reforms can be understood from the fact that in 1953–54, according to the National Sample Survey (NSS), the top 10 per cent of households owned over 52 per cent of the land. In contrast, the bottom 40 per cent owned merely 1.25 per cent of land. Of course, the top 10 per cent of households were mostly upper caste or, in some cases, Muslims.

The passage of the bill, however, was far from harmonious. Congress chief minister Shri Krishna Singh and revenue minister K.B. Sahay had to face stiff opposition from feudal and land-owning upper caste groups. The land-owning castes of Rajputs and Bhumihars accused Sahay, a Kayastha, of caste bias. The Raja of Ramgarh, Kamakhya Narain Singh, an influential landlord from South Bihar, even threatened to launch a secessionist movement if zamindari was abolished. Some landlords also formed private senas to oppose the abolition movement.

Zamindari abolition was soon followed by the passing of the Land Ceiling Act in 1956, which established a land holding ceiling of 30 acres for plain areas and 50 acres for hilly areas.[50] However, influential landholders found ingenious ways to retain large portions of their land. The most common of these was to hold benami land (properties held through proxies, or even in the name of non-existent persons), besides transforming lands into ponds, gardens and cold storages or opening libraries and temples on such land. To prevent such transfer of surplus lands, the state enacted the Ceiling on Landholding (Amendment) Act in 1972. However, the total amount of surplus land acquired was much smaller in comparison to the potential for acquisition. When this land was distributed among lakhs of landless families, the resulting landholdings were so small that they were economically unviable. Doubts were also raised on the quality of land distributed in these initiatives.[51]

While these reforms couldn't be taken to their conclusive end, legislations like zamindari abolition and movements like the Bhoodan Movement led to some chinks in the upper-caste grip over land.

Power Shift

Bihar, rarely politically complacent, was among the eight states where Congress first failed to get a majority in the 1967 elections. The political instability that followed led to Bihar witnessing ten changes in chief ministership during the next five years, including a brief period of President's Rule.

The state saw its first OBC chief minister in 1968; Satish Prasad Sinha came to power, albeit for a brief tenure of five days. He was succeeded by B.P. Mandal but only for a slightly longer tenure of thirty days. Mandal would go on to serve as the chairman of the Second Backward Classes Commission—popularly known as the Mandal Commission. While Sinha belonged to the Koeri caste, Mandal belonged to the Yadav caste, both from the trio of upper OBC castes of Kurmi–Koeris–Yadavs. This marked the first step of OBC assertion in Bihar politics, even if for a brief period.

B.P. Mandal was succeeded by Bhola Paswan Shastri in March 1968, as the first Scheduled Caste chief minister of Bihar. By now, however, political instability had crept deep into Bihar, and it would continue till 1990 when Lalu came into power. Bhola Paswan could serve as the chief minister for only a hundred days in his first stint. By the way, the first non-Congress government in 1967 also had Karpoori Thakur as the deputy chief minister. Thakur belonged to the Nai community, a Scheduled Caste whose traditional occupation had been barbering. Thakur would later go on to serve as the chief minister of Bihar thrice, including in the Janata Party government in 1977. He would be hailed as the messiah of the downtrodden for having implemented reservations for backward classes in government jobs in 1978.

While these political offices held great symbolism, the actual transformation on the ground came about as a result of growing awareness among the lower castes of the disadvantages they faced, accompanied by a simmering discontent. They began to see caste structures as the handiwork of the privileged sections of society rather than be resigned to fate. The seemingly trivial yet hugely significant initial signs of reawakening appeared with the adoption of new names by lower castes, other than those generally given to them by privileged others. The new names were also coupled with changes in behaviour and the adoption of cultural rituals generally practised by the upper castes.[52] The legitimacy of the traditional system of social stratification was now under attack.

The dissatisfaction with the established social order led the lower castes to organise themselves and seek redressal of their grievances. The first definitive outcome of these associations was the dismantling of differences between castes and subcastes which were accorded similar status in the social order. The constitutional grouping of OBCs and SCs gave this grouping phenomenon both structure and psychological legitimacy.

This consciousness and organisation were also influenced and shaped by the two major movements of the time: communism and socialism. An uprising took place in Naxalbari in West Bengal in 1967 of landless labourers against the landlords. Known as Naxalism, the ideology soon spread to other parts of West Bengal and Bihar, too. Simultaneously, socialists such as Ram Manohar Lohia, Jayaprakash Narayan and Vinoba Bhave continued to work at the grassroots to empower marginalised communities and encourage them to demand their fair share. Lohia's slogan of '*Pichde paayen sau me saath*' (Backwards should get 60 out of 100), highlighting that representation should be proportionate to the population of communities, found quick resonance with the numerically significant backwards.

The changes driven by newly formed caste associations functioned initially in the realm of social change. However, it subsequently also led to the foundation of a strong political identity for these groups. When the drive for recognition and aspirational fulfilment of these groups was resented and, in many cases, resisted by the hegemonic castes, it also created feelings of antagonism between caste groups. The desire of the lower castes for social advancement, however, was limited by the scarcity of opportunities in Bihar and hence found its escape in the political space. Political space as a tool for allocating power and prestige had become the vehicle of individuals and social groups to achieve their social as well as political aspirations.

However, political rivalry between the upper castes still remained the main driving force behind Bihar's politics. The upper castes remained serious contenders for political power, each in their own right. As a result, the upper castes continued to receive the lion's share of political rewards and privileges.

TOTAL REVOLUTION

If the Quit India Movement characterised India's most significant political event in the pre-Independence era, it would be Jayaprakash Narayan's call for a 'Total Revolution' that takes the limelight in the post-Independence era.

The 1970s marked one of the most politically turbulent periods in India, particularly for Bihar, which experienced significant instability. The decade began with the 1971 India–Pakistan war resulting in the formation of Bangladesh. A severe drought in 1972 lead to a sharp increase in food prices. The middle years from 1975 to 1977 were marred by the Emergency, leading to the first-ever non-Congress government at the Centre, which came to a disappointing end in 1980.

However, the Emergency was not an isolated event in itself; two major protests or movements leading to the Emergency can be associated with the states of Gujarat and Bihar. The two movements, known respectively as Navnirman Andolan and the Bihar Movement, commonly had students at their forefront. The Navnirman Andolan started in December 1973 as a small protest by students at L.D. College of Engineering in Ahmedabad against a 20 per cent hike in hostel food fees.[53] Soon, however, students from other universities joined in. So did middle-class people, factory workers and even professionals like lawyers, against a pervasive economic crisis and corruption in public life. The movement finally led to Gujarat's chief minister, Chimanbhai Patel's resignation on 9 February 1974.[54] It became the first and only protest in Independent India to force an elected government to resign. Meanwhile, as Gujarat's protest was gathering heat, a similar movement led by students in started in Bihar.

The Bihar Movement

Bihar was already reeling under the effects of poor economy, practically non-existent law and order and deeply entrenched class struggles. It had essentially become a den of corrupt officials, criminal-turned-politicians and landlord-cum-moneylenders. According to the 1971 census, four-fifths of the total working force was deployed in the agricultural sector, owing to severely low productivity. Between 1964–65 and 1969–70, the agricultural production in Bihar declined by 1.8 per cent per annum, compared to the 1.4 per cent increase nationally.[55] The declining agricultural production combined with a stagnant industry in the Chhotanagpur belt and intensified exploitation and oppression of the rural poor had led Bihar to a precarious political situation.

A rebellion was imminent in Bihar. The students in Patna became the torchbearers of the imminent political movement. The Bihar movement was notably led by a unified front of ideologically variant student outfits such as the Akhil Bharatiya Vidyarthi Parishad affiliated with the Jan Sangh, the Samajwadi Yuvjan Sabha connected with the Samajwadi party, and the Communist Party of India's (CPI) All India Students Federation. The Bihar Movement marked its beginning with the formation of the Bihar Chhatra Sangharsh Samiti at a convention organised by students of Patna University on

18 February 1974. Lalu Prasad Yadav was chosen as the president of the body to spearhead the agitation. Standing alongside Lalu were student leaders who would go on to play significant roles in Bihar's political landscape, such as Sushil Kumar Modi, Ramvilas Paswan and Basistha Narayan Singh. Nitish Kumar would be recalled as somebody who was a part of the movement but not as significant then as he would be later, starting in the late 1980s.

The student agitations had fireballed into massive demonstrations across the state in March and April 1974. Blockades of roads, strikes and damage to public property were becoming a common feature. The protesting students had called for a gherao of the Bihar Legislative Assembly on 18 March 1974. Some agitators set fire to the house of former education minister Ramanand Singh during the frenzy that followed. The Bihar government, led by the then Congress chief minister Abdul Ghafoor, came down heavily on the protesters. Deaths were reported in a police firing during the 'Paralyse the Government' protest in Gaya.

With the student agitation gathering momentum, JP was approached and requested to lead the movement. Popularly known as JP, Jayaprakash was a freedom fighter born on the banks of the Ghaghra river in the village of Sitabdiara in 1902. Interestingly, Sitabdiara is a large village spread across two states and three districts—Saran and Bhojpur in Bihar and Ballia in Uttar Pradesh. He studied in various universities in the United States and, influenced by the Russian Revolution, returned to India as a Marxist in 1929. He joined the Congress at the request of Jawaharlal Nehru and was mentored by Mahatma Gandhi. Eventually, he formed the Congress Socialist Party, a Left-wing offshoot of Congress, and played an important role in the Quit India Movement.

JP subsequently founded the Praja Socialist Party and went on to fight the 1952 general elections against the Congress. However, Nehru, who greatly admired JP, made several requests for him to join his cabinet. JP turned them down and, soon after becoming dissatisfied with party politics, announced in 1954 that he would devote his life exclusively to the Bhoodan Movement. This movement started by Vinoba Bhave urged bigger landlords to donate land to be distributed among the landless.

JP had almost receded into oblivion by 1974. He was also withdrawing himself from an active role in the Bhoodan Movement. JP, however, agreed to lead the student movement, though he put some conditions on the form and rules; for instance, he stipulated that only non-violent methods would be used in the movement. The movement would subsequently turn into the biggest anti-corruption movement in the history of India. JP's call for Sampoorna Kranti or Total Revolution, at Patna's historic Gandhi Maidan would go on to symbolise the struggle against Indira Gandhi's Emergency imposition.

JP attacked the government for failing to live up to people's expectations and questioned its moral right to continue in office. He urged the incumbent chief minister, Abdul Ghafoor, to resign. Ghafoor refused to resign from his post and almost sarcastically reverted to JP's call, 'After consulting my conscience as advised by JP, I have decided not to quit at this critical juncture as that would be an act of cowardice.'[56]

Mrs Gandhi viewed JP's movement as aimed personally at her. She criticised JP, calling it unfortunate that some people, including social workers, had lost interest in rural upliftment and were now trying to plunge themselves into active politics. She once remarked, 'Does he want to be a saint or a martyr? Why does he refuse to accept that he has never ceased to be a politician and desires to be prime minister?' JP retorted that she was living in a 'fool's paradise'. Notably, JP had close family ties with Nehru, (whom he used to call 'bhai') which also extended to his fondness for Indira Gandhi, whom he would often refer to as 'Dear Indu' in his letters to her. Interestingly, the salutation would change to 'Dear Prime Minister' after JP was interned by Mrs Indira Gandhi during the Emergency.

JP led a silent procession in Patna on 8 April 1974 in which over ten thousand protestors participated with their lips sealed with pieces of saffron cloth and handkerchiefs and their hands tied behind their back. Many carried black badges on their arms and some carried placards.

Firing the Prime Minister for a Traffic Ticket

Amidst all of this, an old legal case that had been lingering for a long time came to decisively define the most important phase of Indira Gandhi's as well as India's future. Indira Gandhi had defeated Raj Narain by over 1.11 lakh votes during the parliamentary elections of 1971. Raj Narain had contested the result and lodged cases of electoral malpractice and use of state machinery for electioneering against Indira Gandhi in the Allahabad High Court. Gandhi was represented by Nanabhoy 'Nani' Palkhivala, while Shanti Bhushan fought the case for Raj Narain. It became a high-profile case with the prime minister being called for cross-examination in the court for the first time in independent India.

The final verdict came on 12 June 1975, with Justice Jagmohanlal Sinha of the Allahabad High Court finding Mrs Gandhi guilty of electoral malpractices and declaring her election from Rae Bareilly null and void. A stunned Mrs Gandhi was present in person in the court. The court gave Congress twenty days to replace Mrs Gandhi in her official posts and also debarred her from contesting elections for six years. Ironically, the court acquitted Mrs Gandhi of serious charges such as bribing voters and election malpractices but found her guilty of charges such as using state police to build a dias and using electricity from the state electricity department. *The Times of India* described the verdict as 'firing the Prime Minister for a traffic ticket'.[57]

Mrs Gandhi challenged the verdict in the Supreme Court, which granted a conditional stay on 24 June 1975. On the evening of 25 June 1975, JP, Morarji Desai, Nanaji Deshmukh, Raj Narain, Madan Lal Khurana and several other political stalwarts addressed a mammoth crowd at Ramlila Maidan in Delhi, calling on Indira to resign. JP roared the words from famous Hindi poet Ramdhari Singh Dinkar in front of a lakh-strong crowd: '*Singhasan Khaali Karo Ki Janata Aaati Hai* (Vacate the throne, for the people are coming).' He also controversially exhorted the police to reject the orders of the government if they were immoral or unethical.

Mrs Gandhi, also sensing the precarious political situation, quickly moved a proclamation of Emergency through a compliant president in the form of Fakhruddin Ali Ahmed. P.N. Dhar, secretary to the prime minister, would later recall the incident in his book *Indira Gandhi, The Emergency and Indian Democracy*:

> On June 24, the Supreme Court gave its conditional stay order on her appeal. That night, at 11 p.m., I was called by the prime minister to her house. The atmosphere in the house was tense. [S.S.] Ray[58] and [D.K.] Barooah[59,60] were there. Ray looked grim, while Barooah wore a huge grin and was trying to look relaxed as usual. Mrs Gandhi told me tersely: 'The situation in the country is very bad. We have decided to declare an internal emergency. There is going to be a cabinet meeting early in the morning tomorrow, after which I am going to broadcast the

decision on AIR.' Having said this, she handed me the draft of the proposed speech.

JP and others who had gathered at the house of one of his aides to formulate plans to force Mrs Gandhi to resign had no inkling of what was going on just a few kilometres away. Subramaniam Swamy, who was at the gathering, wondered if Indira could declare martial law. Both JP and Morarji Desai, however, shrugged off the possibility, saying that Nehru's daughter would never think of doing such a thing.[61]

JP's door was knocked on at 2 a.m. the same night. He surrendered at the Parliament Street police station, making a much-reported comment: '*Vinaash kaale, vipreet buddhi.*' Chandra Shekhar, a future prime minister, too, was arrested from Rivoli Theatre in Connaught Place, where he was watching a late-night movie with B.P. Koirala, Nepal's former prime minister. George Fernandes, who was in Gopalpur, a small fishing village by the sea in Odisha, escaped in the nick of time, clad in his lungi, before police could arrive.

The proposal for a declaration of Emergency under Article 352, citing 'internal disturbance', was moved without any discussion in the Union Cabinet, only to be ratified the next morning on 26 June. None of the cabinet ministers, including the stalwart Dalit leader from Bihar, Babu Jagjivan Ram, and Y.B. Chavan or Home Minister K. Brahmananda Reddy, voiced any objections. The Maintenance of Internal Security Act (MISA) had already been used in the early hours of 26 June to arrest over a hundred people, including JP and Chandra Shekhar, who were opposed to Mrs Gandhi. Others included Morarji Desai, Raj Narain, Atal Bihari Vajpayee and Lal Krishna Advani. The electricity supply to all major newspapers was cut off within the next few hours. Organisations such as Rashtriya

Swayamsevak Sangh and Jamaat-e-Islami, as well as some political parties, were banned.

The government devised a twenty-point economic programme to be run during the Emergency. Mrs Gandhi's eldest son, Sanjay Gandhi, declared his own five-point programme, which included the infamous family planning campaign. Sanjay Gandhi launched a compulsory sterilisation programme in the September of 1976 to limit population growth. This led to 8.3 million sterilisations in 1976–77; most of them forced.[62] Sanjay's enthusiastic spree of urban renewal also led to large-scale demolitions of slums in Delhi, displacing almost 700,000 people.[63] Besides the several changes in law, made mostly through ordinances, the 42nd Constitutional Amendment brought extensive changes to the letter and spirit of the Constitution.

Emergency and the Rise of New Leaders

The proclamation of Emergency allowed Mrs Gandhi to 'rule by decree'. It meant suspension of elections, curbing of civil liberties and a virtual free hand for Indira Gandi and her elder son, Sanjay Gandhi, who had virtually become the No. 2 in the Congress party.

An ailing JP was interned at the Postgraduate Institute of Medical Education and Research (PGIMER), Chandigarh, where he underwent treatment in custody. He continued writing letters to Mrs Gandhi and other Congress leaders like Giani Zail Singh, the then chief minister of Punjab, and Sheikh Abdullah, the then chief minister of Jammu & Kashmir, who were known to be close to Mrs Gandhi but disagreed with the Emergency. Because of his failing health, JP would later be shifted to Jaslok Hospital in Mumbai.

Vajpayee was arrested in Delhi on the night of 26 June and flown to Bangalore Central Jail. Other Jan Sangh leaders such as L.K. Advani and Madhu Dandvate were lodged in the same jail.

The JP Movement was deeply rooted in Bihar and gave Bihar its second generation of politicians. Most of the senior political leaders of the Hindi heartland today flaunt some connection with the JP Movement. This is true for leaders across party lines and ideologies.

George Fernandes was one such leader who became a romantic symbol of resistance against the Emergency. Originally hailing from Karnataka and with no prior connection to Bihar until the Emergency, he would go on to become an integral part of the state's politics for the rest of his life. His picture in handcuffs, raising his hand in defiance, became one of the most enduring images of the era. Fernandes's past was as colourful.

Fernandes spent his childhood in Mangalore before being sent to a seminary at the age of sixteen to be trained as a Catholic priest. He left the seminary two years later for Bombay, disillusioned by what he considered to be the hypocrisy of the church. It was in Bombay that he spent nights on the benches at Chowpatty and became a rebel and an activist, fighting for the rights of the unheard. Influenced by socialist leader Ram Manohar Lohia, Fernandes became actively involved with the Socialist Party and the trade union movement.

By the 1950s, Fernandes had already become the undisputed leader of the taxi drivers' union in Bombay. Often bringing the bustling Bombay to halt with his calls for bandhs, Fernandes would be jailed several times for his activism. His soaring popularity became obvious when he trounced veteran Congress leader S.K. Patil in the 1967 general elections to the South Bombay parliamentary constituency. He earned the nickname 'George the Giant Killer'.

While JP was leading the protests in Patna, Fernandes called for a nationwide railway strike on 8 May 1974, for workers' salaries and other grievances. Fernandes had taken over as the chairman of the All India Railwaymen's Federation just six months ago. The strike was soon joined by electricity department workers, taxi drivers and other transport workers. The railways, as well as other modes of transport, came to a screeching halt. The government retorted ruthlessly, and the strike was soon broken, but still, a statement had been made.

When he was visiting his in-laws in Orissa, Fernandes heard of the Emergency on the radio. He quickly slipped away to escape arrest and kept moving around the country in disguise and mobilising popular support for the movement. To oppose the fascist government in power, Fernandes advocated acts of defiance, which may even be violent but shouldn't result in casualties. His slogan, '*Jab tak bhookha insaan rahega, tab tak dharti par toofan rahega* (As long as people are hungry, there will be turmoil on Earth)' reflected his concern for the marginalised.

Fernandes was apprehended on 10 June 1976 in Calcutta, where he had taken refuge in a church, following a tip from an anonymous source. However, leading up to his arrest, two of Fernandes's closest associates, Snehlata Reddy, a reputed actor in theatre and films, and Lawrence, his brother, had to face the police's cruelty. Snehlata was detained under MISA and met with inhuman treatment before being released on medical grounds. She died soon after of a massive heart attack. Lawrence too was tortured in police custody and needed both mental and physical rehabilitation upon release.

In what came to be known as the Baroda dynamite case, Fernandes was charged by the Central Bureau of Investigation (CBI) with smuggling dynamite to blow up railway tracks, bridges and other government establishments. Fernandes prepared his own arguments for the trial and declared once, with his chained hands raised in the air: 'The chains that we bear are symbols of the entire nation which has been chained and fettered.' He ended his plea to the judge with the words, 'Sir, I am proud, very proud indeed, that when Mrs Gandhi became a dictator, my comrades and I behaved like men.'[64]

The Emergency was called off and elections were announced while Fernandes was still in jail. Though Fernandes was sceptical of the fairness of elections, he was fielded in absentia from the Muzaffarpur constituency in Bihar on JP's insistence. Fernandes swept the polls with his supporters campaigning with his photograph.

Fernandes still, however, carried the pain of the losses from the Emergency.

'How can I ever forget or forgive JP's kidneys, the torture of my brother Lawrence, the death of Snehlata?'[65] he said when Morarji Desai talked about the need to forget and forgive post-Emergency.

When Fernandes was assuming the chairmanship of the railway workers' union, Lalu, in Patna, assumed the mantle of general secretary of the Patna University Students Union. When the students' protest broke out in Patna, Lalu was at the forefront of it. He had already become a crowd-puller through his witty oratory and buffoonery. His street-smart ways had brought him close to JP, too. His detractors, however, maintain that JP was aware of Lalu's passing on of information to the Congress camp, and so, he never included him in the core group meetings.

Lalu, by the end of the Emergency, had stood out as one of the most visible outputs of the movement—somebody who was active in student politics before the movement but was catapulted onto the national political scene by the movement. Lalu was fielded from Chhapra, in Bihar, in the parliamentary elections post-Emergency. He swept the polls at the mere age of twenty-nine.

Another leader from Bihar to be interned during the Emergency was Sushil Kumar Modi, who later went on to become the deputy chief minister of Bihar. In his book *Beech Samar Me*, Modi recalls the nineteen months of his internment as a nightmare. He recalls, 'I was handcuffed and my waist tied with a rope by policemen while being taken to a jail in Samastipur district where I was kept among criminals and insane prisoners.' He goes on to describe how he had to miss his sister's wedding even after he was released on parole. This happened when, after being released on parole, he went to meet the then Hazaribagh deputy commissioner to apprise him of the difficulties he faced in the jail. The deputy commissioner, a haughty young man, when approached by Modi, started beating and abusing him before interning him in another made-up case.[66]

Sharad Yadav, who won the 1974 parliamentary by-election from Jabalpur at the peak of the JP Movement, was arrested and jailed for nineteen months in various jails in Madhya Pradesh. Yadav would keep shifting his political constituencies in Madhya Pradesh and Uttar Pradesh before settling in Bihar politics in the early 1990s.

Another socialist and a Dalit leader whose prominence in Bihar's politics was cemented in the 1977 parliamentary elections was Ram Vilas Paswan. In political circles, he had already earned a name for himself after defeating a prominent Congress leader to win the Alauli assembly seat in the 1969 state elections. Paswan was greatly influenced by JP and became an integral part of the Bihar Movement and later the JP Movement. Paswan spent almost the entire Emergency period in various jails of Bihar. When he was released, JP wanted him to contest from the Hajipur parliamentary constituency. However, some confusion led to the Janata Party declaring Ram Sundar Das as their candidate from Hajipur. When JP came to know of it, it enraged him. He immediately called his personal secretary, Ibrahim, and asked him to get 10,000 posters printed with his personal appeal and signature on them. The poster:

> *Hajipur me Janata Party ka umeedwaar kaun hai, main nahi jaanta; par JP ka umeedwaar Ram Vilas Paswan hai* (I don't know who the Janata Party candidate from Hajipur is. JP's candidate is Ram Vilas Paswan).

The people of Hajipur were surprised to see these posters on the boundary walls, shutters of shops and electricity poles the next morning. When the Janata Party leaders came to know of this, they realised the seriousness of the issue and the disastrous implications for the Janata Party candidate from Hajipur. It was quickly decided to allot the party symbol to Ram Vilas Paswan and withdraw Das's candidature. When the results of the elections were announced, Paswan had won from Hajipur with a margin of over 4,46,000 votes, a world record entered into the *Guiness Book of World Records*. JP's personal appeal had accentuated what may have been one amongst several Janata Party victories of 1977.

Janata Rule: Hope and Despair

On 18 January 1977, Indira Gandhi called for fresh elections to be held in March. The darkest phase of India's democracy was seemingly coming to an end.

The opposition parties across the spectrum formed a united front, the Janata Party, to fight the Congress. This included the Bharatiya Jana Sangh (BJS), Charan Singh's Bharatiya Lok Dal, Raj Narain and George Fernandes's Socialist Party of India and

Congress (O).[67] The overarching appeal of JP—who was seen as the ideological leader of the anti-Emergency movement and was now the mentor of the united opposition—had helped unite the various parties with diverse and often conflicting ideologies. The Janata Party swept the elections, winning 298 of the 542 seats. The Congress was reduced to its lowest ever tally of 153 seats, 92 of which came from the four southern states. It couldn't win a single seat in the two largest states of Bihar and Uttar Pradesh. Indira Gandhi as well as Sanjay Gandhi lost their seats. The results were a verdict against the authoritarian high-handedness of Indira Gandhi. It had restored the common man's faith in Indian democracy.

Morarji Desai was sworn in as the prime minister of the new government. The government had JP's blessings and carried the hopes of crores of Indians to usher India out of the dark memories of the Emergency.

Among others, one of the first things Morarji Desai did upon assuming charge was to dismiss the state governments in the ten Congress-ruled states. It was argued that the ruling party had been rejected by the voters and must seek a new mandate. Fresh elections were held in these states. The Janata Party assumed power in seven, including Bihar. Karpoori Thakur, a socialist and a leader from the backward community, was made the chief minister. One of the most contentious decisions of Thakur was the implementation of the Mungeri Lal Commission report. It recommended reservations for backward castes in government jobs. This immediately rocked the state, with caste violence spreading across all the important towns and universities of the state. Thakur eventually had to pay the price for the radical move when he lost his chief ministership in April 1979. Ram Sundar Das, a Dalit leader, replaced him as the new chief minister. Though both Thakur and Das were socialists, Das was considered to be more moderate and accommodating by a large number of upper-caste MLAs.

At the Centre, the political and ideological divisions among various Janata Party constituents had started surfacing. The first and most important of them was the issue of dual membership of Jana Sangh members. Members of the erstwhile Bharatiya Jana Sangh, such as Vajpayee and Advani, were asked to choose between remaining in the government and being members of the RSS. Vajpayee and Advani chose to remain members of the RSS and resigned from their ministries. By 1979, Morarji Desai was also taking the heat from his own party as well as the other eclectic Janata Party constituents for worsening economic conditions, as well as allegations of corruption and nepotism involving Desai's own family members. Charan Singh, the Lok Dal leader, already had an acrimonious relationship with Desai ever since he was trounced by Desai in the race to become prime minister. The government fell after Charan Singh, as well as some other socialist factions, withdrew their support. Desai resigned on 19 July 1979.

Charan Singh was sworn in as the new prime minister on 28 July 1979. The government was supported from the outside by Indira Gandhi's Congress (I), the sworn enemy of the Janata Party. The government lived lesser than even the most pessimistic predictions. Charan Singh resigned after just three weeks in office.

The Janata Party was a hasty amalgamation of various political groups with the sole aim of defeating the Emergency regime of Mrs Gandhi and restoring democratic rights. It had a unique agenda that, once achieved, could not contain the antagonisms and conflicting ambitions of various constituent political groups.

The experience of Indians with the first non-Congress government in the country was far from satisfactory. People became increasingly disillusioned with the constant in-fighting within the government, its inept handling of the economy, ineffectiveness to take Emergency atrocities to conclusion, charges of corruption and finally its short-lived tenure which resulted in another midterm elections.

THE DEMISE OF THE CONGRESS

The fall of the Janata Party government at the Centre and the public's disillusionment with the Janata rule of 1977–80 set the stage for the revival of Congress party. The Congress campaigned in the 1980 midterm elections shouting the slogan, 'Elect a government that works', to capitalise on the frustration towards an unstable government at the Centre. Indira Gandhi apologised for the mistakes made during the Emergency. She was also able to garner support from respected leaders such as Vinoba Bhave. The Congress (I) won 353 out of the 542 seats in the 1980 general elections and came back into power.

Indira Gandhi did a *la-Morarji* by dismissing nine state governments in February 1980. Ram Sundar Das's government in Bihar was dismissed, too, despite the fact that he comfortably enjoyed a majority support in the assembly. Elections were held and the Congress was back in power. Jagannath Mishra was sworn in as the new chief minister of Bihar.

Setting the Stage for a Non-Congress Government in Bihar

The post-Independence political history of Bihar can be segmented into three phases. The first phase (1947–67) was marked by the complete dominance of the Congress party, with upper castes at the helm of affairs. The second phase (1967–90) can be designated as a transition period with a gradual decline in the influence of both the Congress and the upper castes and a gradual rise in power of the middle castes—Yadavs, Koeries and Kurmis. The third phase (post-1990) became an upturned version of the first phase with the marginalisation of the Congress party as well as upper castes in state politics.[68]

The Congress in the 1950s, with its dominant role in the freedom struggle, became a natural choice for voters in Bihar, as in other states of independent India. The Left parties, with support in pockets such as Begusarai, Muzaffarpur, Sitamarhi and Gaya, couldn't consolidate their mass base further. The Congress was virtually without a competitor. The absence of an organised opposition, the towering leadership of its chief minister, Shri Krishna Singh, and a low voter turnout had helped Congress monopolise the political space until 1962. It had formidable support from the coalition of the landed upper castes, SCs and Muslims. The party itself was dominated strongly by upper castes, namely Brahmins, Bhumihars, Rajputs and Kayasthas, and thus was their natural choice of support. The SCs owed their loyalty to the Congress because of its long history of fighting for the abolition of untouchability and fighting for their dignity under Mahatma Gandhi. Even constitutional provisions such as reservations in education and employment were seen by Dalits as Congress' gifts to them, and they rallied behind the party. The Muslim support for the Congress was largely in the absence of any other alternative. The Muslims carried the burden of proving their loyalty post-Independence, and, despite the fact that they weren't represented well in the Congress party or in the ministries, they had no choice but to go with the Congress.

Although based on the strong support of the upper castes during this honeymoon period, the Congress also took a reformist approach by abolishing the zamindari system and implementing land reforms. The upper OBC castes—Yadavs, Koeris and Kurmis—were mostly the tenants of these upper castes and stood to gain the most out of the zamindari abolition. These castes tried to carve their way into the Congress' power pie but couldn't get any significant hold through most of the 1950s and 1960s. The upper-caste-heavy Congress', dislike for these upper OBC castes was no secret.[69] Efforts such as the formation of Triveni Sangh—an alliance of Yadavs, Kurmis and Koeris, as well as backward caste mobilisations by Lohiaites in the 1960s—had some effect, but didn't really prove to be a major challenge to the Congress hegemony. It was only in 1970 that Daroga Prasad Rai, a Yadav, was made the Congress' first backward chief minister in the state. This sent feelers to the upper OBCs that the Congress was now willing to share power with them. However, his removal through a plot by the upper-caste Congress leaders did permanent damage to the OBCs' support for the Congress.

During the 1970s, the OBCs kept oscillating between different parties and mostly dispersed with their political choice hinging on individual candidates. The 1970s also saw the rise of Jagdeo Prasad, a charismatic Kurmi leader popularly known as the 'Lenin of Bihar'. He was brutally killed by the police while leading a peaceful protest of 20,000 people during the Bihar Movement in 1974. Fingers were pointed at a Bhumihar minister in the Congress government. Jagdeo Prasad's murder further alienated the OBCs from the Congress.

Owing to the growing disillusionment and the Sampoorna Kranti movement led by Jayaprakash Narayan, the Congress was dislodged in Bihar during the 1977 elections. The Janata Party won decisively, and Karpoori Thakur, a backward caste candidate from Samastipur, became the chief minister.

However, the disillusionment caused by the Janata Party and its shoddy coalition management led people to bring back the Congress at the Centre and in most states by 1980. The decade of the 1980s was ruled by the Congress, both at the Centre and in Bihar. Indira Gandhi came back to power at the Centre, riding on the failure of the Janata Party to provide a viable political alternative. The 1980 assembly elections brought back the Congress in power and Jagannath Mishra as the returning chief minister. He had earlier been the chief minister during the Emergency period between 1975 and 1977. Affectionately called 'Doctor Saheb', Mishra became one of the most powerful leaders in the Bihar Congress after his brother, L.N. Mishra, the Minister of Railways in the Indira Gandhi government, died in a bomb explosion at Samastipur Railway Station in 1975.

A populist leader with a huge mass appeal, Jagannath Mishra had earned popularity among the teachers, when during his first stint, his government took over hundreds of private primary, middle and high schools across the state. However, he also took flak for the controversial 'Bihar Press Bill' that he introduced in 1982. The bill was intended to significantly censor the press. Having learnt from their experiences during the Emergency, the press retorted with a shutdown of most of India's ten thousand newspapers in protest. Mishra finally had to withdraw the bill. In an interview later in his life, Mishra would confess that he had brought the bill to keep the then prime minister, Indira Gandhi, in good humour.

Another significant bill, which earned him the name 'Maulana' Jagannath, was making Urdu the second official language of Bihar, right after he became the chief minister in 1980.

Falling Out of Favour

In 1983, Jagannath Mishra had to pave the way for someone handpicked by Indira Gandhi: Chandra Shekhar Singh—different from Chandra Shekhar, the future prime minister. This was after Mishra publicly criticised the Centre for its stance of low royalty on minerals mined from the state and the inadequate role of financial institutions in the state's development. Despite the continued rule of the Congress, he didn't return as the state's chief minister until the fag end of the decade.

After Indira's death in 1984, Chandra Shekhar Singh was picked up by Rajiv Gandhi as the petroleum minister in his cabinet. This vacated the position of chief minister in Bihar and paved the way for Bindeshwari Dubey to become the next chief minister. Dubey was a freedom fighter and closely associated with the trade union movement. However, his three-year tenure as chief minister from 1985 to 1988 remained highly controversial and marred by rising lawlessness and corruption.

Dubey's tenure wasn't just marked by administrative and external challenges but also by rebellion within the party. The multiple power centres made a concerted effort to dislodge him from the chief ministerial position. These efforts were primarily led by Jagannath Mishra. The battleground was Dhanbad, the coal capital of India, and the hold on the trade union there. Dubey had antagonised the Rajput mafia leaders of Dhanbad ever since the 1985 assembly elections by denying some of them tickets. He had also launched an offensive to break their stronghold on government contracts in the region. The mafia retaliated in unison, with the active support of Jagannath Mishra. The two warring groups tried to wrench control of the Rashtriya Colliery Mazdoor Sangh (RCMS), one of the largest trade unions in Dhanbad. Dubey had been the president of an

Indian National Trade Union Congress (INTUC)-affiliated union in the past. Dubey initiated the much publicised 'Mafia Trial' in 1987 to tackle the mafia in the coal belt. A court was specially constituted for the purpose, and five public prosecutors were appointed for it. The 'Mafia Trial' was to hear forty-two cases involving the most infamous dons of Dhanbad: Suryadev Singh, Raghunath Singh, Shakaldev Singh and Satyadev Singh. Amongst these, Suryadev Singh, a Janata Party MLA and known as the 'Don of Dons' was the uncrowned mafia king of Dhanbad with over twenty cases pending against him. His terror spread far and wide, and his house, 'Singh Mansion', was a court of sorts for resolving all kinds of issues.

It was alleged, however, that the trial was farcical and was initiated by Dubey merely to target his rivals. However, the one blunder Dubey committed in his fight was not finishing the mafia completely.[70]

His first major setback came when the then deputy commissioner of Dhanbad failed to arrest Suryadev Singh. In a comical move, Singh admitted himself to hospital at the last moment, feigning a heart attack. The combative mafia soon came back to haunt Dubey, and he had to sack his excise minister, Indernath Bhagat, after Bhagat opposed the auction system for liquor shops and sanctioned raids on some shops. Amidst all this, Jagdish Narain Pandey, a trade union leader close to Dubey, was murdered.

The criminals during Dubey's tenure seemed to have a field day. Crimes were pervasive and the police and administration were conspicuous by their absence. Corruption had seeped into every possible corner of government offices. Mass killings and police firings on innocent people made Dubey's tenure utterly controversial too.

The Tumultuous Years

In the midst of his tenure in 1988, Dubey had to soon make way for Bhagwat Jha Azad. Azad, the father of cricketer-turned-politician Kirti Azad, was a freedom fighter and a lifelong Congressman. He tried to take on the mafia groups from the beginning, but soon got pulled into the quagmire of the nexus of crime and politics. Azad could barely survive a year of chief ministership.

This paved the way for Satyendra Narayan Sinha, another freedom fighter and JP's companion during the Emergency. S.N. Sinha was the son of nationalist leader Anugrah Narayan Sinha, who was also a participant in Gandhi's Champaran satyagraha. He was fondly known as 'Chote Saheb' and wielded considerable clout in Bihar politics. However, Sinha could hardly change the existing anarchy in Bihar. During his rule, the state was rocked by the murder of Triloki Harijan, a Congress MLA. Triloki was murdered on 6 July 1989 in his village of Bahuarwa in west Champaran while the assembly was in session. He was murdered by the infamous gang of dacoits, Pathal Noniya, and his body was thrown into a canal near his village. It was later learnt that Triloki had made repeated requests for protection from the DGP to the district authorities but didn't receive one. Another former MLA from Dhanha in west Champaran was incidentally kidnapped on the same day on which Triloki was murdered, albeit by another gang. However, Sinha's ultimate nemesis came in the form of the Bhagalpur riots.

Bhagalpur Riots

Bhagalpur lies on the eastern periphery of Bihar, on the banks of the Ganges. The district's claim to fame is its handloom industry, which traditionally employed a large population of Muslims. On 24 October 1989, a religious procession of Hindus called 'Ramshila' was passing through Tatarpur, a Muslim-dominated area. The Ramshila procession was aimed at collecting *shilas*, or bricks, for the proposed Ram temple in Ayodhya. Processions from various parts of the district were to congregate at the Gaushala area, from where they would proceed to Ayodhya.

Tensions were already running high because of some slogans raised in the procession, such as '*Hindi, Hindu, Hindustan, Mullah bhago Pakistan*' (India is for Hindus, Mullahs go away to Pakistan) and '*Babur ki auladon, bhago Pakistan ya Kabristan*' (Children of Babur, run away to Pakistan or to the graveyard). On 24 October, the district magistrate of Bhagalpur, Arun Jha, was escorting the procession through sensitive areas. When he reached Tatarpur, the Muslims refused to let the procession pass and suggested that it take an alternative route. While Jha was still talking to the Muslims from Tatarpur, some miscreants threw crude bombs at the procession from a nearby Muslim high school building.[71] No one was killed, but eleven policemen suffered injuries. When the police opened fire to disperse the crowd in Tatarpur, some Muslims hurled bombs at the officials, including at the district magistrate (DM) and superintendent of police (SP). Two people were killed in the retaliatory police firing.

Bhagalpur had already been sitting on a precarious balance. All the elements required to fuel a riot—communal rivalries, criminal rivalries and political rivalries—were present there.[72] The incident in Tatarpur triggered riots in Bhagalpur, which were unprecedented in scale and gruesomeness since Partition.

While a curfew was imposed immediately in the afternoon of 24 October, the Hindu procession that had retreated from Tatarpur had turned into a mob. The mob went on a rampage, attacking and looting shops owned by Muslims, destroying their property and turning to a locality called Parbatti, where at least forty Muslims were massacred.

The riots assumed greater proportions over the next few days, with massacres in several Muslim localities and villages, the destruction of several mosques as also the handlooms and powerlooms owned by the Muslims. The worst massacres took place in the villages of Chanderi and Logain in Bhagalpur.

In Chanderi, Yadavs from neighbouring settlements, who were already disapproving of the construction of a mosque in the village, attacked the Muslims on the evening of 27 October. This area, including Chanderi, was being watched by a Jammu and Kashmir Light Infantry regiment led by Major G.P.S Virk during the riot period. When Major Virk reached the village, he found it deserted; around 125 Muslims were hiding in a large house belonging to one Sheikh Minnat. He deployed some policemen at Minnat's house and promised to be back by morning to evacuate the Muslims to a place of safety.

However, when he returned the next morning, he found the house vacant. Around sixty-one mutilated bodies were recovered from a nearby pond. The house was attacked in the early hours by attackers who pretended to have come to evacuate the Muslims. When the Muslims came out, they were attacked; some were killed on the spot; others were taken to the nearby pond, where they were chopped off.

At Logain, 116 Muslims were killed by a mob led by a police officer, Ramchander Singh. The bodies were buried in fields, and cauliflower was grown over the mass grave to hide the evidence. Ramchander Singh, along with thirteen others, would be convicted and sentenced to rigorous imprisonment seventeen years later, in 2007.

The Indian Army was called in on 26 October and Bhagalpur Superintendent of Police K.S. Dwivedi was ordered a transfer on the same day by Chief Minister Satyendra Narayan Sinha. Dwivedi was deemed incapable of containing the riots and was also held responsible for police atrocities, further fueling the violence. However, Rajiv Gandhi, during a tour of the riot-affected areas, overruled the transfer of Dwivedi at the request of policemen and Hindu groups.

The riot affected Bhagalpur town and almost 250 villages around it. According to official figures, 1,070 people were killed, and around 48,000 were displaced. The destruction of 600 powerlooms and 1,700 handlooms dealt a huge blow to the flourishing weaving industry.

In the aftermath of the riots, Chief Minister Satyendra Narayan Sinha, who had come under fire from the Muslims as well as his colleagues for his handling of the riots, stepped down. In a bid to pacify the Muslims, who had been the Congress' vote bank for long, Jagannath Mishra was brought back as Bihar's chief minister. Mishra had struck a chord with the Muslims during his second term as chief minister in 1980, when he made Urdu one of the official languages of the state.

However, far from being pacified, the Muslims accused the Congress government of failing in not just stopping the riots but also in providing adequate relief or rehabilitation. The Muslims, who had traditionally been Congress voters, would soon shift their loyalty to a new social coalition formed by Lalu and stick to it for a long time.

Rajiv Gandhi: Quick Rise, Quicker Fall

The Congress, led by Rajiv Gandhi, had won a full majority in the 1984 general elections, riding on a sympathy wave after

Indira Gandhi's assassination. However, Rajiv Gandhi's term was marked by major controversies and scandals such as the Bofors scandal, the strengthening of the Khalistan movement in Punjab and India's controversial role in the civil war between the Liberation Tigers of Tamil Eelam (LTTE) and the Sri Lankan government.

One of the harshest critics of Rajiv Gandhi's government was Vishwanath Pratap Singh. Born as the third child of a Rajput zamindar family in Allahabad, Singh was adopted by Raja Gopal Singh of Manda and became the heir-apparent. He became the Raja of Manda in 1941, at the age of ten. V.P. Singh started his political career in the Uttar Pradesh Legislative Assembly after winning the Soraon constituency on a Congress ticket in 1969.

He was elected to the Lok Sabha in 1971 and served as the minister of commerce in Indira Gandhi's government from 1976 to 1977. After the Janata Party's interlude at the Centre, when Indira Gandhi came back to power, V.P. Singh was appointed as the chief minister of Uttar Pradesh in 1980. He earned much praise for tackling the growing menace of dacoity, especially in areas of Uttar Pradesh adjoining Chambal. With a long and illustrious political career, V.P. Singh was called to serve as the finance minister in Rajiv Gandhi's government in 1984. However, V.P. Singh treaded dangerous waters by getting raids conducted on famous and powerful names such as Dhirubhai Ambani and Amitabh Bachchan. Rajiv Gandhi was forced to move him from the finance ministry to defence.[73]

Once he moved to South Block, V.P. Singh started getting into the details of murky defence deals, including the purchase of 410 field howitzers from the Swedish arms manufacturer, Bofors. The Bofors contract raised a huge furore and allegations were made that Rajiv Gandhi's friends and associates had received kickbacks in the deal.[74] While no evidence of Rajiv Gandhi's personal gains came to light, opinion polls showed that the public at large believed Rajiv Gandhi was guilty.[75] Word had also spread that V.P. Singh possessed certain classified information that could embarrass the prime minister.[76] He was removed from the defence ministry at this point. In response, he resigned from the Lok Sabha and Congress membership, projecting himself as an anti-corruption crusader.

V.P. Singh soon launched a political frontier named Jan Morcha to fight corruption with others who disagreed with Rajiv Gandhi's ways, particularly Arun Nehru and Arif Mohammad Khan. Rajiv Gandhi had reshuffled his cabinet more than a dozen times since taking over in 1984. Amidst talks of scandal, several of his close advisors had either quit or were forced to. However, Rajiv Gandhi made all efforts, including putting out a statement in Parliament, to quell the rumours that he had a secret Swiss bank account. He said in Parliament in July 1987, 'I categorically declare, in this highest forum of India's democracy, that neither I, nor any member of my family, has received any consideration in these transactions.'[77]

M.J. Akbar, then the editor of *The Telegraph*, wrote about Rajiv Gandhi:

> It has nothing to do with what he is. Rather, it is the peculiar history that made him Prime Minister. People don't relate to him. They like him, they want to believe him, but there is a subconscious uneasiness about his identity. He can overcome this, but it may take a long time.

On 11 October 1988, on the birthday of Socialist leader Jayaprakash Narayan, V.P. Singh launched the Janata Dal through the merger of Jan Morcha with other parties—Janata Party, Lok Dal and Congress (S)—as a coalition of parties opposed to the Rajiv Gandhi government. However, V.P. Singh knew that if he was to put up a formidable fight against Rajiv Gandhi in the 1989 elections, he would need the support of other parties. He thus reached out to regional parties such as Dravida Munnetra Kazhagam (DMK), the Telugu Desam Party (TDP) and Asom Gana Parishad (AGP) to form the National Front, as an alternative to the Congress. V.P. Singh was declared the convenor of the National Front and N.T. Rama Rao as the president.

Rajiv Gandhi, who was on the backfoot due to corruption scandals and a deteriorating economy, also made some campaign blunders. He started his 1989 campaign from Ayodhya, promising 'Ram Rajya' in a bid to appease the Hindus. However, in the process, he lost the trust of the Muslims.

The National Front fought the 1989 Parliamentary elections after forging an electoral understanding with the Left parties and the BJP to help unify the anti-Congress vote. This could be termed as V.P. Singh's greatest political achievement. He successfully forged coalitions at multiple levels, even with those he wasn't aligned with ideologically. The three levels of coalition to form the Janata Dal first, National Front next and then an electoral understanding with ideological opposites—the BJP and the Left—speaks volumes of it. His discomfort with the BJP was clearly reflected in the fact that in some places where he would campaign with the BJP, V.P. Singh and the BJP leaders were seen addressing the public from two different stages.[78] Singh made corruption and Bofors a poll plank and promised an independent investigation into the Bofors deal if elected.

When the results of the elections were declared, the National Front formed a government at the Centre, after earning a simple majority along with its allies. The Congress party, which emerged as party the single largest party with 197 seats, shrank to less than half its previous poll tally of 404 seats in 1984. The BJP, which jumped to 85 seats, riding on the Ram Mandir issue, and the Left decided to support the government from the outside.

The Congress fared badly in Bihar too. It was reduced to a mere four seats out of fifty-four. Two members of Parliament from Bihar were sworn in as cabinet ministers in V.P. Singh's government. George Fernandes, contesting from Muzaffarpur, became the railway minister while Ram Vilas Paswan from Hajipur was made the cabinet minister for labour and employment. Sharad Yadav, the MP from Badaun who would later choose Bihar as his political arena, became the minister of textiles. The other significant wins were those of Lalu from Chhapra and Nitish from Barh.

However, V.P. Singh served as the prime minister for less than a year. The coalition he was leading had nothing other than anti-Congress sentiment uniting them. The Centrist government depended on the support of the ideologically right BJP as well as the Left parties. Besides, V.P. Singh had many rivals within his own party, the Janata Dal, which he had helped form.

However, the period he served defined India's socio-political space for decades to come. Besides taking controversial decisions such as posthumously awarding the Bharat Ratna to Dr B.R. Ambedkar, two other significant events stood out during his prime ministership. The first was the implementation of the Mandal Commission report and second, the Ram temple issue. The latter eventually led to the fall of his government.

Change of Guard in Bihar

From 1980 to 1990, the Congress ruled Bihar continuously, albeit with five changes in the chief ministership. The ten-year period was a lull phase for non-Congress leaders. The opposition largely revolved around Karpoori Thakur, the respected Lohiaite leader. Hence, when Thakur died in February 1988, it created a huge vacuum. This would be filled by Lalu in the years to come. Sankarshan Thakur, writing about this equation, says:[79]

> Thakur had a huge following among the backward and Dalit communities of the state. While Lalu would later go on to far outstrip Thakur's popularity and appeal, it was Thakur who took Lalu under his tutelage during the years. Thakur was instrumental in getting Lalu a Lok Sabha ticket in 1977, in the post emergency elections as also a Lok Dal ticket for Bihar Assembly thereafter.
>
> Thakur died in February 1988, leaving a huge vacuum in the opposition ranks. He was the leader of opposition in Vidhan Sabha which suddenly lay vacant. Lalu used this opportunity craftily to lay claim as Thakur's successor and the leader of opposition in Vidhan Sabha. While publicly Lalu would hail him and seek the blessings of the departed soul to follow in his footsteps, Lalu didn't have a high opinion of Thakur. In fact, in private conversations, Lalu would refer to him as 'Kapti (Cunning) Thakur'. For all initial worship of Thakur, Lalu let the promise of a Thakur memorial languish. It became more and more clearer later that Lalu didn't want himself to be overshadowed by Thakur's image and would rather let his name vanish from people's memories. Lalu wanted to go down in history as Bihar's tallest leader, the true leader of the backwards and Dalits.

The elections to the Bihar Assembly were conducted in February 1990. With the 1990 elections throwing up a hung assembly, Bihar was headed for another shaky government. The Janata Dal emerged as the single largest party with 120 seats in the 323-seat assembly. The biggest loser turned out to be the Congress (I), which could garner just 70 seats.

As it became clearer that the Janata Dal would be forming the next government in Bihar with the help of the Left and other parties, the race for chief ministership started. The three main contenders for the post were Lalu, backed by central leaders such as Devi Lal and Sharad Yadav; Raghunath Jha, a favourite of Chandra Shekhar's; and Ram Sundar Das, the most probable candidate backed by the central high command, including V.P. Singh and also acceptable to the Left parties and Jharkhand Mukti Morcha, the allies.

The central Janata Dal leaders, including the then railway minister George Fernandes, Uttar Pradesh's chief minister Mulayam Singh Yadav, and Ajit Singh, tried to resolve the leadership issue initially through discussions. However, when the attempts failed, the leadership question was put to a vote. Nitish Kumar was instrumental in enlisting support for Lalu in his bid for the chief ministership, and mobilised MLAs from backward castes in Lalu's favour. Lalu comfortably outmanoeuvred Das and Jha, owing to his role in distributing tickets earlier to many Janata Dal victor MLAs. Interestingly, 33 of the elected 120 Janata Dal MLAs belonged to the Yadav caste.

The 1990 assembly also saw a large number of criminal elements entering the Vidhan Sabha. A large number of them were from the Janata Dal. Lalu had backed them saying, nobody is a criminal until convicted.

The defeat of the Congress in 1990 marked the end of an era in Bihar's politics, which can be best described as 'feudal democracy'.[80] The Congress had failed to deliver on the promises of poverty alleviation, land reforms, ending discrimination and providing dignity for Dalits and OBC. Moreover, the Bhagalpur riots made it lose its ever-loyal Muslim vote bank too.

THE SOCIO-POLITICAL UPHEAVAL

'The only way to deal with an unfree world is to become so absolutely free that your very existence is an act of rebellion.'

—Albert Camus

BHURABAL SAAF KARO

Lalu took oath as the chief minister of Bihar on 10 March 1990. The rise of Lalu was one of the most significant turns in the socio-political landscape of Bihar since JP's Total Revolution. However, it wasn't a singular event that changed Bihar in one go. Changes had been occurring throughout the 1970s and 1980s in various parts of Bihar, led by local leaders, the mafia, social movements and a changing demography in general.

The social structure in Bihar can be outlined by categorising castes and communities into three broad social groups. The first group consists of the so-called twice-born upper castes, namely the Brahmins, Bhumihars, Rajputs and Kayasthas. Their higher caste status is also correlated with their class privileges as being landed and economically better off. Their numerical strength, however, is barely 15 per cent of the total population.

The second group consists of the backward castes, which can be further subdivided into the Other Backward Castes (OBCs) and Extremely Backward Castes (EBCs). The former consists of 30 of the relatively better-off backward castes and comprises almost 27 per cent of Bihar's population. The group includes the politically dominant Yadavs, Koeris and Kurmis. The Yadavs derive their economic strength from dairy activities and agriculture, while the Kurmis and Koeris are considered expert agriculturists and also take up a major portion of the tenancy work in Bihar. The EBCs, more numerous in strength, consist of around 112 castes and constitute almost 36 per cent of Bihar's population.[81]

The third and most marginalised social group consists of the lower castes or the Dalits, such as Paswan or Dusadh, Bhuiyan, Dom, Ghasi, Halalkhor, Kanjar, Musahar, Rajwar and Turi.

These caste groups can also be fitted neatly with the class structures in Bihar, with the upper castes forming the landed and relatively more prosperous segments of the population. The OBCs fit between the upper castes and Dalits in terms of their wealth and landholding. The Dalits with no social status are generally bereft of any land or material wealth.

In what may be called hidden apartheid, almost every other village in Bihar remains segregated by caste. The segregation in these villages itself gives away the stark nature of discrimination in the state—the Dalit tolas are invariably on the outskirts of the villages, with a clear demarcation between them and the main settlement. These tolas are often named after the caste groups residing there, such as Bhuntoli for the Bhuiyas, Musahartoli for the Musahars and Dusadhtoli for the Dusadhs.

While untouchability is punishable by law, it remains ubiquitous in Bihar. Sadly, it is present not just in rural areas or the hinterlands but right in the heart of Bihar's biggest cities, including Patna. In villages, untouchables cannot cross the Laxman Rekha—forbidden line—dividing their settlements from those of the upper castes. They cannot visit the same temples, use the same wells or sit on the same chabutra (platform for social congregation). Children from Dalit communities are often made to sit separately in or at the back of the classrooms.

Dalits are also relegated to the most degrading of tasks such as manual scavenging, removal of dead animals and human waste, leather work and sweeper work. Women from these castes face the triple burden of caste, class and gender. They often have to face sexual abuse and violence at the hands of the landed class and sometimes the police too, often in a bid to teach them a 'lesson'.

The Social Assertion

One of the first major decisions that Lalu took after coming to power was to implement the Mandal Commission report. To make sure that the rules of reservation were not transgressed, the government made violation of caste-based employment quotas a punishable offence.[82] The government opted to keep positions vacant if qualified backward-caste candidates were not available, rather than filling them up with upper-caste candidates. Such a style of governance has been termed the 'politics of state incapacity' by Mathew and Moore.[83]

This was also in sync with the call of *Bhurabal Saaf Karo*, meaning eliminate Bhurabal—an acronym for the four upper castes, viz. Bhumihar–Rajput–Brahmin–Lala (Kayastha). The origin of the contentious phrase has often been attributed to Lalu.

However, the 'policy of state incapacity' wasn't universal and had caste-based exceptions. The case of cooperatives in Bihar clearly demonstrates this approach. Lalu's government set about systematically dismantling the cooperatives, which were largely dominated by the upper castes. The cooperative statutes and elections were first suspended, and these organisations were put under the control of select public servants. The state, however, turned out to be truly determined and supportive when it came to benefiting the core voting constituents of Lalu, such as the highly significant dairy cooperative sector. In contrast to the stories of other cooperatives, the Bihar State Cooperative Milk Producers Federation (Comfed), whose members were mostly cow herders and dairy farmers, was a clear success.[84] It wasn't a mere coincidence that most of the members, because of their traditional occupation, belonged to one caste: the Yadavs. The membership of the cooperative grew from 66,000 households in 1987–88 to 213,000 households in 2002–03.[85]

Similarly, the state's intent and capacity were visibly demonstrated in the protection of Muslims, which constituted a solid vote bank for Lalu. In his memoir, *Gopalganj to Raisina*, Lalu recounts how he travelled to and dissipated communal tensions in Sitamarhi during the Durga Puja of 1992. Clashes had erupted between two communities on the issue of the immersion of the idol of Durga. Lalu recalls that he stood in a moving vehicle, holding the megaphone and announcing that a curfew had been imposed.

The electoral indispensability of the Muslims, besides the higher moral ground of constitutional protection for minorities, made Lalu passionately look to prevent any Hindu–Muslim riots.[86] However, Lalu did provide a sense of security and protection to the Muslims, which won him their unfettered support over the next fifteen years of his rule and even beyond.

Lalu had also challenged a long-standing style of governance and bureaucracy that was inherently elitist. For generations, access to the hallowed doors of politicians and bureaucrats was granted exclusively to those in power. The others, the commoners, the poor and the Dalits, were asked to come through the 'proper channel', a term which essentially meant that the doors were closed to them. This proper channel thus prevented any access to the system by those from outside the elitist circle and also protected the insiders with a veil of secrecy.

If the British-era bureaucracy showed inefficiencies in other parts of the country, in Bihar it had come to occupy the role of nothing less than kingship. A district magistrate would be colloquially referred to as the king of his district, and he could do whatever he pleased.

However, it was usual for Lalu to humiliate bureaucrats in public, punish them with frequent and arbitrary transfers and postings, and often overrule their decisions. Power suddenly seemed to have shifted from the immaculately dressed, elite bureaucrats to rustic, kurta-clad politicians. Access, which was based on class, seemed to have shifted towards caste. A Yadav now, young or old, rich or poor, would get a seat in police stations and the offices of the tehsildar and circle officers. So was the case with hitherto other marginalised castes.

The reduced dependence on and open disrespect for bureaucracy wasn't without design or cause. While the composition of the Bihar Legislative Assembly tilted favourably towards the OBCs and lower castes during the 1990s, the bureaucracy remained dominated by the upper caste, and there was no way Lalu or his coterie could change its composition. There was always a simmering tension between this group of upper caste-dominated bureaucrats and Lalu's government, the origins of which are difficult to specify but easy to conjecture.

In his memoir, Lalu writes:[87]

> Even the bureaucracy didn't support my efforts. In the initial phase of my chief ministership, barring a few officers, most of the bureaucrats felt uncomfortable with my ideas. I didn't have enough IAS officers who were committed to the rights of the marginalised and those of the economically and socially backward. [...] The conditions worsened after some newspapers alleged that I was promoting officers from my caste in the bureaucracy. This was completely baseless.

However, the bureaucrats have a different story to tell. Lalu would mistreat even the most senior officials publicly and deride their entire clan. He would call the chief secretary of the state as

Bada Babu—a term generally used for the Station House Officer (SHO) of a police station, often a daroga; similarly, the Director General of Police (DGP) was called Munshi Ji—the clerical employee at a police station. Officers would often complain that they were pressured into employing unjustified and often illegal means, and the ones not compliant would be punished through transfers, punishment and harassment. Such was the discontent that a total of 144 out of 384 IAS officers posted in Bihar in 1991–92 requested a central deputation.

S.K. Sinha, held the portfolio of managing director of Bihar Tourism Development Corporation in 1994 when he was ordered by the Patna High Court to award the Rajgir Ropeway Project to a company acquired by the Bihar government. The tourism minister, who wasn't happy with the court's decision, asked Sinha to dilly-dally on the issue and not comply with the court's order. Sinha expressed an inability to comply with the minister's direction. Sinha was first transferred to a position that was lower than his rank and one that lacked even an office or provisions for salaries in the budget. To top it off, he was made to report to an officer junior to him. When this transfer was challenged and termed unjustified by the Tribunal, Sinha was transferred to a position that had ceased to exist. When this was again quashed by the Tribunal, the state government appealed against the Tribunal's order in the Supreme Court. The Supreme Court upheld the Tribunal's decision, but Sinha was neither reinstated in his previous position nor was his salary released, which had been held back since 1992. Even his medical support and insurance were stopped. Even repeated Tribunal warnings couldn't move the state government into compliance. A frustrated Sinha wrote to the central government for a transfer to any other state than Bihar. This, however, is not an isolated story but the story of every upright or uncompromising officer in Bihar in the 1990s.

The bureaucrats and officers were also targeted and discriminated against for being from particular castes. This is also evident in the way postings and transfers were made from the beginning of Lalu's rule. The result invariably was a deep mistrust between the two most important cogs of administration—the legislature and the executive. However, even with his inclination for posting conformists in all important positions, Lalu couldn't find enough IAS officers from the SC, ST, OBC or Muslim backgrounds to be posted as district collectors in all of Bihar's districts. The state secretariat, too, was filled with bureaucrats from the upper caste. In 2002, almost 60 per cent (133 out of 224) of the IAS officers in the state belonged to the four upper castes—Brahmin, Bhumihar, Rajput and Kayastha. Only seven officers belonged to the upper OBC castes—Kurmi, Koeri and Yadav—and only four of them were Yadavs. Interestingly, all four had entered the IAS through promotion from the state administrative services.[88]

A picture that would often appear in newspapers would have Lalu sitting on his lawn with his feet on a centre table with bureaucrats lined up in front of him. This was a powerful symbol with class as well as caste connotations. His voters loved such images, and Lalu knew that well.

This, in turn, made the bureaucracy withdrawn, ineffective and vulnerable to the demands of their political masters. One section of bureaucrats, ready to toe the line, bent itself to Lalu's whims in a bid to reap the benefits of new spoils. The compliant ones were often given extensions of tenure, keeping all rules at bay. The deputy director of the Ranchi Animal Husbandry department, Shyam Bihari Sinha, was given an extension despite the fact that Income Tax officials had recently raided his house and found property far beyond his sources of income. Sinha would later go on to be known as the kingpin of the multi-crore fodder scam. Similarly, an officer of the fisheries department, Prem Shankar Prasad, was thrice given extensions to secure his position. A Ranchi-based executive engineer of the Bhavan Nirman department, Naval Kishore, was charged multiple times with the misuse of government treasury. He was soon given an extension of office because of his deep contacts in the government. This pushed an ex-MP of the Janata Dal from the Kosi belt, Taslimuddin, to comment that Lalu Prasad needs 'corrupt officers' to carry out illicit activities with their help.

The state of the education department was as deplorable. The Patna University and Bihar University Amendment Bills were passed in August 1993, which reserved 50 per cent of the senate and syndicate seats in these universities for the OBCs.[89] This was a visible strike on the most entrenched power seat of the upper castes—higher education. Most of the new appointees for vice chancellorship and directorship of educational institutions now came from OBCs. This deeply impacted the character and nature of these educational institutions, which were monopolised by the upper castes until then.

It had also become common practice for college lecturers, professors and school teachers to get salaries after several months of delay. By 1997, the universities in Bihar were in deep financial distress. The teachers had already been drawing only two-thirds of their salary, with even their Provident Fund contributions in danger. The government owed crores of money to the universities. The Magadh University alone was reported to be owed Rs 111 crore.[90]

Lalu's Electoral Charisma

The Janata Dal's victory in the 1990 Bihar Assembly elections could hardly be attributed to Lalu. It was the party's win, driven largely by a strong anti-incumbency against the Congress both at the Centre and in the state. Lalu surely outmanoeuvred the other contenders to win the chief minister's position. However, the 1991 Parliamentary elections would give Lalu a chance to prove his mettle.

An ebullient Lalu declared at the start of the campaign that no other party except the National Front–Left alliance would win a single seat. In the year since Lalu had taken over, he had been able to establish himself as a champion of the backwards and Muslims during the Mandal protests and Ram Mandir movement, respectively. The electoral genius of Lalu started to become evident during the campaign.

He would declare in his quintessential Bihari Hindi while flying in the state helicopter: 'See, this *udan khatola* [flying machine] was purchased by Jagannath Mishra, but I am the one flying in it.' On being probed on how he could use a state helicopter for electioneering, he would let his disdain be known, 'Why shouldn't I campaign in a state helicopter? Isn't Mulayam using one? Rajiv has three. Chandra Shekhar has his *jet-va* [jet]. *Hum chief minister hain, paidal chalenge kya?* [I'm the chief minister, will I walk?]

Therein lay Lalu's secret to being the hero of the marginalised. He would project himself as anti-establishment and an underdog even while holding the chief minister's position. Lalu stated unapologetically that he once was as vulnerable as they were and still was, but he had taken it upon himself to fight the oppressors. He would quickly switch his tone to display his bravado, 'Congress (I) says suspend Lalu's government. *Hum koi daroga hain* [Am I a sub-inspector] who you can suspend at will? *Karke dekhiye.* [Try doing it.]'

It worked. When the results were announced, the Janata Dal coalition won all but five seats, which went to the BJP. Accusations were made of large-scale booth capturing and rigging of elections. It, however, didn't disturb Lalu. He was basking in the glory of his spectacular win. This time, he deservedly took the credit too.

Ek Dhakka Aur Do

Lalu had successfully stopped Advani's Rath Yatra in 1990, which had earned him accolades both within Bihar and across the nation as secularism's new poster boy. But little did he know that his efforts to reign in Advani and the Ram Mandir movement would be short-lived.

It would be just over two years later that the karsevaks would reach Ayodhya for their annual karseva and return, not empty-handed but with the debris of the fallen Babri Masjid. Around 150,000 karsevaks of the VHP and the BJP had congregated in Ayodhya on the eve of 6 December 1992. The VHP and BJP had given assurances that no harm would be done to the disputed structure of Babri Masjid and that it would be a ceremonial karseva.

L.K. Advani, Murli Manohar Joshi, Uma Bharti and others reached around 10 a.m. on the day to address the crowds and perform karseva. However, within minutes of the leaders reaching the dias, the restless crowds started pushing the police cordons placed around the disputed structure. Slogans such as '*Mandir yahin banayenge*' (The temple will be constructed here) started gaining voice amidst the crowds. The Uttar Pradesh police and Central Reserve Police Force (CRPF) personnel on guard around the mosque could hold off the crowds somehow only till noon, when a young boy managed to sneak past the cordon and reach the top of one of the three domes, waving a saffron flag. The crowds saw this as a signal to march to the structure, and so they did. The police personnel, who were vastly outnumbered, gave in after a strong pushback from the mob. Most of them chose to flee the scene or act as bystanders. The mob attacked the structure with hammers, axes and whatever else they could lay their hands on, bringing the entire mosque down before the sun set on the day.

The demolition was followed by large-scale riots across the country. Mobs of Hindus and Muslims attacked each other, burning and looting homes, shops and places of worship. Over 2,000 people were killed in the ensuing riots.[91] The worst hit was Mumbai, which recorded around 900 deaths in communal clashes over the next two months.[92] Several BJP leaders were arrested, and a ban was put on the RSS and VHP, though only for a brief period.

During this tumultuous period, however, one state that surprisingly or by careful design remained unhurt was Bihar. With the scars of the Bhagalpur riots barely forgotten, Bihar seemed to be a potential hotbed for communal clashes following the Babri demolition.

However, Lalu, with his strict warnings to the DMs and SPs across the state, made sure that there was no laxity wherever any chances of communal flare-ups arose. He would gloat while explaining how his district officials had arrested returning karsevaks before they could reach their towns and villages. Lalu, being the shrewd politician that he was, didn't let this feather in his cap go unnoticed. In a National Front–Left rally at Patna's Gandhi Maidan, barely two months after the Babri demolition, Lalu thundered amidst an eclectic starcast of Chandra

Shekhar, Jyoti Basu, CPI(M)'s Harkishan Singh Surjeet, Mufti Mohammed Sayeed, George Fernandes, Sharad Yadav and Ram Vilas Paswan. The last three, though local political rivals to Lalu, couldn't help but heap praise on him.

Lalu's heightened status was clearly evident from the life-size cut-outs on the eve of the rally in Patna, which depicted him as Krishnavatar—reincarnation of Lord Krishna—with Janata Dal's symbol, the wheel, as his Sudarshan Chakra. Lalu couldn't help congratulating himself, 'Bihar may be a zero in every field, but it has emerged as a national hero in the field of communal harmony.' He didn't stop before berating the BJP and its leaders for insincerity in their religious pursuits in his usual rustic tone: '*Man na rangaye, rangaye jogi kapda; dadhia badha ke ban gaile bakra*' (Since their hearts can't match Ram's colour, the jogis have coloured their clothes; by growing beards they have become fools).

Lalu, who till recently was running a shaky government with all-round rebellion within his party as well as its allies, was suddenly looking forward to marching to Delhi. The charges of administrative failure and economic mismanagement were now forgotten or had taken a backseat in the new social equations. The Babri debacle also helped him cement his carefully crafted Muslim–backward-caste coalition, that was developing chinks.

While Lalu did everything possible to avert religious divisions from endangering his social coalition, he systematically alienated the upper castes. Lalu drew up a plan to appoint Harijans and Adivasis as priests in temples. He declared that this was going to break the Brahmanical hold over society. In addition, Lalu and his supporters also let the word go round that the pages of Manusmriti and other scriptures, in which they were treated as untouchables, would be publicly burnt by Harijans and Adivasis.

The former Bihar chief minister, Jagannath Mishra, said, 'Lalu has converted communalism into casteism. In the name of his Sadbhavna campaign, he is nakedly destroying social harmony by inciting caste passions just to remain in power.'[93] It didn't seem too far from reality.

The Dissent

While Lalu kept rising in stature and popularity, both within the party and among the people of Bihar, not everyone was happy with the way Bihar was being governed. Lalu's political career was intertwined with several other young leaders who had risen through the JP Movement. Some of these leaders, such as Nitish Kumar, Ram Vilas Paswan and Sharad Yadav, were also instrumental in Lalu's ascendancy to Bihar's top post.

Each of these leaders would later go on to play a significant role in the politics of Bihar as well as national politics. However, the one who would turn out to be the most significant by the turn of the century would be Nitish Kumar. His political career began alongside Lalu Yadav and Ram Vilas Paswan's with the JP Movement, but not with the same bang.

An engineering graduate from the Bihar College of Engineering, he joined the Bihar State Electricity Board, but soon moved to politics. In the 1977 general elections, Lalu, Paswan and a host of other leaders from the JP Movement won in the anti-Congress wave. Several other leaders won in the soon-to-follow state assembly elections. However, Nitish Kumar lost both the 1977 parliamentary as well as the 1980 assembly elections.

Nitish Kumar would later say this in an interview:

> I took an engineering degree and joined the State Electricity Board, but almost half-heartedly. My first day in the office

was my last. Political life has always interested me. I am not in politics by fluke.[94]

Nitish Kumar tasted his first electoral success in the assembly elections in 1985, even in a strong Congress wave riding upon Indira Gandhi's assassination. He went on to win the parliamentary election in Barh in 1989, later becoming a minister in the short-lived V.P. Singh government. Nitish Kumar played a pivotal role in getting Lalu the chief minister's chair.

However, he was soon disillusioned with Lalu's antics and his flippant approach. Nitish and Lalu had risen together through university and Lohiaite politics. However, Nitish found Lalu moving away from the socialist ideals they had vowed to follow.

Nitish Kumar had a belief that Mandal implementation would truly empower the backward sections of Bihar. However, he also realised that most of the benefits of reservation would flow to the existing dominant constituent of the OBC segment in Bihar. At a memorial function on Karpoori Thakur's anniversary, Nitish cautioned Lalu against ignoring the Bihar-specific recommendations that the late Thakur had proposed in the Mandal formula.

However, Lalu's social coalition was perfectly cast by then. The Yadavs and Muslims combined accounted for around 30 per cent of the electorate. Along with a few OBCs in the fold, he had an unchallenged forte. Whenever Nitish Kumar would try to reason with Lalu and remind him of their promises to the electorate, Lalu would quip, '*Tum humko raaj-paat sikhaoge? Governance se power milta hai ka? Power milta hai vote bank se, power milta hai people se, kya governance rat-te rahte ho*'. (You will teach me how to rule? You think governance brings one to power? Power is derived from the vote bank, the people. Why do you keep harping on governance?)[95]

However, it was an ugly spat at Bihar Bhawan in Delhi in 1992 that led Nitish to take the final call to part ways with Lalu. The details of the incident have been chronicled by Sankarshan Thakur, a senior journalist and the author of biographies of both Lalu Prasad Yadav and Nitish Kumar.

In the late months of 1992, Nitish went to see Lalu with a few other Janata Dal leaders with a list of things to discuss. The leaders included Shivanand Tiwari, Brishen Patel, Lalan Singh and Saryu Rai of the BJP. Rai wanted to discuss the issues of irrigation and power with agitating farmers in the Nalanda and Son regions. None of the leaders who were present there recall how within minutes of their entry into the chief minister's suite, the meeting turned into a raucous exchange of cursing and fisticuffs. Lalu started screaming at Lalan Singh to get out of his room. '*Nikal bahar, bahar nikal, saala*' *(Get out, get out, you rascal!).*

As the commotion reached the corridors, Saryu Rai, who was waiting in the other room, came rushing to check what the matter was. Barrages of abuse were clearly heard in the corridor. Amidst the jostling at the VVIP door, Lalu was heard calling for his security, '*Pakad ke phenk do bahar, le jao ghaseet ke*' (Throw them out of here, drag them out).

Thakur opines that Lalan Singh, with his characteristic harshness of tongue, may have said something that would have triggered Lalu. Nitish walked away from the scene with a pithy statement, '*Ab saath chal paana mushkil hai*' (It is difficult to walk together now). He asked Saryu Rai to draft a letter, listing out the reasons for the parting that could be made public. The letter lay buried, however, for years before senior journalist Srikant could lay his hands on it, with the last page missing.[96]

Nitish began the letter with:

> It is not possible to speak to you any longer because you are not, to my mind, earnest about discussing serious or important

> issues. Your attitude towards the party, the government and democratic institutions, and your current company is such that there is no space or occasion for meaningful dialogue [...] I stood by you rock-like in your election as leader of the Opposition and as chief minister of Bihar. I have been protecting your government and working for it.

Further, Nitish doesn't mince words in exposing the nefarious modus operandi of Lalu and his government.

> But this government has belied all our expectations; it has become the playground of power cliques around you. It is clear that you are bent on showering the benefits of government appointments and contracts on people from a particular caste group. Such discrimination among backward communities is discouraging non-Yadav groups [...]
>
> [...] There is widespread misuse of funds and financial indiscipline, welfare programmes are suffering as a result, governance is at a standstill [...] Genuine workers of the party are demoralised and angry and alienated because you are not prepared to listen to them. You have now turned to insulting senior colleagues, you want to keep yourself surrounded by sycophants. [...] This is not what many of us expected when we helped put you in power.

The last page of the letter, which has been reported missing, is said to contain Nitish's unambiguous announcement of severing ties with Lalu and going separate ways. However, it would take Nitish another two years before he would publicly announce his departure from Lalu's camp and form his own party with George Fernandes.

Lalu's belief in his invincibility at this point, backed by his caste-based vote bank, was sky-high. This was also evident from the way political spoils were distributed in his reign. From government appointments, government contracts, liquor and transport licences to lucrative administrative and police postings, all were cornered by influential Yadavs. These were more often than not be facilitated by Lalu's brothers-in-law, Sadhu and Subhash Yadav. The Yadavs had become the new Brahmins. The Muslims grabbed some of the spoils in areas dominated by Lalu's cronies such as Shahabuddin and Md. Taslimuddin.

Lalu didn't even fear alienating some of the OBCs. The most important of these were the Kurmis. The Kurmis are agrarian people and are arguably the most upwardly mobile of the backward castes in Bihar. The word 'Kurmi' is considered to be derived from *krishi karmi*, meaning agriculturalist. Despite constituting barely 3 per cent of the population of Bihar, their influence on Bihar politics has been disproportionate to their numbers. While the Kurmis regarded themselves as Suryavanshi Kshatriya and traced their ancestry to Lord Ram, the Rajputs never accepted them as equals or as Aryans. In a manner of compromise, the Kurmis and their kindred caste, the Koeris, opted to consider Luv and Kush as their progenitors, respectively. Nonetheless, the Kurmis always played a significant role in the socio-political space of Bihar, while also earning notoriety for incidents such as the Belchi massacre in which eleven Dalits were brutally murdered and tossed into a mass pyre by a Kurmi gang from the neighbouring village.[97] The rise of Lalu in 1990 had given them the hope of an equal space in the power structure and the state's politics. However, just a few months into the term, it was clear that backwards for Lalu meant just one caste when it came to sharing power and political spoils. The Kurmis resented Lalu for his conspicuous bias against them when he appointed Yadavs to several important positions, such as the heads of the Bihar Public Service Commission, the Bihar State Electricity Board, the Bihar Secondary Education Service Commission and the Bihar State Development Corporation.[98] In fact, Lalu had let the rumours fly that Kurmis and Koeris would be taken off the reservation list.

The Rebellion

The hopes of Kurmis were dashed. They felt further insulted when Lalu allegedly derided them as 'kukkurs' (dogs) and looked down upon their demands for a share of power. As a culmination of this, the dissenters, including those from within the Janata Dal, gathered in a massive protest rally at Gandhi Maidan in February 1994. They had gathered under the aegis of the Kurmi banner. Nitish, dissenting from Lalu and also a Kurmi, seemed the natural choice to lead them. Nitish, who was then housed in his friend Vijay Krishna's Chhaju Bagh ministerial quarters, just a stone's throw away from Gandhi Maidan, was unsure of taking Lalu head on. Just days before the scheduled rally, Lalu had conveyed to Nitish that the latter's participation in the rally would be considered an act of treason. Nitish was also wary of associating with a caste-based movement, even if it were his own. Even later in life, the risk-averse Nitish would have to be prodded to pick up the rally as his bugle against Lalu's anarchy. Finally, Nitish attended the rally and roared to an impatient crowd of lakhs of people, '*Bheekh nahi, hissedaari chahiye ... Jo sarkaar hamare hiton ko nazarandaaz karti hai, woh satta me nahi reh* sakti' (We don't want charity, we want participation ... The government that ignores our interests cannot stay in power). The crowds responded with equal fervour: '*Nitish tum aage badho, hum tumhare saath hain*' (March ahead, Nitish. We are with you).[99]

Emboldened by the response at the Kurmi rally, Nitish openly tore into him at a subsequent Janata Dal parliamentary meeting in Delhi. In a scathing attack, Nitish called Lalu a 'power-drunk autocrat'. He said that if a change in leadership was not made in Bihar, future generations would hold them accountable for imposing such a corrupt leader on them. In a rare instance of being unequivocal, he declared that he wasn't ready to share that blame.

Another Janata Dal leader who by then was disgruntled with Lalu was George Fernandes. Having played a major role in anti-Emergency protests and being a one-time mentor to Lalu, he was lately sidelined by Lalu just like everyone else who Lalu thought wouldn't fall in line. Fernandes would soon become the face of the revolt against Lalu and the main leader of the new outfit, the Samata Party. In its call of 'Bihar bachao', the party was also joined by fourteen Janata Dal MPs and leaders such as Abdul Ghafoor, Shivanand Tiwari, Bhola Prasad Singh and Brishen Patel. The party came into existence in October 1994, just a few months before the next assembly elections. The prevailing disgruntlement with Lalu and the overwhelming response received by Fernandes and Nitish made them believe that they could challenge Lalu's forte, or rather break it. Politics has rarely been that predictable, though. Both leaders would soon learn that and face the biggest existential dilemma of their political lives.

THE BALKANISATION OF BIHAR

Lalu's rise in Bihar politics was nothing short of spectacular. So was the rise of his close associates, cronies and political partners in different parts of the state. If the 1990 election was historic in terms of ushering in a new era in Bihar politics, it was also significant in the way it brought a number of people with criminal background into politics. While politics and crime had links going far back, it got institutionalised in the 1990s.

Being an agrarian society, and wealth being measured by possession of land, henchmen were often used to wrest control of land in Bihar. The role of henchmen was expanded when they began to be used to intimidate rivals and to capture voting booths by politicians across the spectrum. In the 1980s and 1990s, these henchmen, having realised their immense clout and crucial role in capturing political power by politicians, decided to contest the elections themselves. This led to the entry of crime into politics and vice versa in a way that the two became virtually inseparable. These new criminal-turned-politicians and the political parties served each other perfectly. The contestants got a party symbol and the legitimacy to fight elections. The parties got candidates who they knew were more capable of winning than any others in their constituencies. The assembly elections in 1990 saw an unprecedented thirty independents win the elections. Most of these were bahubalis, whose terror reigned in their areas. While the growing criminalisation of politics was not unique to Bihar, the impunity with which these criminal-turned-politicians ruled their fiefdom looked unparalleled in a modern democratic state.

The decade of the 1990s turned out to be the deadliest phase of rivalries and battles for dominance that the state had ever seen. The law-and-order situation became such that it was tough to comment if and how much of Bihar was actually under the control of the government. By the end of the millennium, Bihar started resembling a deeply divided African nation, with each area being the fiefdom of a local gang lord.

This made it easy for the government too, which didn't have to go through the hassle of maintaining law and order. Often when a certain crime would gain too much prominence and need the chief minister's intervention, a phone call would be made to the reigning 'king' of the area to handle the matter. So, it surprised few when, in a leaked phone call between Lalu Yadav and jailed criminal-turned-politician Shahabuddin, Lalu was heard telling Shahabuddin: '*Suno u bahute pareshan kar raha hai, kuch karo uska.*' (Listen, he is troubling me a lot. Do something about it). Shahabuddin, a loyal soldier in jail, answered in Bhojpuri on the call: '*Chinta mat karin, okar kaam ho jayi.*' (Don't worry, he will be handled.)

The stories of each of these bahubalis are unique, and yet, in a way, they bear a striking similarity to the trajectory of each other's rise in the Bihar of the 1990s. While their fiefdoms were clearly demarcated, their paths often crisscrossed on the treacherous route to politics. The struggle against the atrocities of one bahubali would often lead to the rise of a new bahubali, which then continued as a vicious cycle. Some of these rivalries ran deep into successive generations of the bahubali's families and go on to define the socio-politics of their regions. They often became part of regional lore.

The Rivalry of Kosi-Seemanchal

The only time one may hear about Kosi is during the season of the annual flooding in the region caused by the eponymous River Kosi, also known as the 'sorrow of Bihar'.[100] The Kosi-Seemanchal covers the north-eastern region of Bihar and is a sub-region of the Mithila region. The Kosi subdivision consists of the districts of Supaul, Madhepura and Saharsa, the last also being the headquarters of the division. To the east of the Kosi division lies the Purnea-headquartered Seemanchal division. It borders Nepal as well as northern Bengal and consists of the districts of Kishanganj, Araria, Purnia and Katihar.

The Kosi-Seemanchal region has been witness to long-standing rivalries between bahubalis looking to establish the region as their fiefdom. The most noteworthy of them is the rivalry between Pappu Yadav and Anand Mohan.

Pappu Yadav started off as a petty extortionist and black movie-ticket seller. He came into the limelight with his alleged involvement in the murder of an upper-caste college student. He was soon brought into the fold of his maternal uncle, Arjun Singh, who used to run a parallel government in Purnea. Pappu Yadav was responsible for bringing youth into the fold of his uncle's gang.[101] However, with his uncle going behind bars, Pappu Yadav soon became the whole and sole of the organisation. Arjun was murdered by a rival Rajput gang in 1987. Pappu Yadav resolved to avenge his death. Thus began a long-drawn war between Pappu Yadav and the Rajput gangs of the region.

Pappu seemed to dominate the war and created for himself the image of a Yadav leader unwilling to surrender to upper-caste hegemony. With rising caste rivalries, Pappu found a loyal caste constituency waiting for him. Pappu Yadav started dictating the terms in the Purnea belt. Doctors would be forced to treat the poor for free, and corrupt officials would be thrashed. Some started looking up to him as a modern-day Robin Hood. The next obvious destination for Pappu was politics. In the meantime, he formed an organisation named Yuva Shakti that continued carrying out criminal activities for him.

He won the 1990 assembly elections from the Singheshwarsthan constituency in Madhepura as an independent candidate. Pappu's debut election win impressed many heavyweight politicians, including Lalu. It is widely believed that Pappu helped Lalu Yadav fetch the support of the eleven independents he needed for a majority in his first stint as chief minister. Soon, Pappu Yadav built armies of supporters, not just in Madhepura but also in the adjoining districts of Purnea, Saharsa, Supaul and Katihar. He started to be seen as a formidable opponent to Anand Mohan, who had become well known as an anti-reservation crusader in the wake of the Mandal protests. The rivalry for dominance in the Kosi belt soon took the form of gang wars, with neither side conceding.

Pappu Yadav quickly became close to Lalu and got a Janata Dal ticket to contest the 1991 parliamentary elections from Purnea. He won the seat by a huge margin. Once Pappu became an MP, the constituency began to receive an almost uninterrupted power supply because he allegedly threatened to burn down the power station if there was a power cut.

Pappu Yadav would go on to win parliamentary elections in 1996, 1999 and 2004. This, however, didn't deter him from his shenanigans and misadventures. On the night of 17 December 1995, a large consignment of arms, including several hundred AK-47s and over 16,000 rounds of ammunition, was dropped by a Latvian aircraft in the Purulia district of West Bengal.[102] This came to be known as the Purulia arms drop case. The chief accused, Kim Davy, later alleged that Pappu Yadav was involved in getting him a safe exit from India. Pappu Yadav, however, escaped unhurt in the trials. He would often boast that there wasn't a jail in Bihar that he hadn't been to. Pappu's relationship with Lalu saw its ups and downs until his conviction and incarceration for the murder of Ajit Sarkar, a popular communist leader from Purnea, in 1998.

The Murder of Ajit Sarkar

Ajit Sarkar had entered politics through the Students' Federation of India, the youth wing of the Communist Party of India (Marxist) (CPM). He went on to represent Purnea in the tumultuous 1980s and 1990s when the poor and Dalits were trying to find their voice against the landed upper castes. However, his political career and life came to an abrupt end when he was gunned down in broad daylight at Purnea's Subhash Chowk on 14 June 1998.

The main accused in his murder was Pappu Yadav.

While he had been charged earlier with several other crimes, the murder Ajit Sarkar proved to be Pappu Yadav's nemesis. He was arrested in March 2004 for his alleged involvement. Pappu was incarcerated for over a decade before being acquitted by the Patna High Court in 2013. Once, when he was released on bail in 2004, he threw a party for his jail inmates, a matter that got highly publicised. His other lavish lifestyle adventures in jail, such as cell phones and other amenities, were also questioned. The Supreme Court soon cancelled his bail, moving him to the high-security Tihar Jail.

However, while Pappu Yadav was in jail, his wife, Ranjeet Ranjan, pitched in to fill the void. She fought elections from Saharsa and Supaul and kept in touch with the public.[103] Pappu Yadav and Ranjan's marriage itself has many interesting anecdotes.

Ranjan, who was born and brought up in Rewa in Madhya Pradesh, Punjab and Delhi, was an active lawn tennis player in the Bihar circuit. It is said that Pappu noticed her on a tennis court in Patna in 1993. He proposed to her, and they eventually got married, but not before a lot of drama, which Pappu chronicles in his autobiography *Drohkaal ka Pathik*. This includes his attempt to commit suicide by consuming sleeping pills because of Ranjan's apathy.[104] Their families finally agreed and they got married. Pappu converted to Sikhism as a compromise.[105]

Pappu's reign in the poverty-ridden Kosi-Seemanchal belt didn't go unchallenged. His growing influence in the area led to the consolidation of the Rajputs, who have a significant presence in the area. This culminated in a massive rivalry between Pappu Yadav and the Rajput strongman Anand Mohan Singh.

The Messiah of the Rajputs

On the eve of the 2014 parliamentary elections, JD(U) leader Sharad Yadav visited the house of a murder convict in Madhepura to seek his mother Geeta Devi's blessings, while the convict was lodged away in Saharsa Jail.[106] The convict was none other than Anand Mohan. Sharad Yadav was contesting from the Madhepura constituency against another of his clansmen, Pappu Yadav, a sworn enemy of Anand Mohan. Ironically, it was Pappu who had helped Sharad Yadav defeat Anand Mohan from the same Madhepura constituency in a by-election in 1991. Pappu had escaped from police custody a fortnight before the election date, helped seal Sharad Yadav's win, and had also famously driven Sharad Yadav's car at the victory procession. Such friendships of opportunism are not unusual in politics. However, for Anand Mohan and Pappu Yadav, their rivalry, once it started in the late

1980s, never waned. The rivalry at one point threw the entire Kosi belt into a civil war.

Anand Mohan was born into a Rajput family in Panchgachiya village in Saharsa district. The grandson of prominent Gandhian freedom fighter Ram Bahadur Singh, he dropped out of college in 1974 to join JP's Sampoorna Kranti movement. This was his first introduction to politics. Ironically, however, Anand Mohan's ways differed strongly from the non-violent methods of Gandhi or JP. He came into the limelight after he displayed black flags before then prime minister Morarji Desai in Saharsa at a public meeting.[107] After the infamous display of the black flag, Anand Mohan became involved in numerous crimes along with a band of criminals. He eluded the police despite the many attempts to capture him, and soon developed a larger-than-life aura about him, owing to his penchant for riding horses and his Robin Hood-style attacks on rich and powerful businessmen.

Anand Mohan himself once said, 'It was the terror unleashed by the politicised criminals against the poor that forced me to pick up the gun at the age of seventeen.'[108] Such was Anand Mohan's popularity that people prevented the police from carrying out his arrest once in his village in Saharsa. By the time he surrendered and was first incarcerated in 1983, his name figured in thirty criminal cases in various parts of Bihar.[109]

Anand also rose politically with his first election to the Bihar Legislative Assembly in 1990 from the Mahishi constituency on a Janata Dal ticket. However, he soon split ways with the Janata Dal's espousal of Mandal politics. Anand Mohan's political rise in the belt became co-terminus with the increasing heat of Mandal politics. He became the champion of his caste for crossing swords with Lalu and the Yadavs. This also brought him into a direct confrontation with Pappu, who had become Lalu's right-hand man, using his firepower for the espousal of Mandal.

After his fallout with the Janata Dal and his staunch opposition to reservation policies, Anand Mohan had not just emerged as a saviour of Rajputs but also the axis of upper caste resentment against Mandal politics in Kosi as well as nearby districts. The period was also marked by Lalu's indiscriminate use of caste polarisation to consolidate his voter base. Caste armies had come up in all corners of the state and affiliations with them were flaunted with pride. To challenge the backward caste assertions and consolidations, especially by Yadavs, the Vaishali-Muzaffarpur belt soon saw a unique Rajput–Bhumihar bonhomie gaining ground.

The Rifle-Bullet Combination

Lalganj is one of the numerous typical market towns in Bihar and also the headquarters of Vaishali district. Close to Hajipur, Lalganj is dominated mainly by Banias, the trading community, and is well known for its timber furniture market. The town is well connected with Muzaffarpur and falls within the touristy 'Buddhist Circuit'. It also boasts of having one of the oldest municipalities in Bihar, established in 1869 during colonial times, and a century-old library, the Sharda Pustakalaya.

Munna Shukla, who rose in the 2000s as a local MLA, installed a big statue of Maharana Pratap at Lalganj's busiest chowk. It was surprising to see a Bhumihar strongman choose to venerate a Rajput icon in a deeply caste-divided Bihar. It perhaps was a continuation of the Rajput–Bhumihar coalition that had been forged in the backdrop of political rise of backward castes under Lalu. It also symbolised Shukla's own deep connection and bonhomie with Rajput leader Anand Mohan.

Tehelka notes in a 2007 article:[110]

> It was his [Anand Mohan's] muscleman image that made Mohan's name synonymous with terror in Bihar's poverty-ridden Saharsa-Supaul belt for the past 20 years. He and Munna Shukla faced several criminal cases, many of them for murder, in various courts across Bihar. While Shukla still remains a dreaded figure around Muzaffarpur and Vaishali districts in north Bihar, Mohan is notorious in the Saharsa-Supaul belt as a criminal and sometimes as a kind of folk hero.

However, the seeds of the Rajput–Bhumihar consolidation, often called the 'Rifle-Bullet' combination for their dominance in politics, were sowed in March 1992 after the murder of a rising Bhumihar leader of the Congress, Hemant Shahi. Shahi, who was the son of veteran Congress leader Laliteshwar Prasad Shahi, was killed by Janata Dal supporters in broad daylight at the circle officer's office. The murder was raised forcefully in Parliament, replying to which Home Minister S.B. Chavan said he had not been able to contact the chief minister who was just not coming to the phone. He later admitted: 'The murder of the legislator in the office of the Circle Officer of Goraul block in Vaishali district is sufficient proof of the administrative chaos prevalent in Bihar.'[111]

When Veena Shahi, Hemant's widow, decided to contest the Vaishali assembly seat vacated by her husband's murder, the Rajputs, including Anand Mohan's wife, Lovely Anand, campaigned for her. Veena Shahi's victory sealed an unsaid Rajput–Bhumihar pact and heralded the birth of a coalition that would soon threaten Lalu's carefully crafted caste equations.

Anand Mohan saw this as an opportunity and formed his own party, the Bihar People's Party (BPP), in June 1993. Within a year, he got an opportunity to prove his mettle and the tenacity of the Rajput–Bhumihar consolidation when a by-election was announced for the Vaishali Lok Sabha seat. Anand Mohan fielded his wife, Lovely Anand, on a BPP ticket. It became a high-profile contest, with the three main contestants being women, all belonging to prominent families in the state. Lalu fielded Kishori Sinha, the wife of former chief minister S.N. Sinha, on a Janata Dal ticket. Given the prestige associated with the seat, Lalu himself accompanied Kishori Sinha to Muzaffarpur to file her nomination papers. The Congress responded by fielding Usha Singh, the daughter of the late Bhumihar stalwart Mahesh Prasad Singh.[112]

The Bhumihars, however, backed Lovely Anand, and the Bhumihar don Chhotan Shukla campaigned for her in the Vaishali Lok Sabha by-elections. Mohan had cleverly brought together two dominant and erstwhile rival communities of Rajputs and Bhumihars, who were equally disenchanted with Lalu. The thirty-year-old Lovely Anand trounced the stalwarts Kishori Sinha and Usha Singh, laid the foundation of the Rajput–Bhumihar alliance. However, the alliance would soon be threatened when its benefactor Anand Mohan, would be accused of the most audacious crime ever heard of.

The Murder of a District Magistrate

The year was 1994. The exact date, 5 December. G. Krishnaiah, the district magistrate of Gopalganj and a 1985 batch IAS officer, was on his way back to Gopalganj after attending a meeting in Hajipur. Krishnaiah's story was an inspiration to lakhs of civil service aspirants in Bihar as well as his home state, Andhra Pradesh. Born to a landless Dalit family, he worked as a coolie alongside his father before working as a clerk and a lecturer and then finally cracking the coveted civil services exam.[113]

His first posting was in West Champaran in Bihar, where he became popular among the poor with his empathetic approach. He was later posted to Gopalganj, Lalu's home district. On 5 December 1994, he was passing through Muzaffarpur when his car was intercepted by a mob from the funeral procession of Chhotan Shukla, a Bhumihar strongman from Vaishali and a criminal-turned-politician.

Chhotan Shukla was a dreaded figure in the Vaishali-Muzaffarpur belt. He had first picked up a gun after his father, Ramdas Shukla, was brutally murdered. Chhotan spread his influence far and wide in the Vaishali-Muzaffarpur region. The Bhumihar gangster had also gained huge popularity among his castemen. Chhotan had campaigned for Anand Mohan's wife, Lovely Anand, in the 1994 by-election to Vaishali and played an important role in her win. The election had also strengthened the Rajput–Bhumihar friendship and given a winning formula in elections to the newly formed BPP. Encouraged by their win in the Vaishali by-election, Chhotan was declared as the future candidate for the 1995 assembly elections from the Kesaria constituency of East Champaran, a district contiguous with Muzaffarpur. On 4 December 1994, while Chhotan was returning from a campaign in Kesaria, his car was stopped near Sanjay Cinema by some men dressed in police uniform. Before Chhotan could ask anything, he and four of his associates were caught at the receiving end of indiscriminate firing from AK-47s. All of them died on the spot. The news of Chhotan's killing spread like wildfire and brought Muzaffarpur to a standstill.

Brij Behari Prasad, a minister in the Janata Dal government, was alleged to be behind the murders.[114] Brij Behari came from the OBC Bania community and was considered close to Lalu Yadav. Brij Behari was feared in the East Champaran to Muzaffarpur belt for using muscle power to influence voters and deciding the outcome of elections. Chhotan's rising political ambitions in the same region had brought him into direct contention with Brij Behari. The murder was also seen in the larger context as an outcome of the ongoing tussle between Chhotan's leader, Anand Mohan, and Brij Behari's master, Lalu Yadav. Some of the supporters of Chhotan also alleged complicity of the police and local administration in his killing.

The next day, on 5 December, Chhotan Shukla's funeral procession was taken out from his home situated in Naya Tola. The procession was also attended by Anand Mohan, the BPP chief, and his wife Lovely Anand. When the procession reached Bhagwanpur, Anand Mohan gave a fiery speech to a 5,000-strong crowd.[115] The funeral procession had turned into a furious mob instigated by speeches from Anand Mohan and others against the DM and SP of Muzaffarpur. Chhotan Shukla's supporters suspected foul play by the DM and SP of Muzaffarpur.

G. Krishnaiah, the Gopalganj district magistrate was on his way to Gopalganj after attending a meeting in Hajipur. When the crowd saw a white Ambassador with a red beacon, indicating the presence of a government representative, it got infuriated. G. Krishnaiah's vehicle was caught in the midst of this fury near Khabra village along NH-28.[116] As G. Krishnaiah's vehicle neared the protest site, the mob started pelting stones at the car, thinking it was the Muzaffarpur DM's car. G. Krishnaiah came out of the vehicle and pleaded that he wasn't the DM of Muzaffarpur. The mob didn't pay any heed.

As per his conviction verdict of 2007, this is where Anand Mohan incited the mob to kill the DM. '*Dekhta kya hai, Bhutkan? Badla le lo*' (What are you waiting for, Bhutkan? Take your revenge).'[117]

G. Krishnaiah was kicked, thrashed and then was literally stoned to death. However, not before Chhotan's younger brother and dreaded criminal Bhutkan Shukla shot him thrice in his blood-soaked head at point-blank range.[118] G. Krishnaiah was just thirty-five when he was killed.

The Patna District Court, in 2007, convicted six politicians for G. Krishnaiah's killing. This included Anand Mohan, his wife Lovely Anand, Munna Shukla, a JD(U) MLA, Akhlaq Ahmed and Arun Kumar (both ex-MLAs). Anand Mohan was sentenced to death, making him the first politician to be handed the punishment.[119] His sentence was, however, commuted to a life term later by the Patna High Court.

An absconding Bhutkan Shukla took over the reins of his brother Chhotan Shukla's gang. He killed several of Brij Behari's men to avenge Chhotan's murder. An agitated Brij Behari retaliated by moving Bhutkan's protégé, Deepak Singh, to his fold. Deepak would soon kill Bhutkan in his own house. The killing of Bhutkan would be soon avenged by a coordinated effort of several gangsters from Purvanchal (eastern Uttar Pradesh) and Bihar.

Brij Behari was shot dead on 13 June 1998, while under treatment in judicial custody at Patna's Indira Gandhi Institute of Medical Sciences. Brij Behari was under probe for alleged involvement in admission scams at technical institutes while he was the state's science and technology minister. While Prasad was taking a stroll outside his ward, surrounded by Bihar military police commandos, a man approached him to ask for his help in securing proper treatment for his relative. Prasad directed one of his men to speak to the concerned doctor and secure proper treatment for him before walking towards a poorly lit section of the parking lot. By the time the commandos approached him towards the parking lot, an Ambassador car stopped near him and unidentified gunners opened fire on Prasad and his men, killing them on the spot. A number of big names in the mafia world, including Chhotan and Bhutkan's younger brother Munna Shukla, Surajbhan Singh and Sriprakash Shukla, were charged for Brij Behari Prasad's murder.

With Brij Behari's killing, the cycle of retribution that started with Chhotan Shukla's killing was brought to a halt. Chhotan Shukla's murder couldn't be solved, and Bihar Police filed a closure report twenty-six years later, in 2020, citing no evidence against any accused.

In Anand Mohan's case, his involvement in the murder of G. Krishnaiah meant more trouble for him. In the 1995 assembly elections a few months later, Anand Mohan fielded around a hundred candidates. Anand Mohan himself contested from three different constituencies and lost all three. He then went on to align with the Samata Party. Nitish Kumar and George Fernandes fielded him from Sheohar in the 1996 Lok Sabha polls. Anand Mohan won the election, fighting from jail. He declared after winning the elections, '*Sandhi nahi, ab rann hoga, sangharsh maha bhishan hoga*' (There won't be a compromise now. This time there will be a war).

He was re-elected from Sheohar in the 1998 parliamentary elections. The highlight of his stint in Parliament was an alleged smuggling of a gun into the House—a charge that was dropped later because of insufficient evidence, as were several other charges in almost twenty-odd cases in Bihar. Even while in jail, Anand Mohan exercised huge influence over the voters, with his wife continuing to be his political proxy in the field.

The Man Who Danced with Bar Girls in Jail

Muzaffarpur is one of the largest towns in Bihar and serves as the headquarters of Tirhut division. It is famous for its litchis, a seasonal fruit. However, it was even more talked about in the

1990s for its gangsters, most of them coming from the Bhumihar community. It became the hotbed of successive rivalries between Ashok Samrat, Chhotan Shukla and Brij Behari Prasad. However, with all three killed in separate incidents by 1998, the name that started doing the rounds was that of Munna Shukla.

Shukla's life, as discussed in the previous section, was closely intertwined with Anand Mohan's life. Vijay Kumar Shukla, better known as Munna Shukla, was the youngest brother of notorious gangsters Chhotan Shukla and Bhutkan Shukla and a co-accused in the murder of G. Krishnaiah.

It was this murder that first brought Munna Shukla to prominence. He soon became the reigning king of government tenders in the Muzaffarpur-Vaishali region. However, Brij Behari Prasad kept posing a staunch challenge to Munna Shukla's hegemony. Munna Shukla was waiting for the right opportunity to strike. He, along with Surajbhan Singh, avenged the murder of Chhotan Shukla by killing Brij Behari Prasad in 1998.

While the rivalry was put to an end, the murder brought fresh troubles for Munna Shukla, who was now actively targeted by the police and administration. It is at this point that he decided to take refuge in politics. In 2000, while lodged in Hajipur Jail, Munna Shukla contested the assembly election as an independent candidate from the Lalganj constituency in Vaishali and won. He shifted to the Lok Janshakti Party in 2005 and subsequently to the JD(U), but retained the Lalganj seat. Munna Shukla, whose influence ran deep in the Muzaffarpur-Vaishali belt, faced seventeen criminal cases at one point. After he was convicted in the Brij Behari Prasad murder case in 2009, he fielded his wife, Anu Shukla, from the same constituency in 2010, who won the seat comfortably.

Munna Shukla, even while in jail, continued to flout rules and run his fiefdom. He would often be spotted out of jail and in public places, meeting people and carrying on business as usual. In 2001, a video surfaced in which Munna Shukla was seen dancing with bar girls in the prisoner ward of Muzaffarpur's Sadar Hospital.

In October 2007, the court of Patna's Additional District Judge pronounced the verdict in the murder case of Gopalganj DM G. Krishnaiah. Munna Shukla was sentenced to life imprisonment. However, in 2008, the Patna High Court acquitted Munna Shukla. In August 2009, the verdict was pronounced in the murder case of Brij Behari Prasad. Munna Shukla, along with nine other accused, was sentenced to five years of imprisonment. In 2014, as ironic as it may sound, Munna Shukla was again acquitted by the high court in this case.[120]

Notably, Munna Shukla's accomplice and co-accused in the Brij Behari murder case, Surajbhan Singh, would script another tale of rivalry in the nearby region of Mokama.

The Rivalry of Mokama

Mokama is a small town located in the eastern periphery of Patna district. Situated on the southern bank of the Ganges, it is considered the junction of ancient Magadh, Mithila and Ang kingdoms. The strip of land along the bank of the Ganges is known as diara in local parlance and is submerged during the monsoons. A significant population of Bhumihars live in the area and thus dominate the local politics.

While the Kosi belt saw the rise of dons like Pappu Yadav and Anand Mohan, fighting with each other and precipitating a virtual Yadav–Rajput war, the region of Mokama saw an intense and violent rivalry between two Bhumihar leaders and, eventually, families.

One of these strongmen was Dilip Singh. Born in the Ladma village of Barh block, as the third of four sons in his family, Dilip

Singh started out as a protege of smuggler Kamdev Singh in the 1970s. He soon rose to become the right-hand man of Kamdev Singh. Then, Kamdev Singh was murdered and Dilip Singh captured his throne. This was the decade of the 1980s when most politicians used henchmen with impunity to capture booths. Dilip Singh had started as a henchman for Shyam Sundar Singh, capturing booths for him during elections. Shyam Sundar Singh 'Dhiraj' was a minister in the state Congress government in the 1980s and represented the Mokama constituency.

However, an ambitious Dilip Singh soon challenged and further defeated Shyam Sundar Singh in the 1990 assembly elections by over 22,000 votes.[121] Dilip Singh also became a minister in the then Bihar government. He again defeated Shyam Sundar Singh in the 1995 elections and established his name as the unchallenged leader of the region. However, Dilip Singh was soon to get a taste of his own audacious foray against his mentor.

A name that had started making rounds in Mokama during the same time was that of Surajbhan Singh. He was born on 5 March 1965 to a family with meagre means. Surajbhan's father wanted him to join the army. However, the company that Surajbhan Singh kept soon brought him into the extortion racket. Surajbhan, who had started with petty crimes in the 1980s, earned a name for himself with the murder of Rami Singh, a resident of Madhurapur village in Begusarai district, on 16 January 1992. When Surajbhan's father, an employee in a local shop, realised that Surajbhan wouldn't give up the crime world, he committed suicide by jumping into the Ganges. Surajbhan's brother, a CRPF jawan, too, killed himself a few days later.[122] Surajbhan Singh, however, was undeterred in his pursuits.

Surajbhan was soon picked up by Dilip Singh to intimidate voters and capture booths for him. However, Surajbhan's name gained wide prominence when, in 1998, he, along with Munna Shukla, was named in the murder of Brij Behari Prasad, a sitting minister in the Bihar government.

Surajbhan Singh had now become a dreaded figure in the Barh-Begusarai region and wasn't ready to play second fiddle to Dilip Singh. Surajbhan challenged Dilip Singh in the 2000 assembly elections as an independent candidate from Mokama and defeated him by a massive margin.[123] By this time, Surajbhan already had twenty-six criminal cases to his credit across Bihar and Uttar Pradesh.

Meanwhile, a defeated Dilip Singh had started withdrawing from political life. He was nominated to the Legislative Council in 2003. His term, however, prematurely came to an end as a heart attack in 2006 proved fatal for him. Surajbhan's dominance, however, would soon be challenged by Dilip Singh's younger brother, Anant Singh.

Anant Singh, the youngest of four brothers, would be the sole one to survive by 2008. While Dilip Singh succumbed to a heart attack in 2006, his other two brothers fell victim to the intense rivalry in the region. Legend has it that Anant Singh swam across a river and gunned down his brother's killers. He was greatly feared as his reputation spread far and wide. The youngest of his brothers, he soon began to be referred to as 'Chhote Sarkar'. Anant Singh would wrest back the Mokama seat for his family in 2005, contesting on a JD(U) ticket and winning it consecutively six times till the last assembly by-election in 2022.

Anant Singh became Nitish's man Friday and continued to be so till 2015, before a fallout happened between the two over the BJP–JD(U) breaking their alliance and RJD, an archrival of Anant Singh, coming into the picture. Nitish, amidst his campaign for a terror-free Bihar, would often be criticised for this association. In a testament to his popularity, Anant Singh contested the 2015 assembly election as an independent and won it. He would go on to win the 2020 assembly elections too on his archrival RJD's ticket. The party symbol didn't matter to him. When he was disqualified in 2022, following his conviction in an arms recovery case, he fielded his wife in the by-election from Mokama. His wife, Neelam Devi, continued the family's winning streak while Anant Singh was incarcerated.

According to his election affidavit in 2020, Anant Singh was facing thirty-eight criminal charges, including seven murders, eleven attempts-to-murder and four cases of kidnapping.[124]

Besides his intimidating look, Anant Singh is also an extremely colourful character. Once, on a visit to Rashtrapati Bhawan, he was impressed by a buggy he saw. He tracked down the man who had built it and had one built for himself. He would then occasionally ride it to Vidhan Sabha in Patna, with his armed men following him in SUVs. Anant Singh also has an eclectic interest in pets. He is often seen flaunting his pets, including an elephant, horses and a python. In 2007, when an NDTV reporter went to interview Anant Singh after his name came up in a rape and murder case, he reportedly held the reporter hostage and beat him up. While thousands of criminals were sent to jail during Nitish Kumar's regime, no one dared touch Anant Singh. After a long list of shenanigans, when Nitish Kumar finally decided to act against his erstwhile friend, under mounting pressure from the opposition as well as his newfound ally Lalu Prasad, he had to send a convoy of 500 policemen equipped with sophisticated weapons and landmine-resistant vehicles to arrest him.

Milan Vaishnav, the author of *When Crime Pays*, asked people in Mokama why they voted for Anant Singh in spite of his criminal background. In a logic relevant to almost all of Bihar, people told him they thought he could protect their interests and rein in the Yadavs in their area. He was thus elected for his criminality rather than in spite of it. His criminality has become his credibility.

I Am the King; My Word is the Law

The first picture that the internet throws up on a Google search for Mohammad Shahabuddin is that of a young man seated on a sofa, dressed in an orange sweater and flanked by half a dozen gun-wielding bodyguards. The image portrays the most ostentatious show of crude power.

Regarded as the most prominent criminal-politician to have appeared on the national scene since the 1990s, few could compare to his levels of notoriety and terror. Born in Pratappur village in Siwan, Shahabuddin started his political career as a youth wing leader of the Janata Dal under Lalu's tutelage. The first case was registered against him in 1986; he was barely nineteen at the time. He soon had a history sheet in his name at the Hussainganj police station and was declared an 'A'-category criminal.

Like some of the other criminal-turned-proteges of Lalu, Shahabuddin started his political career by winning the assembly elections in 1990 and repeating the winning streak in 1995. Lalu further gave him a ticket to contest from Siwan in the 1996 parliamentary elections on a Janata Dal ticket. He won the elections comfortably. However, it was marred by heavy pre- and post-poll violence. Shahabuddin's men killed a BJP leader after the polls, including five people on the day of polling. They weren't even deterred from making an attempt on the life of the SP of Siwan, from which he managed to escape.

Shahabuddin surrendered a few months later under mounting political pressure and to save Lalu Yadav from further embarrassment. However, with much fanfare. He arrived at the court accompanied by Public Health Engineering Minister Awadh Bihari Choudhary in a convoy of cars and high-pitched sloganeering by his minions. After his bail was rejected, he was moved to prison in Choudhary's official car. Shahabuddin had twenty-four criminal cases pending against him when he was finally interned.

With the split of the Janata Dal in 1997, and Rashtriya Janata Dal (RJD) coming into power in Bihar, his stars continued to move northward. So did the audacity of his crimes. It hardly mattered that he had become an MP in 1996.

One such crime that elicited national attention was the murder of political activist Chandra Shekhar Prasad. Born in Siwan, Chandra Shekhar Prasad was raised by a single mother after his father's death at a young age. He had graduated from Jawaharlal Nehru University (JNU) and served as the president of the Jawaharlal Nehru University Students' Union. He was a popular student activist and leader. Influenced by the ideology of the Communist Party of India (Marxist-Leninist) Liberation [CPI(ML) Liberation], he is credited with having single-handedly built up the All India Students Association (AISA).

With a desire to venture into and clean up politics, Chandu, as he was fondly called by his friends, moved back to Siwan after completing his M.Phil. He was deputed as the leader of the CPI(ML) Liberation in Siwan. Chandu started campaigning against the rampant corruption and criminalisation of politics. He quickly rose in popularity and began to be widely considered a serious candidate for the Siwan constituency in the upcoming elections.

On 31 March 1997, Chandu, with some of his colleagues, was addressing a *nukkad sabha* on J.P. Road in Siwan. They were protesting the rampant corruption and murders in the state.

Little did he know that it would be his last such act. He was shot along with another of his comrades, Shyam Narayan, and killed on the spot.

Chandu's assassination triggered unprecedented protests on college campuses across the country. Siwan witnessed a march held by thousands of young men and women from Chandu's village to the site of his assassination, J.P. Chowk in Siwan. The size and passion of the crowd was unprecedented. Chandu's mother was offered a compensation of one lakh rupees by the then prime minister, I.K. Gujral, which she refused to accept. Her words reflected her real pain.

> It will be an insult to accept money in exchange for my son. I curse those who have put a cost on my son's life. The only compensation for a mother whose adult son has been murdered and who knows the murderer is punishment for her son's killers [...] Let Shahabuddin out of the political fortress and either hang him or let the masses shoot him.[125]

Notably, when the students of JNU marched to Bihar Bhawan in Delhi, demanding a dialogue with Lalu Prasad Yadav, they were greeted with bullets. The shooting was ordered by Lalu's dulara (dear) brother-in-law, Sadhu Yadav. [126]

Shahabuddin was the prime accused, along with five other members of his party. Three accused in the crime were convicted and sentenced fifteen years later in 2012 by a CBI special court. Shahabuddin, however, wasn't even chargesheeted for the crime, let alone be convicted. This is despite the fact that one of the convicts, Dhruv Jaiswal, was nabbed from the RJD MP's home.[127] Shahabuddin was rather rewarded with what he desired the most. He came to be even more dreaded by the public.

Shahabuddin, who was fond of saying, 'I am the king, my word is the law,' didn't stop at Chandu's assassination. He selectively targeted the CPI(ML) Liberation and its members to check their growing influence in the Siwan and Gopalganj regions. In 1998, he bombed the office premises of CPI(ML) and brutally beat up their office secretary, Keshav Baitha. He is believed to have kidnapped and killed another CPI(ML) activist, Chhote Lal Gupta, in February 1999. While it could be established that Chhote Lal Gupta was kidnapped by Shahabuddin and his gang—a witness was able to identify him—his dead body was never recovered, and so, Shahabuddin couldn't be charged with murder.

By the year 2000, Shahabuddin had established himself as the undisputed mafia king of Siwan. He was considered a law unto himself and ran a parallel government. He held Khap panchayats to hear people's grievances and redress them. He would adjudicate even on matters as complex as land disputes and marital issues. His judgement would be final and couldn't be appealed against. He considered himself no less than a court, admitting public interest litigations (PILs), and would pass on orders fixing the fees of doctors and ticket prices of cinema halls.

Shahabuddin had literally wiped out any party or person who could offer him any competition. No party would dare open its office or its members dare hoist its flags atop their houses. Local shops would often have a picture of him, mostly to show their allegiance.

The police, in most of the cases, either acted as Shahabuddin's servile associate, managing cover-ups or, at best, stayed indifferent. Shahabuddin often threatened or thrashed police and administrative officials. However, this reached epic proportions in March 2001.

The police had gone to execute an arrest warrant on Manoj Kumar Pappu, a local RJD leader. Shahabuddin objected to it and slapped the lead officer, Sanjiv Kumar. Shahabuddin's men beat up the policemen accompanying Kumar. The police soon sent for reinforcement and raided Shahabuddin's house. An extensive fire exchange followed, which took the lives of eight of Shahabuddin's men but not before two policemen were killed. Three police Jeeps were also set on fire. The police recovered three AK-47s from the spot. However, Shahabuddin escaped with Manoj Kumar Pappu and his men, and couldn't be arrested for a long time after.

An enraged Shahabuddin declared: '*Agar Bachchu Singh Meena ko Rajasthan tak bhi dauda kar maarna hoga to maarenge, lekin maarenge zaroor*'[128] (I'll kill Bachchu Singh Meena even if I have to chase him to Rajasthan). Meena, a 1996 Indian Police Service officer, was the then Siwan police chief and had ordered the police raid.

Shahabuddin was arrested a few months before the 2004 general elections. However, using his power and influence, he got himself shifted to Siwan Hospital where a whole floor was assigned to him. It was barely an incarceration for him, with meetings and visits continuing unabated. 'Saheb' would hold his daily *janta darbar* at 4 p.m. where he would hear out people and settle their grievances. The toughest of jobs got done with just a phone call.

In the same year, another gruesome crime committed by Shahabuddin made national headlines. The three sons of Chanda Babu, a businessman in Siwan, were abducted by Shahabuddin's men after a minor altercation with them. While the youngest, Rajeev, managed to escape, his two elder brothers, Girish and Satish, were doused with acid and killed. Rajeev, who was a witness in the case, was shot dead in 2015, days before his deposition at the court. He had been married just eighteen days ago.

None of this, however, had any effect on Shahabuddin's political career. The 2004 general elections saw large-scale violence and booth capture in almost 500 booths in Siwan. While Shahabuddin won again, the JD(U) opponent did give him a tough fight. As a retaliation for putting up a fight, nine JD(U) members were killed within a few days; several others were beaten up. A mukhiya of a village where the rival candidate had polled well was murdered at a government office. Not even the rival candidate, Om Prakash Yadav, was spared. Several bullets were fired at his house after which he was provided security.

But, Shahabuddin's fortunes changed quickly after the end of Lalu's reign in Bihar. In 2005, a raid was conducted by the joint team of SP Ratn Sanjay and DM C.K. Anil at Shahabuddin's home in Pratappur. What the police recovered wasn't the usual corruption money and some illegal rifles but automatic weapons such as AK-47s, laser-guided guns, night-vision goggles and other military weapons authorised for possession only by the army. Some of these arms had the markings of the Pakistan Ordnance factory. Shahabuddin had long been alleged to have links with Pakistan's Inter-Services Intelligence (ISI), which was also mentioned in a raid report by the then Bihar DGP, D.P. Ojha.

The police were finally able to arrest him only in November 2005. The Supreme Court, while denying his bail, commented during the trial:[129]

> By virtue of being an MP, are you entitled to keep these weapons, including a night vision device, when even the police, CRPF, and other security agencies do not have them and only the army possesses them?

The Long List

The list of bahubalis and the story of their rivalries is fodder enough for an entire book to be dedicated to them.

The rivalry between Ashok Mahto and Akhilesh Singh in the Sheikhpura belt is one such story filled with twists and turns. The book *Bihar Diaries* written by IPS officer Amit Lodha and its Netflix series adaptation *Khakee* are loosely based on Ashok Mahto's hide and seek with the police. The Ashok Mahto gang was a caste army of the Koeris and Kurmis in the Nawada-Sheikhpura belt and was responsible for killing a large number of forward-caste people in the late 1990s and early 2000s.[130] It is this initial rivalry between Ashok Mahto and Akhilesh Singh to wrestle control over sand mining and sand lifting in the area, that turned into a full-blown caste war between the Bhumihars and Koeris. The ensuing rivalry affected almost 100 villages in the Nawada-Sheikhpura-Nalanda belt and took 200 lives between 1998 and 2006, including 130 in Nawada alone.[131] Ashok Mahto was also wanted for the murder of three policemen during a Nawada jailbreak in 2001 and that of veteran Congress politician and sitting MP Rajo Singh in 2005.

Mahto was finally arrested in 2006. He was paraded across the town with a garland of slippers around his neck, and the police thrashed him from time to time in full public view before being produced in court. A large number of onlookers who had lined up along the road hurled abuse and threw rotten eggs at the gangster. Photographs showed a half-naked Mahto being held by his hand by Special Auxiliary Police (SAP) jawans in a jeep while blood dripped from his wounded upper lip.[132]

REALITY STRIKES

I shall be an autocrat: That's my trade.
And the good lord will forgive me: That's his.
—Catherine the Great

THE VANISHING ILLUSION

By the end of fiscal year 1994, Bihar's GDP per capita had reached Rs 1,019 or 40.7 per cent of the national average.[133] Bihar's income gap relative to the national average would continue to fall, reaching its lowest in 2005 at 29.5 per cent of the national average.[134] Interestingly, this year would also mark the end of the Lalu-Rabri rule in Bihar. Some other indicators of the same year paint an even more grim picture of the condition of Bihar. The extent of human deprivation in Bihar became exceptionally high, even when compared to other states within the country. Bihar, by 2005 had the second highest share of population below the poverty line. In the same year, Bihar was placed worst in terms of Human Development Index (HDI) as also having the highest proportion of population with 'multi-dimensional poverty'.[135] Had Bihar been a country, it would have figured in a 'low HDI' category somewhere between Myanmar and Yemen, with only 12 countries out of 169 worse than itself.[136]

The Reality of Social Justice

On 19 July 1994, Ramendra Kumar, a member of the CPI, raised the matter in the state legislative assembly of a local DSP caught while accepting a bribe of Rs 300. The state transport minister, Sitaram Singh, accepted the complaint as rightful. However, to everyone's surprise, Lalu rose from his seat and immediately countered the complaining member as well as his own minister. He said that the SP's report could not be taken at face value since the DSP was his trustworthy man and could do no wrong. He then summarily rejected the allegation as a political conspiracy. The stunned opposition listened to Lalu in disbelief. Lalu informed the house that the 'poor' DSP was posted in Hazaribagh following the principle of 'social justice'. What Lalu implied was that under his 'social-justice'-style of governance, officers from certain sections of society were allowed to accept bribes with impunity. In any case, it was known that even if the officer were tried and convicted, nothing would happen to him unless Lalu allowed it.[137]

Lalu exhorted the OBCs and, particularly, the Yadavs to assert themselves in every way possible. This not only included the traditional power plays in politics and social relations but even in crime and illegal occupations. This often went too far to even undermine the administration, the institutions, and at times even the judiciary. The backwards were made to understand that the rules didn't favour them, and hence whatever needed to be done to contest the entrenched hegemony of the privileged upper castes was justified. The enthused class of hitherto marginalised would respond to every call of Lalu to overthrow the unjust system. Walter Hauser commented on this, saying 'democracy thrived but governance collapsed'.[138] Lalu had deliberately and purposefully adopted a 'conflict approach'. This approach had noise, mayhem, chaos but no new purposeful end in sight. It seemed Lalu didn't even want that! Bihar thus had a new 'democratically endorsed non-governance'.[139]

However, this social churn and chaotic revolution wasn't without its victims. More often than not, the victims were the ones this revolution intended to empower. The most depressed

SCs saw little change in their lives and often had to pay the price for demanding what was rightfully theirs. The state machinery rarely stood by them. It was members of these vulnerable castes that were killed in the largest numbers during the caste massacres throughout the 1990s. What actually could have benefitted these castes, such as land and tenancy reforms, were never brought in, for the fear of facing backlash from the landed OBCs. So, while the truly marginalised Scheduled Castes were exhorted by Lalu to fight for their rights, little was done to help them when they did. The legislative initiative to help them was even more meagre. The declining state capacity to provide basic public goods, such as health and education, also affected these vulnerable groups disproportionately. The SCs and EBCs, therefore, continued to work on fields belonging to others for meagre sums and, when even that wasn't available, they continued to migrate to the fields of Punjab and new industrial centres in metropolitan cities. The only thing that the successive railway ministers hailing from Bihar ensured was an ever-increasing number of trains from Patna to these metros.

Thus, what Lalu had essentially done was to overturn the existing social order, which obviously had its flaws. However, he didn't replace it with anything new. In fact, it seemed like he didn't know how to channelise the energy and anger of hitherto marginalised classes, after he had stoked them using every possible trick in his bag. The youth, while wanting to be a part of the change, didn't find avenues for the same.

It was also during this period that politics became a popular mass vocation, triggered by the de-elitisation of politics and the entry of hitherto common men into politics. However, the motivation was not altruistic but rather to gain benefits through political and bureaucratic contacts. Lalu and his party, which never believed in building local-level cadres, did, however, lure a large number of rural, unemployed and jugaadu youth into politics. This was further aggravated by the appropriation of government jobs mostly by the upper caste youth, which pushed the OBCs and Dalits further into exploring innovative avenues of money-seeking, both legal and illegal. Roaming around the block offices and getting the work done for the needy, such as the issuance of birth certificates, caste certificates, getting their pension or even writing and submitting the applications with an assurance from the office 'babu', became a daily routine for a large number of young, aspiring politicians. Some others would be present at other nerve centres of the town, such as at bus stands, managing and even dictating the terms as agents. Some others would flock around thanas and local courts and get petty issues resolved in return for a fee. Their politics thrived under a government marred by nepotism, corruption and the complete breakdown of the state apparatus.

Seshan ka Saand

Sushil Modi, the then deputy chief minister of Bihar, commented in a May 2019 *Indian Express* article, 'The period [1990 -2004] must have a special mention in the Guinness World Records for registering the maximum number and probably worst forms of electoral violence perpetrated in this state [Bihar].' [140] He wasn't wrong.

The 1995 elections, more than a contest between parties, became a contest between the existing Janata Dal government and the Election Commission led by T.N. Seshan. Seshan was an Indian Administrative Service (IAS) officer of the Madras cadre who had also served as cabinet secretary under Rajiv Gandhi. He was appointed the chief election commissioner in 1990 and had come to be known for his tough electoral reforms.

With the upcoming Bihar elections in 1995 and having known the notoriety of elections in this part of the country, Seshan was hell bent on getting the elections conducted in a fair manner. The election was rescheduled four times before being conducted in five phases. The elections ran over a month, and the final counting took over a week.[141] Seshan hired commandos from Punjab to ensure that the polls ran without booth capturing, intimidation and violence, which had become a norm in Bihar elections.

Lalu would complain in his usual accent at his morning durbars at his home: '*Seshan pagla saand jaisa kar raha hai, maaloome nahi hai ki hum rassi baandh ke khataal me band kar sakte hain*' (Seshan is acting like a raging bull, he doesn't know that I can tie him up and lock him in the cow shed).[142]

However, Seshan's opponent in this pursuit wasn't just the incumbent government, but the Naxalites and musclemen, too, each with their own motives. The 1995 elections to the state assembly saw a spate of murders in their wake, including some high-profile ones. Congress candidates from Gopalganj and Tarapur and a CPI(ML) candidate in south Bihar were murdered. In post-election violence, Ashok Singh, a prominent Janata Dal MLA from Mashrak (Saran) was murdered just a few months into Lalu's second term. Singh was shot dead by a visitor at his well-guarded official residence—5, Strand Road—in Patna, a stone's throw away from the chief minister's residence. Ashok Singh's one-time political mentor Prabhunath Singh was the main accused in the crime. Prabhunath Singh was a former MLA from Mashrak and had been switching political sides in the past few years. Starting as an independent MLA from Mashrak, he fought on a Janata Dal ticket in 1990 but lost fighting on a BPP (Bihar People's Party) ticket to Ashok Singh in 1995. Unable to digest his defeat, he often remarked, 'It is better to be dead than to be called an ex-MLA.' He allegedly also threatened to avenge his defeat by killing Ashok Singh within three months. He kept his word.

Lalu Prasad Yadav emerged victorious in the 1995 elections, with a thumping majority. When Lalu confidently announced before the elections that he was going to secure a two-thirds majority, others dismissed it as another of his hyperboles. The Janata Dal secured 167 seats out of 324, securing a clear majority. The decisive factor that played out in Lalu's favour was a formidable combination of support from backward communities—specifically the Yadavs—and Muslims, coupled with a split opposition. The 28 per cent vote share secured by Janata Dal didn't sound like a decisive mandate but when converted to seats, it certainly did. Lalu had carefully crafted a social coalition in the five years of his premiership, which was based more on the call of social justice and dignity than development. Hence, when Lalu secured such a decisive victory, it surprised the pundits who didn't understand why the poor and backward would vote for Lalu. He had hardly done anything for them in five years. That Lalu didn't take any concrete steps such as land redistribution to break the upper-caste hegemony hardly mattered to them. Lalu was their messiah who could say or do no wrong.

The backward caste vote bank was consolidated further in reaction to the deep animosity of the upper castes towards Lalu. The landed gentry kept accusing Lalu of destroying the social fabric and the fine balance that existed in the countryside. Lalu, rather than being apologetic, turned more militant against them, at least in his rhetorical speeches. This further enthused the poor and backward to throw their weight behind Lalu in his supposed fight against the oppressors.

The Samata Party, which was formed just before the elections and which some thought could pose a real challenge to Lalu's social coalition failed badly. It secured just 7 seats out of the 310 that it contested. Led by George Fernandes, the party was conceived as a potent backward–minority coalition minus the Yadavs. It had also hoped to rope in some upper-caste votes by projecting itself as moderate and far removed from Lalu's style of anti-upper-caste stance. However, when the final results came out, it seemed not to have enjoyed the full confidence of either the Koeri-Kurmis nor the upper castes. The Koeri-Kurmis grew disillusioned with Samata Party's association with upper castes, while the upper castes, having burnt their fingers with Lalu's backward coalition, reverted to traditional voting patterns, supporting the Congress and the BJP. Samata Party's alliance with CPI(ML), which was entering parliamentary politics for the first time, also proved disastrous. In hindsight, it was obvious that the landed Koeri-Kurmi base of Samata Party and landless labourers of the CPI(ML) cadre would never align on the ground. In fact, they had always been at each other's throats.

The CPI(ML) led by Vinod Mishra won just six seats.

Lalu, on the other hand, understood and used the social combinations perfectly, even in ticket distribution. An example of this was Mohan Ram, whom Lalu summoned during his swearing-in ceremony for the second term. What was unique about Ram was that he belonged to the Holokhor community and had nothing else to show other than his eclectic collection of degrees and a dilapidated hut in his village. The Holokhor community, believed to be the lowest in the caste hierarchy, would still engage in carrying night soil as headload, a practice punishable under law. Ram, with a double MA, B.Ed., LLB and a doctorate degree, was highly qualified for a member of his community. He got the Janata Dal ticket to contest from a rural

Darbhanga seat after a serendipitous meeting with Lalu at an airport before the elections.

March to Delhi

If you walk across the corridors of any office building in Patna, the one striking similarity you would find is the corners covered with stains of paan juice. It is true for even the most high-profile buildings, including the secretariat, the high court and the Vidhan Sabha. Sometimes the signages prohibiting spitting in the premises themselves are covered in red with the stains and hence, are illegible. A typical muscle man from Bihar will often keep chewing his paan and will speak only after one of his lackeys picks up the spitoon for him to spit out his paan juice.

Lalu had made a resolution to give up on his paan-chewing habit on New Year's Day in 1996, but the political tension seemed to have broken his will. However, his stars seemed to be at their peak at this time. After conquering Bihar formidably, Lalu's eyes were set on Delhi and the parliamentary elections of 1996. He didn't fail to openly express his desire for the prime ministerial position. Lalu's elevation as the Janata Dal's president also raised his and the hopes of others.

Lalu had sequentially demolished anyone who was and could become a challenge to him. He first sidelined his long time rivals Ram Sunder Das and Ramai Ram—both Dalits—to party posts. However, when they grew strong as state party chiefs, they were kicked out to be replaced by another of Lalu's cronies.[143]

He had started declaring in the rallies: '*Koi mai ka laal ab aapko Dilli par kabza karne se nahi rok sakta*' (No power on earth can stop you from capturing Delhi now). His enthusiasm was shared by his supporters who devised ingenious slogans and songs to appease their master, such as this one:

Ab Dilli tohe bulawe
Chadhaiya karba na

Now Delhi beckons,
Go and conquer.

The 1996 parliamentary elections were fought against the background of an unpopular Congress government at the Centre and a fragmented Congress party. Narasimha Rao's government was rocked by several corruption scandals, with seven of his cabinet ministers resigning during his term. Rao himself didn't remain untouched by these charges. The final year of Rao's government was dragged through the mud by the Vohra report, which highlighted a virtually parallel government being run by a politician–criminal nexus and escalating violence and unrest in Kashmir and Punjab. When it seemed that the problems on the government front couldn't get any worse, the party suffered further heavy setbacks. After a series of splits and factional squabbles, two stalwarts of the Congress, Arjun Singh and Narayan Datt Tiwari, decided to break away and form their own party, the All India Indira Congress (Tiwari). Plagued by scams, internal squabbles and defections, the Congress went into the 1996 elections woefully low on confidence.

The other parties also sensed that no party was going to get a decisive victory and hence political formations started coming into force even before the elections. In Bihar, the one-year-old Samata Party aligned with the BJP. The National Front, which had collapsed after 1990, tried to regain its presence as a viable alternative, albeit in a different form. It now comprised the Janata Dal, the Left front and the Telugu Desam Party. It was later joined by the Samajwadi Party with the simple goal of keeping the Congress and the BJP out of power. The Congress went alone in Bihar, but aligned with parties such as the All

India Anna Dravida Munnetra Kazhagam (AIADMK) in the south. Thus, a significant feature of the 1996 elections and a few others after it was the realignment of political parties to form viable coalitions in the absence of clear mandates.

In Bihar, the coming together of the BJP and Samata Party had made it tricky for the Janata Dal, which had an emphatic victory under Lalu's leadership just a year ago. When the results were declared, the myth of Lalu's invincibility was demolished. The results were a mandate on the growing arrogance of Lalu and his coterie, too. The Janata Dal, which had come to power on the pretext of social justice, kept increasing its reliance on Lalu's charisma and alienating itself from people. Corruption and anti-people practices had lately become a hallmark of Lalu's government, manifested by several scams. The well-knit social coalition of Lalu also developed chinks with the coming together of the BJP and Samata Party. Lalu and his coterie had overemphasised the Muslim–Yadav combination, thereby alienating other backward castes, most significantly the sizable Koeris-Kurmis. The EBCs that constituted a significant 30 per cent of the state's population also got little representation in the power structure. These factors combined with a viable alternative in the form of BJP-Samata brought the combine a total of 24 seats out of 54. Janata Dal was reduced to a tally of 22 from the previous figure of 31. Lalu was hurt but still not broken.

THE SCAM THAT SHOOK INDIA

The year 1997 marked the beginning of Lalu's decline. Mind you, just the beginning—Lalu would go on to hold the reins of Bihar for years to come even without holding an office. It was a sharp contrast from the situation just two years earlier when Lalu had been viewed as a credible contender for the position of prime minister.

Lalu had just returned as the chief minister of Bihar in March 1995. He was the only sitting chief minister to have returned to power since Bihar's first chief minister, Sri Krishna Sinha, in the 1950s. Two other factors that made it even more significant were Lalu's party and his caste. Lalu didn't come either from the Congress or any forward caste—the two features common among most of Bihar's chief ministers since Independence.

Lalu had certainly developed an astute political understanding on the right mechanisms to sway public opinion and their votes. Political pundits tried making sense of Lalu's political success and simplified it into the acronym 'M-Y'—the Muslim–Yadav combination. But it was far beyond that. Lalu had, for long, carefully cultivated an image of himself which seemed to characterise and stand for the poorest and the most vulnerable in Bihar. He spoke of the economic rights of the poorest, the socio-cultural rights of the marginalised and the hegemony of upper castes. People and often Lalu himself had started quipping by his second term:

> *Jab tak rahega samose me aaloo, tab tak rahega Bihar me Lalu.*
>
> As long as there are potatoes in samosa, Lalu will continue to rule Bihar.

In short, Lalu had started looking invincible. The one destined to rule, against all odds.

Till 25 July 1997.

The summer of 1997 in Patna was the tensest it had been in years. Rumours had begun circulating in the farthest corners of Bihar that Lalu might face arrest for corruption related to a fodder scam.

Those who hated him cursed him in their hearts, quoting the cliched:

> *Bhagwan ke ghar me der hai, andher nahi.*
>
> God does answer prayers, however late it may be.

Those who loved him rejected any such possibility:

> *Arre police ka itna aukaat hai ki Lalu ko giraftaar kar lega. Aajtak uska chhotka chela Shahabuddin ke ghar me ghus hi nahi paaya.*
>
> The police don't have the gumption to arrest Lalu. They haven't even been able to touch his stooge Shahabuddin in all these years.

When the rumours started getting stronger, however, they started praying, still hopeful that their messiah would pull some last-minute trick and avoid his impending arrest. The mastermind did pull a trick that even his opponents couldn't have anticipated but couldn't avoid his arrest.

Lalu was finally arrested for fodder scam and sent to jail on 25 July 1997. However, the arrest took extensive investigations, willpower, political machinations, negotiations and years of work, the links to which went as far back as the 1980s.

Roots of the Fodder Scam

Vijay Shankar Dubey was an IAS officer of the 1966 batch, who would later go on to become the chief secretary of both Bihar and Jharkhand. Known as a no-nonsense officer, he was posted as the principal secretary of the finance department in July 1995.

Dubey recounts the events to a News 18 reporter:

> By the year 1995–96, the financial condition of the Bihar government was so bad that even government employees were not getting their salaries [...] Since we were not in a position to pay the salaries of employees, it struck my mind that where the money is going.[144]

On further investigation, Dubey discovered that the Animal Husbandry Department (AHD) was spending more than five times its budgetary allocation. He immediately faxed a one-liner to all district collectors to check the last three years' expenditure for AHD.

Dubey also received an office memo from the Comptroller and Auditor General of Bihar on 20 January 1996, expressing concerns on the magnitude and manner of withdrawal from various treasuries.[145]

Dubey further recounts in the same interview:

> On 20 January, I dispatched one of our additional secretaries to Ranchi to find out where the money was spent during the last three years, and the very next day, on 21 January, he reported back saying, 'They have not only exceeded budget limits but all

the vouchers and bills, against which the money was withdrawn, are fake.'[146]

On 27 January 1996, Amit Khare, the then district collector of Chaibasa, raided the AHD and treasury offices in Chaibasa under instructions from Dubey. The documents seized by his team indicated the involvement of a large nexus of officials, politicians and businessmen in embezzlement of funds. The raid marked the unearthing of the massive scam that would come to be known as the Fodder Scam.

Following the unearthing of the scam, the state government formed two one-man commissions to probe the irregularities. However, the credibility of both these commissions came under the scanner when the lone member of the first commission, Phoolchand Singh, began featuring in the same chargesheet.[147]

The state BJP president and leader of opposition in the state assembly, Sushil Modi, filed a PIL in the high court on 11 March 1996. The court ordered a CBI probe into the scam, which was later upheld by the Supreme Court under stiff resistance from the state government.[148]

An enquiry by the CBI was initiated under the leadership of Joint Director U.N. Biswas. As the investigation proceeded, the CBI team unearthed linkages of the scam to the serving chief minister, Lalu Prasad Yadav. It formally made a request to the then governor A.R. Kidwai to prosecute Lalu Prasad Yadav. Since the enquiry was being conducted under the supervision of Patna High Court, the court enquired why the governor's permission was being sought. The CBI replied that it was just a 'precautionary measure'.

However, a lot had been transpiring amidst all this between the political circles in Patna and Delhi. I.K. Gujral had just taken over as the prime minister of India on 21 April 1997 after the fall of the H.D. Deve Gowda government. The Congress, which had been supporting Deve Gowda's United Front government from the outside, decided to withdraw its support after citing concerns of marginalisation in decision-making. Gujral was elected as the new leader of the United Front government as a consensus candidate from a list that also included Mulayam Singh Yadav and Lalu Yadav. Incidentally, Gujral and Lalu went a long way back. Lalu had helped Gujral get elected to the Rajya Sabha in 1992 after his election from Patna in the 1991 Lok Sabha elections was countermanded.

Governor Kidwai sanctioned the prosecution of Lalu on 17 June 1997. People from other parties as well as from within Lalu's own party, Janata Dal, started raising demands for his resignation. With growing pressure from his own party colleagues, Lalu formally parted ways to form his own party, the Rashtriya Janata Dal (RJD), on 5 July 1997.

It was a sign of Lalu's personal charisma that he took with himself almost all of Janata Dal members in the Bihar Assembly. RJD continued supporting the Gujral government, which was under continued pressure from the trio of Janata Dal leaders—Sharad Yadav, Deve Gowda and Paswan—to oust the RJD ministers from cabinet.[149] The other United Front leaders such as Chandrababu Naidu of the Telugu Desam Party (TDP) and Harkishen Singh Surjeet of CPI(M) also called for action against Lalu and dismissal of the RJD leaders.[150]

Lalu, in a bid to pacify Gujral, offered him a quid pro quo to run from any Lok Sabha constituency in Bihar.[151] Gujral, who was caught in a crossfire between the two sides, decided to take the middle path and that middle path involved India's premier investigation agency, the CBI. It was alleged that Deve Gowda during his prime-ministership had pushed CBI director Joginder Singh for Lalu's prosecution. He was returning the favour for the time when Lalu had insisted that Deve Gowda step down as the prime minister during internal squabbles in the coalition.[152]

Lalu would later confirm in a 2008 interview to NDTV's Shekhar Gupta:

> I went to him at his 7, Race Course Road residence and told him, 'Why are you hanging me? I will not be able to work in Bihar.' He was rude and I was also hyper. We said a lot of bad things to each other. He started weeping and fainted.[153]

Lalu went on to comment in the same interview that it was a 'mistake' to make Deve Gowda the prime minister.

While Deve Gowda allegedly used the CBI to target Lalu, it was Gujral's turn now to use the CBI in a diametrically opposite way. However, the scam had become too big for it to be fully contained. Gujral asked the CBI chief, Joginder Singh, to go slow on the prosecution.

Joginder Singh later went on to say in an interview:

> When I informed Mr Gujral about the issue, he asked me to go slow. I told him to give it [the order] to me in writing. He [I.K. Gujral] said: 'You know I am the prime minister?' I said yes and added that you are not supposed to know what is going on between me and the Patna High Court.

Joginder Singh further added that the matter didn't stop there and he got another call from the then home minister, Indrajit Gupta, asking him to go slow and save himself and his job.[154]

The Fodder Scam not just marred the reputation of Lalu and the careers of several others but it also marked a huge setback in Bihar's ever-slow bureaucratic decision-making. The officials became risk-averse and grew reluctant to sign any expenditure-related files. Many of the key initiatives or schemes were put on the back burner.[155] Lalu would confess in 2006 that the

Fodder Scam destroyed his chances of ever becoming the prime minister.[156]

From Housewife to Chief Minister

Amidst all the cacophony and a veritable sword hanging over his head, Lalu still kept a tight grip on his Machiavellian politics. First, breaking up the Janata Dal to form the RJD and saving his government and next, appointing his unlettered wife as the next chief minister of Bihar.

Rabri Devi's appointment as Bihar's chief minister was not just unexpected and surprising but it was also an artful move by one of the shrewdest politicians in the Hindi heartland. Rabri who was illiterate and had served no other role than being a dedicated housewife to Lalu till then suddenly arrived on the national scene.

Born to a small farmer, Shiv Prasad Chaudhary at Salar Kalan village of Gopalganj district, she was married at a young age to Lalu. Rabri recounts the family drama involving her marriage.

> *Shaadi me khoob ladai hua. Kahe ki baaki teeno behen ka shaadi accha zameen jyadad wala pariwaar me hua tha aur mere saasuraal me khali ek jhopdi tha.*
>
> There was a massive brawl during my wedding. This was because my other three sisters were married into well-to-do families with substantial properties, while my in-laws just had a thatched-roof hut.
>
> Everybody kept asking my father why he was handing out his daughter to a *bhikhmanga* (beggar).[157]

Over the next two decades, Rabri and Lalu's partnership resulted in nine children, seven of whom were girls. This was supposedly the couple's unique mode of protest against Sanjay Gandhi's forced sterilisation campaign during the Emergency. The couple even named their first child Misa after the infamous Maintenance of Internal Security Act, which was used to confine Lalu and several other leaders during the Emergency.

Rabri's appointment not only drew criticism but also piqued the curiosity of the general public. Everything, from her atypical name to her sister's even more atypical name, 'Jalebia', became the talk of the state. Political pundits stated varied opinions on the long-term viability of such an arrangement. The cynics quoted that she would meet the same fate as MGR's widow, Janaki Ramachandran, or N.T. Rama Rao's widow, Lakshmi Parvati; the claims to political legacy of their husbands were rejected by their state electorates.

Rabri was suddenly catapulted from the corners of the kitchen at 1, Anne Marg, the chief minister's residence, to being the official occupant of it. Her journey ahead wouldn't be easy as became evident at every public appearance that she had to make immediately afterwards. Having seen her falter thrice while taking her oath, the focus of Lalu's lieutenants shifted to solely managing Rabri's public appearances and making sure she didn't make any blunders.

Later, Rabri would vividly recollect her first journey to Patna post her wedding, while the entire district was locked under curfew. She had taken a steamer at Pahleja Ghat in Sonepur to reach Patna on Basant Panchami in 1974. She also recalls how she had to tackle the police who would come looking for Lalu at their Veterinary College peon quarters while Lalu was evading arrest.

Twenty-three years later, Lalu was not evading but avoiding arrest again. She was handed the charge this time under a more complex scenario than just to fend off policemen. Rabri's immediate challenge was to face the house and prove her majority. In her maiden speech in the Bihar Assembly, Rabri read her prepared speech carefully and haltingly. The speech ended before it even started.

The opposition led by Sushil Modi, which could barely wait to attack the ruling party and the mockery of democracy made by Lalu, jumped to its feet. Undeterred by the ruckus, Rabri sat composed in her pink sari. With no bows in her quiver, she picked the most emotional appeal just a few moments later. She rose to address Sushil Modi, whom she knew as Lalu's companion since the days of the Emergency. 'I have always considered you my elder brother.' The political novice's desperate appeal jailed to calm the raging opposition.

Sushil Modi continued his attack on Lalu and advised Rabri to throw the criminal out of her house. Rabri, who seemingly realised that house debates were no more than usual debates on *doora*—porch of the house—in Bihar's villages, retorted, 'I will send him to your house.'

The assembly erupted in laughter. The task of replying to the debate was left to Raghunath Jha, the parliamentary affairs minister.

After having proved her majority on the floor of the house, Rabri addressed reporters in what appeared to be a carefully practised line: 'I will do whatever my husband says but will not follow his *galat aadesh* (wrong advice).'[158]

In the months following her swearing-in, Rabri became adept at the few lines she was supposed to use every time she was posed with the inevitable questions on Lalu. 'My husband is not a chor (thief). He is being harassed because he fights for the Dalits and the poor' would be Rabri's usual retort. On being asked about her own ownership of the family's disproportionate assets, she would declare, '*Hum log koi chori kiye hain kya ki jail jayenge?*

Sirf kursi ki ladai hai' (Have we committed theft that we should go to jail? It's just a fight for the chair).

On the change in her role from a housewife to the chief minister of the state, she would grudgingly accept that she felt burdened but that it wouldn't change her role as a wife and a mother. 'Even as chief minister, I will continue to cook for my husband and children,' she would proudly declare. However, when pushed further to list out her priorities in governance, she wouldn't falter on using the phrases that had kept Lalu long in power, viz. social justice and dignity for the poor and women.

While Rabri followed every word of 'Saheb' carefully in matters of politics, she proved that she wouldn't be cornered when it came to family matters. Rumours were abuzz in political circles of Lalu's relationship with Kanti Singh, the union coal minister and Lalu's chief confidante. After failing to pacify Rabri Devi with explanations, Lalu had to simply give in to her dictum that Kanti Singh was not welcome in their house anymore.[159]

While Rabri was quickly learning the ropes of politics and administration, questions were raised on a slew of issues, even as trivial as her Independence Day speech. However, the bigger concerns were Bihar's slide into the abyss of administrative mismanagement and the ever-growing clout of the mafia.

Saale Sahab ki Sarkar

Lalu's infamous brother-in-law duo, Sadhu and Subhash Yadav, had gained notoriety much before their sister Rabri became the chief minister. Referred to as S2, Sadhu and Subhash Yadav had assumed pivotal roles in the running of the state as soon as the family shifted to 1, Anne Marg, the official residence of the chief minister.

Just a few years earlier, Sadhu had assaulted even Lalu's elder brother, Mahavir Rai, with whom Lalu used to stay in his days of struggle. Subhash wasn't far behind and had been charged with preventing the wife of a senior IAS officer from exercising her vote in Patna in the 1995 assembly elections.

Concerns were raised about the role of the Yadav brothers as soon as their sister Rabri became the chief minister. The concerns were not unfounded, as it soon turned out. The brothers became Rabri's eyes and ears. Sadhu even played a key role in distributing portfolios in Rabri's new cabinet of seventy-four members. However, the ministry didn't have even a single member from Gopalganj, the first family's home district. This was supposedly to avoid any alternative power centre in their 'fiefdom'.

Sadhu and Subhash's growing clout made them increasingly ambitious. Sadhu was already occupying an official bungalow on Kautilya Marg, which got regularised later by an administration keen to oblige. He went so far ahead as to rename his official bungalow '10, Janpath' in a show of importance that must be accorded to his residence. Sadhu's audacious misadventures went as far as assaulting an IAS officer, N.K. Sinha, at his chamber in 2001. Sinha, the then transport secretary, was allegedly assaulted by Sadhu and his supporters when he refused to follow Sadhu's order to transfer one of his men to Gopalganj, his home district. His growing audacity led Sadhu to a misadventure when he tried to stage a coup and dislodge Rabri. He went and collected signatures of fifty MLAs. But he didn't get too far. The incident brought down his stature in the family and paved the way for the rise of the younger brother Subhash.

Subhash Yadav had graduated from Magadh University in 1993. He soon secured a job as a class III employee in the Bihar state assembly, helped by Lalu. Subhash was soon retrenched, however, with many of the other illegal appointees in 1996. But his role changed when Lalu was arrested and Rabri replaced him as the chief minister.

Subhash, unlike his mercurial brother Sadhu, was calculating, even when aggressive. He became an important link between Lalu, the party and the government. He would often visit his brother-in-law in jail and execute his orders dutifully. Soon, Subhash's trips to the jail became more frequent and his role in the party and state administration more active. Subhash would play the lead role in organising Lalu's rallies and yatras, whether it was in Patna or Ranchi. Subhash's loyalty is reflected in his often quoted statement: '*Hum wahi karenge jo jijaji kahenge, aur kuch apna mann ka bhi karenge kahe ki unka saala hain*' (I will do as my brother-in-law [Lalu] says, and then some more, since I am his brother-in-law).

Subhash Yadav formed his own strong political base using all his groundwork and his proximity to the chief minister's residence. Subhash's growing clout was evident from his meddling with administrative decisions and his role in all transfers and promotions in the state, along with Sadhu. In 1998, he publicly abused a city SP for raiding a liquor shop, seizing stock and arresting eleven people for violating ban orders. Subhash and his men set free the arrested people after recovering the seized stock. He was soon rewarded with a nomination to the legislative council and a massive government bungalow behind the chief minister's residence on King George Avenue.

Soon after becoming a member of legislative council (MLC), his burgeoning wealth and misadventures triggered the opposition to demand his resignation. Newspapers frequently reported instances of his threatening public officers into complying with his decrees. The leader of opposition, Sushil Modi, spelt out the modus operandi in his charges against this all-powerful brother-in-law of Lalu. Sushil Modi claimed that

Subhash controlled three major moneyed departments, namely excise, transport and personnel. He handled all transfers and postings via Lalu and Rabri. It was also alleged that he ran a fleet of buses and his wife acted as a front in contract and toll collection businesses.

Once Shankar Prasad Tekriwal, a minister in the RJD government who was expelled from the party because he dared to rebel against the goings-on, alleged that in Bihar there were two treasuries—the official one that was empty and the private one that was full to the brim. He said two parallel governments ran in Bihar, one of the titular head Rabri and the other of her power-hungry brothers.

Lalu remained unperturbed by such allegations and rather enjoyed the one-upmanship between his two brothers-in-law. He would not fail to show his fondness for them in public. 'They are in fact my spies and keep me informed about dissident activities.' Subhash, in fact, also assumed the role of Lalu's alleged link with criminal-turned-MLAs, whose support remained instrumental in keeping Lalu's rule intact.

Rabri's worries didn't stop at her brothers alone. Her own role in the disproportionate assets of her family was on the radar after Lalu was firmly in the clutches of the CBI. As a pre-emptive measure, she deposited Rs 2.73 lakh as personal income tax for the period 1986–96. This brought her under the income tax radar. She was also accused of using the hospitality of a travel agency, the owners of which were Lalu's co-accused in the Fodder Scam. When placed under scrutiny, Rabri declared that she and her family possessed agricultural fields and dairy farms and the wealth had accrued from these sources. However, she rambled when asked about the exact location or the mode of acquisition of these farms.

The 1998 parliamentary elections also threw up a complex family issue for Lalu and the party. Both of Lalu's brothers-in-law decided they wanted to contest from Gopalganj. The elder, Sadhu, seemed determined to contest at any cost. While Sadhu declared that he had nursed the constituency for twenty-three long years and expected Rabri didi's aashirwaad (blessings), Subhash, the younger but seemingly more mature one, pinned his hopes on Lalu. '*Hamare liye saheb hi sab kuch hain. Saheb hi faisla karenge ki kaun umeedwar hoga*' (Saheb is everything for me. It is for Saheb to judge who will be the candidate). However, the waiting period couldn't deter Sadhu, who along with another RJD MLA, Munajir Hasan, beat up some of Subhash's supporters. Apparently, the duo was drunk.

The seat, however, wasn't allotted to either of them, and a politically shrewd Lalu allotted the ticket to the incumbent MP, Lal Babu Prasad Yadav.

THE CASTE WARS

We owe respect to the living,
To the dead, we owe nothing but the truth.

—Voltaire

EYE FOR AN EYE

Barra is a small sleepy village in the Tekari block of Gaya, a district situated in central Bihar of the then undivided state. A village with around fifty houses, mostly belonging to upper-caste Bhumihars, it rose to prominence on the fateful night of 12 February 1992. Television and radios the next day were abuzz with reports of a gruesome massacre in which thirty-five villagers, all Bhumihars, were killed.

A mob of around 500 people led by the heavily armed Maoist Communist Centre (MCC) cadres had surrounded the village from all sides and attacked it at around 10 p.m. as soon as the 300-odd villagers had gone to sleep. The MCC, a Left extremist organisation, had been actively strengthening itself in the region for a few years. The villagers were jolted out of their sleep by loud bomb explosions. The marauders set a number of houses ablaze and began pounding on doors in search of Ramadhar Singh and his lieutenant Hardwar Singh. Ramadhar Singh, a Bhumihar, was the commander of Sawarna Liberation Front (SLF), one of the numerous caste-based groups that arose during the period and which catered to narrow caste interests. Some of the marauders, dressed in police uniforms, demanded the villagers open their houses for a search, assuring them they wouldn't be harmed.

Some other mob members kept shouting slogans such as 'MCC zindabad!' and '*Jo humse takrayega, choor choor ho jayega'* (Whoever clashes with us will be shattered to pieces). The madness soon made way for the method, and the male members were herded and taken to a nearby canal. Their hands and feet were tied and non-Bhumihars were asked to identify themselves in the crowd. Four Bhumihars who posed as Brahmins were let off. Two other Dalits were also freed. Women and children were then asked to leave the place. What followed was a bloodbath, in which the throats of the tied captives were slit and they were left to bleed to death.

Sunil Kumar, the Gaya superintendent of police, received wireless messages from his police party after they noticed the fire blazing in the village and tried to rush to the spot. The police had to face roadblocks, gunfire and heavy resistance before they could reach the spot. The Maoists had cleverly cut trees and laid them on the roads to serve as roadblocks for anyone who may try to reach to help. By the time the police reached, what was left was thirty-five butchered bodies, as many inconsolable widows and an even larger number of orphaned children.

It was seventeen years later in 2009 that three accused, out of a total of 35 named and 100 unnamed in the chargesheet, would be convicted and sentenced to death by a Terrorist and Disruptive Activities (Prevention) Act (TADA) court in Gaya.

Barra was neither the first nor the last in the series of caste massacres to happen in central Bihar in the last century. The period from 1990 to 2001 saw 59 recorded incidents of caste massacres, resulting in the death of 571 people.[160]

There had been a spate of massacres in Bihar in the previous two decades; however, the outrage that the Barra massacre evoked was unprecedented. It was the first time that the Bhumihars, who had been one of the most influential and powerful caste groups in the state, were targeted in a systematic manner. Leaders across party lines visited the site of the massacre with a level of urgency never shown before, not even in the recent Dalit massacres in Savabigha or Mein-Barsima, just a few kilometres from Barra. Bhumihar MLAs of Jehanabad lobby—Ramjatan Sinha, Abhiram Sharma, Ramashray Prasad Singh and Jagdish Sharma—all from the Congress (I), were the first to rush to the village. As per a CID (Central Investigation Department) report, some of these MLAs, too, were accused of being involved in recent massacres in central Bihar.[161] Four former chief ministers, including three-time chief minister Jagannath Mishra and Bindeshwari Dubey, also paid a visit to the site. These former chief ministers, whose own tenure had been marred by several massacres, held the Lalu government responsible for the deteriorating law-and-order situation in Bihar and demanded its dismissal.

However, the Barra massacre didn't happen overnight and the seeds of it were planted in the events that preceded it, most of which revolved around the SLF and its commander Ramadhar Singh. Before taking over as the chief of SLF, Ramadhar Singh was an assistant in a mofussil college at his native Laali village in Gaya. SLF, which allegedly was funded by the notorious Dr Mahendra Prasad, also known as 'King Mahendra', would later become a mobilisation front for Bhumihars in the Gaya-Jehanabad region, against the organised mobilisation of agricultural labourers by the CPI(ML).

King Mahendra's own history is worth mentioning here. Mahendra Prasad, a Bhumihar originally from Jehanabad, a constituency he represented in the Lok Sabha from 1980 to 1984, was a pharmaceutical tycoon and owner of two companies, Aristo Pharma and Mapra Laboratories. King Mahendra, with a net worth of over Rs 4,000 crore, had been a Rajya Sabha MP since 1985 and was often referred to as the richest MP.[162] As an avid traveller, according to his profile on the Rajya Sabha website, he had travelled to every country in the world except Somalia. Interestingly, while King Mahendra was allegedly involved in the mobilisation of Bhumihars and gathering support for groups such as the SLF, he was also elected to the Rajya Sabha on a Janata Dal ticket in 1993, at the height of the rivalry of the Bhumihars with Lalu and his party, the Janata Dal.

Ramadhar Singh, the SLF chief, in the year leading up to the Barra massacre, often proclaimed openly to have got at least around hundred Naxalites killed. He would say, '*Mera itihaas mazdooron ki chita pe likha jayega*.' (My history will be written on the pyres of labourers.) In 1991, he went on a rampage in the Gaya-Jehanabad region, leading the SLF to commit the Savanbigha massacre, in which six Dalit Indian People's Front (IPF) sympathisers were killed. He also orchestrated the Mein-Barsima massacre, which took place three kilometres from Barra and resulted in the deaths of eleven Dalit labourers who were demanding minimum wages.[163] Ramadhar Singh, also known as 'Diamond' among Bhumihars, was chargesheeted as the prime accused in the Savanbigha case, but no action was taken. Ramadhar Singh had thus waged a war on Leftist groups like the Maoist Communist Centre (MCC), Mazdoor Kisan Sangram Samiti (MKSS) and the Indian People's Front (IPF).

The MCC, the most militant of the three organisations mentioned, had been seeking vengeance for a series of Dalit killings in Mein-Barsima for a long time. On the ominous night of 12 February 1992, it was fed the misinformation that Ramadhar Singh and his lieutenant Hardwar Singh were sheltered in Barra. Ramadhar Singh was in Patna at the time. The MCC mobilisation was allegedly fuelled by Surendra Yadav, the notorious Janata Dal MLA from Belaganj in Gaya district. Surendra Yadav, who had established a reign of terror in the Gaya region was at loggerheads with the district's new officials.

The trio of DM Rajbala Verma, SP Sunil Kumar and the DIG, Magadh Range, Balbir Chand, had succeeded, in a short time, in checking the criminal activities of Surender Yadav. A sure shot way to get these officers transferred was to organise a massacre, since Lalu had made it a practice to transfer the DM and SP in the event of a massacre. Yadav used the ongoing feud between MCC and SLF to this end. He organised a public meeting near Barra to draw people's attention to the lax attitude of the administration towards catching the perpetrators of the Mein-Barsima massacre. He further exhorted people to do something to get the officials transferred, who he said were obstacles to 'social justice'. He reminded people, 'Bhumihars have engaged our womenfolk as farm-labourers. Unless we get Bhumihar women to work for us, we will not get justice.' Audio tapes of the fiery speech were circulated in the area.[164] Barra, a Bhumihar-dominated village just three kilometres from Mein-Barsima, became an obvious target, particularly after the MCC cadres were fed the misinformation about Ramadhar Singh's presence in the village.

Ramadhar Singh 'Diamond' who was camping in Patna at the time of massacre openly declared his intent for vengeance by vowing to kill ten Dalits for every life lost in the Barra massacre.

The Seeds of Caste Wars

To understand the origin of caste wars in Bihar, one must first understand the social and economic roles played by caste and land, respectively, and the interplay between the two. The caste wars of late twentieth-century Bihar were the culmination of decades of simmering social and economic tensions.

The relation between the caste and class components of agrarian structure in Bihar has been outlined by Andre Beteille.

> [...] there are two kinds of relationships between caste and the agrarian class structure. The first is what we call a surface relationship which is revealed by the fact that landowners belong predominantly to the upper castes and the landless to the lower castes. The second is a deeper relationship in which the hierarchical values of caste are sustained and legitimised to an unequal relation among landowners, tenants and agricultural labourers.[165]

Bihar had been a strongly feudal society that remained so even after Independence. There were major inequalities in society that weren't just economic but social as well as political. Often, these inequalities were highly correlated with caste identities. The economic, political and social scenes were highly dominated by the forward—Bhumihars, Brahmins, Rajputs and Kayasthas—and the so-called middle castes—Yadavs, Koeries and Kurmis—throughout the latter half of the nineteenth century.

An extremely disproportionate authority was and still is wielded by the largest landowner in the village. This affected not only agrarian issues but also the daily social lives of villagers. The exploitative agrarian system had enslaved the vast majority of peasants in a lifelong debt trap and informal bondage. Thus, a large section of society's marginalised landless strata was forced to surrender their freedom and dignity in order to serve the more pressing goal of economic survival.

The state did witness some land reform movements in the pre-Independence era led by leaders such as Swami Vidyanand and Swami Sahajanand Saraswati. Under the leadership of Swami Sahajanand Saraswati, the Bihar Provincial Kisan Sabha (BPKS) raised issues such as begar (forced labour), abwab (illegal exactions) and bakasht land (land originally belonging to the *raiyats* (tenants and cultivators) but taken over by the landlords in lieu of rent arrears), among others. The BPKS grew from 80,000 members in 1935 to over 2,50,000 in 1938, making it the largest such movement in India.[166]

The most important demands of these movements were the abolition of the zamindari system, the grant of ownership rights to peasants, the cancellation of agrarian debt and tax exemption for low-income families. The BPKS fizzled out after Sahajanand's death in 1950 and the abolition of the zamindari system which was BPKS's most staunch demand.

In post-Independence Bihar, Acharya Vinoba Bhave's Bhoodan Movement soon followed these land reform movements. Based on the Gandhian notion of trusteeship whereby the rich are merely the custodians of wealth and not its owner, Bhave urged the landed class to give up surplus land for redistribution.

By March 1966, the movement claimed to have distributed only 3,11,037 acres of land to the landless families in Bihar.[167] Apart from its insignificant impact, the Bhoodan Movement in Bihar has been criticised for its misuse by several landlords to circumvent land reform measures such as land ceiling and consolidation.[168]

The subversion of land reforms, the continued oppression of the landless, alongside a rising political and social consciousness, led sections of the marginalised class to rise up against the oppressive regime. The gradual awakening of the lower castes was catalysed by extreme events such as the famine of 1966–67 and the Leftist movements against agrarian excesses.

The discrimination and dominance along with the economic exploitation by the oppressive caste order were resisted by the agitating lower castes. Sexual molestation of Dalit women was resisted aggressively, and it was only in the second stage of the movement that the struggle turned to economic issues such as the demand for higher wages.[169] These basic demands later provided an impetus to the land grab movement in the 1970s. The Naxalite Movement led to intermittent clashes in isolated incidents before it became organised through armies and counter-armies.

The Naxal Movements

The Naxalite Movement owes its origin to an armed uprising of peasants and labourers against the region's landlords in the village of Naxalbari in West Bengal. The year was 1967. During the protests, the peasants forcibly harvested standing crops, captured the granaries of the landlords and burnt outstanding debt records.

The upsurge led to the formation of CPI(ML) in 1969, one of the major communist factions in India. Its ideology of armed revolution and electoral boycott, found many takers among the youth and masses, particularly the poorest and most exploited. However, the party eventually split into several factions, almost sixty of them.[170]

The earliest Naxal uprisings in Bihar took place as isolated incidents in the Mushahari region of Muzaffarpur district, as well as in parts of Bhojpur and Patna. However, these struggles, which were modelled after the Naxalbari uprising, were unable to maintain their initial gains.

In many of these cases, the struggle was not for wages or for economic empowerment but for basic rights and human dignity. The Dalits would be often addressed condescendingly with an 'arey' or other derogatory names loaded with caste connotations. Wearing clean or neatly ironed clothes, walking with their heads held high or looking into the eyes of upper-caste men were out of bounds for Dalits. They couldn't sit in a chair or on a cot in front of upper-caste men; they were required to take their place on the floor. The Naxalite Movement that spoke of justice, rights and equality struck a natural chord with hundreds of youth suppressed by existing hierarchical caste and class structures.

A sustained movement first took root in the 1970s in Bhojpur's Ekwari village where Jagdish Mahato, a local teacher, led a protracted struggle against exploitative landlords. Mahato received support from Naxalite leaders who had come from West Bengal and went on to expand the CPI(ML) (Liberation). From Bhojpur, the influence of CPI(ML)(Liberation) spread to the adjoining districts in central Bihar and subsequently to parts of northern and southern Bihar (present-day Jharkhand).[171]

Since its inception, the movement was dealt with a heavy hand by the administration and nearly silenced by police and paramilitary operations. The movement was able to gain ground in the late 1970s, when many of its leaders and cadres were released from prisons after the Emergency. The 1980s saw a resurgence of the movement on the back of popular concerns such as land rights, minimum wages and social justice.

When travelling through Bihar, it was commonplace to spot a red flag firmly planted in the middle of a field. Such flags declare the right of Naxalites over the land. The Naxalites usually stake such claims over surplus land (above ceiling limits), misappropriated gair majarua (common) land or lands of absentee landlords. However, at times, it was also used to settle land disputes in cases where one of the contestants would be a Naxal sympathiser or belonged to a Naxalite group. Such red flags and letters were often sent to landlords, warning them to evict the land or face dire consequences. Prolonged battles would often ensue, resulting in loss of lives and property, till one of the sides would give up the untenable battle. The Naxalites, if they won the land, would redistribute it among local Dalits for agriculture or housing purposes. In some cases, the land would remain in the hands of the party, which would then lease it to the organisation members on a sharecropping basis. The Naxalites also attempted tenancy reforms and enforcement of batai—equal share for landlord and tenant—in some areas, but not without problems.

Minimum wages was another contentious issue. Though an official minimum wage has existed in India since Independence, its knowledge and enforcement in Bihar's agrarian sector is far from realisation. The Naxalites took it up as an important issue in central Bihar post the 1970s with considerable success. However, this wasn't without bloody battles or, in more benign forms, wage strikes and *arthik nakebandi*—economic blockade—against a landlord. Such strikes would lead to a boycott of a landlord and his family by wage labourers of other castes, including those from nearby villages, making it impossible for the landlord to hire labourers. This would result in the land being left fallow for many years. The situation would often then turn violent. Prior to wage strikes, the harvester labourers used to receive one bojha (headload) for every twenty-one bojhas as wages. It rose to one bojha for every ten bojhas by the 1990s.[172] The cause of wages turned out to be a successful campaign for the Naxalite movement for multiple reasons. For instance, it could be taken up by mass fronts of the party without dependence on underground or armed support; it could draw and unite labourers from across castes on a class basis, and the long overdue increase in wages accorded it a good chance for success. The increased rates benefitted not just the casual daily wagers but also halwahas (tillers) and bandhuas (bonded labour), who were tied more loyally to landlords.

The first uprisings, however, were neither for land rights nor minimum wages. In fact, they were against the violation of dignity and termed as *izzat ki ladai* by the Naxal groups. They asserted their right to being treated as human and their right as individuals to common spaces such as village ponds and schools. The Naxalite Movement raised a voice against instances of rape of lower-caste women, arbitrary beatings of Dalits and oft-accorded public humiliation. What may look obvious in a free world—things like selling their labour to whoever they chose, wearing clean clothes, sending their children to schools and even sitting leisurely on khatias in front of their homes—had to be fought for.

The mobilisation of masses by the Naxalite groups was met with formidable resistance through caste militias of landlords. These caste militias, formed and supported not just by the upper castes but also the upper backward castes, aimed to develop intra-caste solidarity instead of a cross-caste cross-class solidarity aimed for by Naxalites. Fourteen such caste armies came to be formed and supported mainly by the Bhumihars, Rajputs, Yadavs and Kurmis in Bihar, mostly during the 1980s and 1990s.[173]

The earliest images of caste wars in this period date back to 1977. Eleven Dalits were killed by Kurmis—also an OBC caste—in Belchi, ninety kilometres from Patna, in what was an inter-gang rivalry. Belchi shot to national prominence with an enduring image of Indira Gandhi riding an elephant to reach the waterlogged village.[174] She had been thrown out of power just six months ago and her quick and courageous trip to Belchi brought her back into prominence.

The caste wars triggered in Belchi didn't slow down till the end of the millenium, by which time almost 856 people had been killed in 90 such attacks.[175] The bulk of these killings happened in the last six years of the millenium, post the formation of Ranvir Sena—the private militia group of Bhumihars mainly concentrated in central Bihar—in 1994.

Naxal Factions and Caste

In the 1980s and 1990s, three of the several factions that had the maximum impact on the Naxalite Movement in Bihar were the CPI(ML)(Liberation), CPI(ML)(Party Unity) and Maoist Communist Centre (MCC). The first two are generally referred to as Liberation and Party Unity (PU), respectively.

The strongest section of the Naxalite movement, after its resurgence post-Emergency, was Liberation. Liberation had a formidable presence in the central parts of undivided Bihar under the leadership of Vinod Mishra. The party had taken the route of mass movements but supported it with armed activities. Its cadre was largely drawn from the peasant class belonging to the SCs. These peasants had to confront not just the upper castes but also the landowning backward castes, such as Kurmis and Yadavs, in their struggle for wages, land and dignity. The Liberation thus had to fight not just the upper caste-backed Brahmarshi Sena (Bhumihars) and Kunwar Sena (Rajputs) but also the Bhumi Sena of Kurmis and Lorik Sena of the Yadavs. The Liberation, with popular support from poor peasants, was soon able to counter and affect the demise of these caste armies. It thus looked like a successful experiment, with a combination of underground armed struggle and overground mass movement in the form of Indian People's Front (IPF). Rameshwar Prasad of the IPF won the Lok Sabha elections from the Arrah (Bhojpur) seat in 1989. The IPF further went on to win seven seats in the 1990 assembly elections. However, the infeasibility of combining parliamentary and non-parliamentary paths led to the demise of IPF and subsequent weakening of Liberation. The IPF was disbanded in 1994 after Liberation itself filed for recognition as a political party. It went on to fight the 1995 assembly elections as CPI(ML).

After the great communist debates of the 1980s, over choosing a parliamentary path versus that of an anti-establishment struggle, the Liberation had subsequently chosen the former. However, two other strong sections of the movement, the PU and MCC chose the path of non-parliamentary movement more staunchly, though not without experimenting with open fronts and over-ground movements.

PU advocated the path of agrarian revolution and protracted people's war.[176] It adopted the twin strategy of selective annihilation and economic blockade of landowners. PU through its land seizure struggles came to be associated with the slogan *Zameen jabtee, fasal jabtee* (Seize land, seize crops).[177] The party vehemently denounced any participation in elections. It was also held responsible for the 1997 massacre of six Bhumihars at Raghopur in Patna district. The house of local MLA Janardhana Sharma was blown up twice in the attack. Greater casualties were prevented as the Naxals hadn't accounted for new phone lines installed in the village a few months earlier. Villagers were able to contact the policemen in the neighbouring Nagahar village, who arrived soon.[178]

However, the one group that had maximum impact on the Naxal movement in Bihar was the MCC. It perceived the struggle to be a movement for appropriating political power. The most brutal of the three factions, the MCC advocated action against 'class enemies'. It conducted a number of massacres in the central parts of undivided Bihar, including some major ones such as the massacre of forty-two Rajputs in Dalelchak-Bhagaura in Aurangabad district in 1987, the massacre of thirty-five Bhumihars in Barra in Gaya district in 1992 and the massacre of thirty-four Bhumihars at Senari in Jehanabad district in 1999. The MCC, too, experimented working with open fronts. However, it soon gave up on the path following heavy police repression and targeting of persons working openly by the police.

While principally the Naxalite movement was primarily based on class, it couldn't remain unaffected by the rise of 'caste politics' in Bihar, which became a dominant factor, especially in the 1990s. Class struggles have often been seen to overlap with caste wars. However, in Bihar class struggle was relegated to the background by the prominence of caste violence.

There was a strong interface in this period, between the Naxalite factions and the castes associated with it. The SCs and EBCs formed the mass base of Liberation. The other two parties, viz. PU and MCC couldn't develop a strong class ideology as Liberation, and remained largely caste-based. While the PU state committee was largely dominated by Kurmis, the Yadavs had a clear dominance in MCC.[179] MCC's Yadav domination also explained their complicity in power and often claimed Lalu's clandestine support to the organisation. MCC's overground leader, Vinay Kumar Arya, accompanied Lalu in the 1995 assembly elections campaign trail, travelling in the same vehicle as him.[180] Lalu cleverly used both these organisations to counter Liberation's growing electoral influence.

The call for boycott of elections given by PU and MCC may actually have helped Lalu. While the call terrorised non-committed opponent voters, it hardly had any effect on the core Yadav voter base of Lalu. The Liberation once alleged the nexus between MCC and RJD. 'MCC used to extend its support to the Rashtriya Janata Dal (RJD) in Bihar and Jharkhand Mukti Morcha (JMM) in Jharkhand.'[181]

One of the first things Lalu did after coming to power was to weaken the Liberation by breaking away its four MLAs and then offering plum posts—chairmanship of boards and corporations—to its influential leaders. The Liberation's front, the IPF, had just won seven seats in its debut election run in the 1990 assembly elections. The Yadavs and Koeris from the weakening Liberation switched their loyalty to Lalu.

Lalu also made good political use of the subsequent massacres of lower castes and landless peasants perpetrated by Ranvir Sena and the retaliatory killings by Naxalite groups. The government often remained a passive observer to such incidents and let the gruesomeness of the sena killings further deepen the divide between the upper castes and landless Dalits, thus consolidating Lalu's own voter base.

This also weakened the Liberation cadres which wanted revenge but grew frustrated with the giving up of violence in 1992. It is then that PU and MCC, with their increased aggression and armed activities, attracted a section of Liberation supporters who had grown disgruntled by Liberation's parliamentary route. They often felt they had been left out in the cold, unarmed and helpless against the armed attack of landowners.

These Naxalite factions had operated hand-in-hand till 1986, to counter private armies such as Brahmrishi Sena, Bhoomi Sena and Lorik Sena of upper and middle castes. Later, they fell out and constantly sought opportunities to display their organisational might or settle scores with each other. PU claimed that Liberation led by Vinod Mishra was 'opportunist and power hungry'. The MCC believed that Liberation exploited the poor and had stooped so low as to bargaining for money, especially during elections. PU clashed with Liberation over control in the Jehanabad region while it clashed with the MCC over control in the Tekari and Konch areas of Gaya region.[182] The internecine clashes among the various factions led to the loss of lives of hundreds of Naxalite cadres.[183]

By remaining silent and letting lawlessness capture Bihar's flaming fields, Lalu showed the SCs that they had no option but to side with him if they wanted to survive. Lalu's favourite tools in his fight for the caste-coated social justice turned out to be indifference, inaction and at times co-option, while the Dalits bled in the central plains of Bihar. Lalu, unlike his predecessors, dealt with the Naxalite movement as a political rather than a law-and-order problem and seeked to benefit from it. The Samata Party and Nitish Kumar sided with the Ranvir Sena—private militia of upper-caste Bhumihars—going to the extent of demanding the removal of the ban on it, thereby polarising and further consolidating Lalu's voter base of lower castes.

The organised struggle of these marginalised sections had not just the landed class as its opponent but also the state whose members came from and seeked to protect the interests of the landed class. A.R. Desai, who has extensively studied the rise of Naxal violence, writes:

> [...] since the state is capitalist in nature, it inherently protects the propertied class. Any move by the marginalised class towards equal distribution of resources is seen as a threat to the state. This also makes visible, the class and caste character of the state.[184]

The first significant attack from the Naxalite groups came in 1987 in the form of the massacre of forty-two Rajputs at Dalelchak–Bhagaura village of Aurangabad district. Aurangabad, a district located in central Bihar, is also known as 'Mini Chittorgarh' because of the presence of a significant Rajput population. The twin villages of Dalelchak and Bhagaura were inhabited by people from varied castes, but most of the land around was held by the Bodh Gaya Mahant and some landlords. There was an ongoing conflict between the Rajputs and Yadavs over the control of such a large piece of government land. This conflict had already led to gun fights, deaths and counter attacks. However, it escalated to its grim peak when 300 to 400 armed men attacked the twin villages on the night of 29 May 1987, went scouting for Rajputs, massacred them and set the village on fire. The MCC, dominated by Yadavs, took responsibility for the massacre. In the aftermath, forty surviving Rajput families fled the village.

Dalelchak–Bhagaura was the biggest massacre in the history of Bihar. It attracted huge condemnation from all quarters and 29 May 1987 got listed as one of the darkest nights of Bihar. However, the real spate of massacres and counter massacres started only after the Barra massacre of 1992. The state saw almost fifty-nine massacres in the eleven years between 1990 and 2001. The ruthless MCC and PU conducted several massacres mainly in the Gaya and Jehanabad districts. The strengthening Leftist organisations didn't just eliminate the landed-class enemies but also the police whom they considered equally responsible for the perpetration of injustice. On 20 January 1996, a 300-strong squad of MCC members descended on Tekari main market in Gaya district and sealed off the area. It is important to note that Tekari was one of the worst affected blocks of Naxal violence and barely five kilometres from Barra village, the site of the 1992 massacre of thirty-five Bhumihars. The Naxalites then surrounded the police station located in the main market, killed the five policemen manning the station and walked away with their weapons. The attack was a retaliation against a recent high court order confirming the death sentence of eight MCC activists involved in the 1987 Dalelchak-Baghaura massacre of fifty-two Rajputs. The attackers put up posters on the wall of the station before retreating, calling the convicts heroes.[185]

It was 3:30 p.m. in the afternoon when the police station located in a busy marketplace was raided. It showed the growing audacity of the Naxals who generally chose nighttime to attack and flee.

Rise of Private Armies

The rise of Leftist movements in central Bihar was countered by the rise of private caste armies. Bihar must be the only state in post-Independence India to have private caste armies, almost fourteen of them at one point.[186] Most of these armies originated in the 1980s with the growing Left influence but gained prominence only in the late 1980s and 1990s. These senas, primarily dominated and financed by the landed groups, spanned across the upper and middle castes. The Rajputs had their first such army in 1979 by the name of Kuer Sena, which operated primarily in the Bhojpur area. Other groups such as Sunlight Sena and Kisan Morcha were also formed by the Rajputs in the late 1980s. The Bhumihars also formed a series of private armies starting with the Brahmrishi Sena in 1984 and SLF in 1990 before settling with the dreaded Ranvir Sena. The Brahmins and Kayasthas didn't have any major armies and lent support to one or the other upper-caste armies. However, such private armies weren't just limited to the upper castes.

The middle castes of Yadavs and Kurmis also experimented with a number of groups to protect their land consolidations, which had mostly occurred after the land reform measures of the government, post-Independence. These middle castes had emerged as the new landlords in the 1980 and 1990s. This had brought them in direct conflict with the landless labourers and Dalits, the core base of Naxalites. The Lorik Sena of the Yadavs and the Bhumi Sena of the Kurmis were both formed around 1983 and were largely active around the Patna, Jehanabad and Nalanda regions. Both were notorious throughout the 1980s.

Despite all other differences, a common thread that ran across all these caste armies was their limited longevity. Most of these senas lacked structure, organisation or even a goal. They had mostly been formed as reactionary armies to Left consolidation in the central Bihar belt. Hence, almost all of these armies followed the same trajectory of a quick decline. The only exception to this was Ranvir Sena, which was formed in 1994 by the Bhumihars in the Bhojpur district of central Bihar. However, to understand the unique circumstances of Ranvir Sena, in terms of longevity and impact, it is important to understand its primary base, the Bhumihars.

Bhumihars: A Peculiar Caste

Often referred to as militant Brahmins, the Bhumihars have a strong affinity with their land and are majorly to be found in Bihar and eastern Uttar Pradesh (Purvanchal). The Bhumihars, purportedly ranked below the Brahmins in ritualistic status, consider themselves as Brahmins involved in agriculture. Two specific characteristics historically separated Bhumihars from the Brahmins. First, they refused to accept charity like the Brahmins did and second, most of them were landholders by profession. The worldview of Bhumihars has been shaped by two contradictory pulls: to get the ritualistic status of Brahmins and to dominate the rural world as Kshatriyas. While their clout has been waning lately with the rising awareness among the hitherto oppressed classes, they have guarded their hierarchical and social status more vehemently than any other upper caste in Bihar. The caste army was one such manifestation and seemed for them to be the last hope of guarding their privileges and making a political comeback to their heydays.

One of the first such experiments was the Brahmrishi Sena, founded by Krishna Singh Sardar, an independent MLA from Bihar. The Jehanabad lobby of the Congress, primarily led by Mahendra Singh alias 'King Mahendra' fully backed him. The sena was active in the Bhumihar-dominated regions of Gaya, Jehanabad, Nalanda and Patna in the 1980s. Brahmrishi Sena was accused of massacres in the villages of Aminabad and Kansara in Jehanabad in 1986, after which it was banned. However, its existence was short-lived, primarily because of factionalism and the elimination of its commanders by Naxal groups.

This was soon followed by Ramadhar Singh's SLF. The landed Bhumihars looked first towards the Brahmrishi Sena and later to Ramadhar Singh to carry their baton of struggle against the Maoists. The Maoists, led by MCC, came strongly against the SLF. Faced with the hostile sena of the Bhumihars, they abandoned the 'class war thesis' and targeted any and every Bhumihar irrespective of their class distinction.

However, the SLF couldn't differentiate itself from the Brahmrishi Sena in terms of its longevity. It soon disintegrated due to the lack of organisational structure and continuous attacks by armed Maoist groups. The final blow to it came in the form of the arrest of its founder, Ramadhar Singh, by the Gaya police in 1992. Allegedly, Ramadhar Singh himself orchestrated the arrest to save his life from the Naxals and the police. Police sources reported that Ramadhar Singh desperately wanted the status of political prisoner, a privilege in Bihar's notorious jails.

After Ramadhar Singh was interned, the epicentre of discontent and rivalry between Bhumihars and Maoists shifted northward to Bhojpur district. It would be here in one of the largest villages of Bhumihars that an organisation would soon be formed, which would go on to become one of the most dreaded upper-caste organisations ever formed. It would unleash a reign of terror over the next eight years that would be unmatched in its ruthlessness by any of its predecessors.

THE RANVIR SENA

Money is considered an important arbiter of society. However, in Bihar, there are several other proxies of power and one of the most prevalent ones is violence. As is the case elsewhere, power flows through the barrels of guns in Bihar.

While the Bhumihars had earlier experimented with the Brahmrishi Sena and Sawarna Liberation Front (SLF), it was the Ranvir Sena that brought them dominance in the caste wars in the central Bihar region. The Bhumihars who formed the base of Ranvir Sena were largely drawn from similar groups such as Brahmrishi Sena of early 1980s in Gaya and SLF in the 1990s in the Gaya-Jehanabad region.[187]

Ranvir Sena was formed in 1994 in Bhojpur district's Belaur village. The name was inspired by a retired military man from the nineteenth century, Ranvir Chaudhary, who was a resident of the same village. He had supposedly protected the rights of the Bhumihars against the domination of the Rajputs and led them to assert their supremacy in the region. The immediate triggers for the formation of the sena are generally not agreed upon. However, it is worthwhile to mention the two separate incidents that are thought to be the immediate causes for the birth of Ranvir Sena.

The first probable catalyst dates back to an incident in Belaur in 1993 when a landlord detained a labourer in captivity for having raised the demand for higher wages. The labourer, however, had to be set free after villagers led by CPI(ML) workers blocked the main road between Arrah and Sahar. The prominent Bhumihars of the village, including the mukhiya (chief), thought that it was necessary to check the growing influence of CPI(ML), and from this group, the Ranvir Sena was eventually formed.[188]

Another incident that has been quoted in *Liberation,* the party newspaper of CPI(ML), sounds frivolous but, given the prevailing caste egos in Bihar, cannot be completely rejected. According to the story, on 11 July 1994, a Bhumihar youth of Belaur village went to a local shop for cigarettes, where the shopkeeper told him that he didn't have any. However, in the evening a Dalit youth from the same village got cigarettes from the shopkeeper. This infuriated Bhumihar youth, along with his friends, thrashed the shopkeeper. Birbal Yadav, a CPI(ML) supporter who tried to mediate in the issue, was also beaten up. The incident apparently escalated the tensions between Bhumihars and Dalits and eventually led to the formation of Ranvir Sena.

The sena was very active in the years from 1994 until 2002, the year in which its chief Brahmeshwar Mukhiya was arrested. Ranvir Sena was different from its predecessors or other caste armies in more ways than one. It was the first such group to have a well-articulated ideological commitment, an organisational and leadership structure and also a robust support system which included landowners, politicians, criminal gangs and caste leaders.

A statement released by the sena made its intentions clear:

> Being forced by the atrocities of CPI(ML), we the kisan putras [sons of peasants], have formed the Ranvir Sena. We have

> taken the pledge to clear the CPI(ML) dogs from their roots in Bihar. We are determined to avenge every killing of peasants by assassinating a hundred Naxalites.[189]

While the sena had the support of Rajputs and other dominant castes in the region, it was primarily led and supported by Bhumihars. The coming together of Bhumihars and Rajputs, two of the most powerful castes and historical foes was as significant as the formation of the sena itself. The common class interests, the anti-Mandal movement and a rising OBC assertion under Lalu's rule were the prime reasons for this bonhomie.

The sena would go on to expand its geographical presence as well as its role much beyond that exerted by any other caste senas. It started to make its presence felt in 1996 through its involvement in two massacres in Bhojpur, in the villages of Khopira and Sarthua. Khopira also gave the sena its main leader, Brahmeshwar Singh, just a few months after its formation. Brahmeshwar Singh, who was reverentially called 'Mukhiya Ji' by his supporters, turned the sena into a paramilitary force and a de-facto political organisation with his guerrilla warfare techniques and great organisational skills. Brahmeshwar Singh is said to have mobilised financial resources from a wide network of sena sympathisers and established a monthly salary-based structure for cadres.[190]

However, the name of the organisation made national headlines when in 1996, it massacred twenty-one Dalits and Muslims in Bathani Tola, Bhojpur district, who the sena alleged were Maoist sympathisers. Among the dead were six children, three infants and eleven women. The massacre gave Brahmeshwar Singh the title 'Butcher of Bathani Tola'. Vinod Mishra, the general secretary of CPI(ML)(Liberation), declared an 'eye for an eye' policy just after the massacre.

Fourteen years later, in 2010, a sessions court in Arrah district convicted and sentenced three people to death and twenty others to life imprisonment in connection with the Bathani Tola massacre. Among the three awarded death sentence, Manoj Singh was charged with the killing of the three-month-old daughter of Naimuddin, one of the prime witnesses; Ajay Singh was charged with the slaughter of ten-year-old Phool Kumari; and Narendra Singh was charged with the brutal murder of two women, Ramratia Devi and Sanjharu.[191] However, all of them were acquitted later by a divisional bench of Patna High Court in 2012, citing 'defective evidence'.[192]

To understand the modus operandi of Ranvir Sena, it is important to understand their ideology that stems from a complex interplay of class, caste and their social and economic implications. The sena, as is apparent from their actions, had been strongly opposed to Maoists organisations. It is not just Maoism but the whole spectrum of communism that they considered antithetical to their own as well as society's interest. The origins of Ranvir Sena may be attributed to the anxiety among erstwhile dominant castes, especially the Bhumihars, about retaining their hegemony over the social and economic landscape of Bihar. However, as it grew and became stronger with support and resources from large quarters of the upper-caste population, politicians and people with vested interests, it also developed structures, processes and ideology like any well-functioning organisational machinery. The sena at its peak had easy access to 17,000 licensed weapons in the possession of Bhumihars. Ranvir Sena claimed in one of its pamphlets: 'The communists have been defeated in Russia and Eastern Europe, now they must be uprooted in India also.'[193]

The Deadliest Period

Ranvir Sena and MCC grew in strength equally, and this led to a never-ending series of bloody reprisals in retaliation to each other's actions. The last five years of the 1990s saw almost forty-three massacres with over 400 victims.[194]

The most chilling of the massacres conducted by the sena is dated to 1 December 1997. Laxmanpur Bathe, a nondescript village of 2,000 inhabitants, is located on the banks of River Son in Jehanabad district. The river, which serves as the lifeline of the village, is also the natural border between the districts of Jehanabad and Bhojpur. There was nothing unusual about the dead silence of the night of 1 December after its residents had gone to sleep.

However, just across the river, a huge group of about 250 men, armed with country-made pistols and knives, had boarded the boats anchored in silent waters, to reach the village. No one saw or heard them as they crossed the one-and-a-half kilometre stretch of river or even when they dispersed in groups upon reaching the village. It was only when bullets started suddenly flying in all directions accompanied by war cries of 'Ranvir Sena Zindabad!' that the inhabitants were shaken awake from their slumber. The sena men forced their way through the huts by breaking open their doors and fired indiscriminately at any human figure they could see sleeping, running, crawling or hiding. The massacre lasted for over three hours, decimating the entire hamlet along the riverside. Two-year-old Sumitra who was sleeping curled up next to her mother was shot in the abdomen. Her elder brother, five-year-old Arvind, had a bullet hole in his head. Their aunt, sixteen-year-old Sita, slated to be married five days later, lay by their side. In a first massacre of its kind, women and children were directly targeted. By the end of the carnage, fifty-eight Dalits, including thirty-five women and children, were killed. The attackers had achieved the highest-ever tally of victims in a caste massacre in Bihar.

The attackers, in a bid to remove the last shred of evidence before disappearing into Bhojpur, slit the throats of the two boatmen who had rowed them back across the river.

Laxmanpur Bathe was selected as a target for a variety of reasons. The sena members believed that the village inhabitants, mostly Dalits, were Maoists sympathisers, who had carried out the Barra massacre of thirty-five Bhumihars in 1992. That the village wasn't guarded unlike neighbouring villages by militant Dalits made Bathe a soft target. It helped the attackers that the village didn't have electricity and the nearest road was four kilometres away. However, the immediate reason may lay, as claimed by the then DGP S.K. Saxena, in a CPI(ML) provocation. The CPI(ML), just a few weeks before the massacre, had called a Jan Adalat. It had passed a decision to forcibly harvest the paddy grown by a Bhumihar landlord on a disputed thirty-acre government land in the village.[195] This was precisely the kind of Naxal threat that Ranvir Sena was formed to counter.

When the news of the massacre hit the headlines the next day, it sent shockwaves across the country. President K.R. Narayanan termed the massacre as a 'national shame'. Around 200 Bhumihar families in the vicinity of Laxmanpur Bathe fled their homes, fearing a reprisal. The accused in the case faced trials at various levels before being acquitted by Patna High Court in 2013 due to 'lack of evidence'.

Ranvir Sena was criticised bitterly for this massacre, particularly for targeting women and children. Many of its own supporters were dismayed at the gruesomeness of the attack. The sena's logic behind the killing of women and children was explained by one of its remorseless commanders to press reporters thus:

> We kill the women because they give birth to Naxalites; when the children grow up, they become Naxalites and kill us. They [Dalits] give shelter to Naxalites. In Bara, they killed 35 Bhumihars and in Dalechek-Bhagaura, 42 Rajputs. We are farmers, but we have decided that if they kill two of us, we will ruin their whole khandaan [family]; we will kill 15 of them.

The incident had occurred within four months of Rabri Devi taking over as the chief minister of Bihar. In the four months leading up to this massacre, 142 people had already been killed in various such instances of caste violence.

The CPI(ML) Liberation was quick to retaliate and avenge the Laxmanpur Bathe killings. At the nearby Rampur Chauram village of Jehanabad, it killed nine Bhumihars who were returning to Arwal after attending the cremation of a fellow villager.

The last three years of the 1990s may be the bloodiest in the history of Bihar or any state in India. Nineteen more massacres were executed by one or the other caste army during this period. Ranvir Sena continued to take a lion's share of this blame and most of the victims continued to come from the backward and Dalit castes. The district of Jehanabad seemed to have fallen into an endless abyss of violence, worse than some of the African nations facing civil war. The state looked helpless and even unwilling to do anything. The sena chief, Mukhiya, carried a bounty of 5,00,000 rupees on his head. The police, in fact, caught him twice in 1998 and 1999, but released him for want of proper identification.[196]

In 1999, while the president was addressing the nation on the eve of Republic Day, twenty-three Dalits, including women and children, were killed by the Ranvir Sena in Shankarbigha in the district of Jehanabad. The killers reportedly belonged to Dhobi Bigha, an upper-caste village just 200 metres away from Shankarbigha. Sixteen years later, a district court in Jehanabad acquitted all twenty-four accused of the killings. All fifty witnesses turned hostile in the court. It isn't difficult to guess why. Bhairo Rajwar who lost five family members, including two daughters, in the massacre had also turned hostile. Rajwar, who had saved his life by hiding on the roof of his hut, explains why.

> I had asked the police for protection, but they refused to ensure any. I told the judge in court, I had not seen anyone clearly that night. Let them take me to Patna and give me some assurance of protection. I will then not hesitate to recognise the accused.[197]

Ranvir Sena conducted another massacre just fifteen days later, on 10 February 1999. Twelve Dalits were massacred in Narayanpur village in Jehanabad. Just a day after the massacre, the Vajpayee government dismissed the Rabri government and imposed President's rule. Ironically, the Ranvir Sena had issued a press release post the carnage, blaming the 'Dalit president' (K.R. Narayanan) for the carnage by citing their previous rejection of President's rule in the state.[198]

However, lacking a majority in the Rajya Sabha, Vajpayee was compelled to reinstate Rabri Devi as the chief minister. The Congress, which was a partner in the Bihar government, refused to withdraw support. The party got all its twenty-three MLAs accommodated as ministers in the government.

Just ten days after the restoration of Rabri Devi's rule, the MCC avenged the Shankarbigha and Narayanpur massacres. On 18 March 1999, hundreds of MCC Naxalites—dressed in police uniform and carrying firearms and other weapons—surrounded Senari village. Senari is located in a twenty-five-kilometre radius of Shankarbigha and Laxmanpur Bathe, the two infamous sites of previous Dalit massacres. The Maoists dragged thirty-four men out of their homes, led them to the north of the village, assembled them at the village thakurbari, tied their legs and elbows, and slit their throats in the Maoist-favoured method of dispatch. Sanjay Sharma who miraculously survived recalls,[199]

> We were crying: Don't kill us. We were weeping, and calling out for God. Then they began cutting throats, and I watched them kill my younger brother. One by one, all of us fell over and were quiet and that's when I fell over too. I hid beneath the corpses, listening to the killers argue. Some wanted to throw a bomb at the bodies, and set them on fire. Some were afraid the police were coming and wanted to run away.

In hindsight, Senari looked like an obvious target for retribution—or maybe not. The Bhumihar-dominated village, a good thirty kilometres away from the Jehanabad headquarters, was connected through what could hardly be termed as roads. The village obviously didn't have any electricity or telephones. But the village had no history of social tensions, and the 200-odd mazdoor families lived in peace with the 70-odd Bhumihar families. The village also had a police picket just a kilometre away, a reason not to include Senari in the list of 292 'extra-sensitive' villages by the government.

Rabri, who had just returned to the chief ministerial helm, refused to visit the village, saying that the Bhumihars were not 'her voters '.

The Senari massacre was soon avenged by the Ranvir Sena, who mowed down thirty-five people in Mianpur in Aurangabad, barely ten kilometres away from Senari. The victims included twenty-six Yadavs and six Dalits.[200]

Central Bihar came to represent the worst of caste conflicts that the state and the country had seen since Independence. Every massacre would trigger a migration of the villagers, especially youth from the 'other' camp. This would be on account of both a fear of retribution as well as their names getting featured in the FIRs and a continued police harassment and torture, just because they belonged to the rival caste. Senari's Dalits were named in the FIR because the Bhumihars were massacred. Similarly, Bhumihars from the same village were named as accused in Shankarbigha and Laxmanpur Bathe Dalit massacres. Village after village emptied out in these districts of central Bihar, with the remaining houses guarded by the women and elderly in the family. The landed castes often refused to employ the labourers in their fields as a punishment after such massacres. The labourers, backed by Maoists, would also often refuse to plough the field of the Bhumihars in their area. The tensions caused such hostility that economic blockades from both sides led to almost seventy-two villages in Jehanabad alone being left fallow in the final years of 1990s.

In most of these villages, residents would take turns doing night patrol from their roofs, lest they were attacked. Even the slightest flicker of a headlight or the faintest sound of a vehicle's engine, even from kilometres away in the otherwise pitch-dark villages, would raise an alert. Villagers would start shouting their agreed-upon codes from their rooftops and men would run to fetch their .303 rifles and country-made firearms. But more often than not, the villagers who actually came under attack would be unsuspecting victims. This gave them little time to react, fight back or even hide.

Some villages that were constantly under threat would be more vigilant and were often able to detect such attacks. Firings would start at the mere sign of any intrusion in the village at night. The attackers would often be held off at the periphery of the village by villagers from their positions on their rooftops.

Bullets and casteist slurs would flow from both sides throughout the night. The aim of the villagers would be to hold off the attackers just till the first light of dawn, when the police may usually arrive.

The village of Bandeya, located in the hinterlands of Aurangabad district in central Bihar, is one such example. Located barely ten kilometres from the block headquarters of Goh, it takes not more than fifteen minutes to reach Bandeya. But that's only a recent phenomenon, thanks to Nitish Kumar's road-building spree. Bandeya in the 1990s didn't have roads, electricity or telephones. To reach the village, one had to walk through muddied fields for at least five kilometres, no matter which route was taken. The nondescript village with barely twenty houses came in the news in the early 2000s when MCC cadres chose to attack it. The target was Ranvijay Singh, a Bhumihar strongman who, the Maoists alleged, was involved in the murder of some Yadavs from the neighbouring village. Singh had been attacked a number of times previously, too, but had miraculously escaped. On that night, when the MCC cadres were planning to ravage the villagers in deep sleep, somebody noticed the flicker of an approaching torchlight. The man soon raised an alarm from his rooftop and the others were quick to run to their own rooftops, guns in hand. What followed was an entire night of firing and curses flying in from both sides. The barely ten-odd firing villagers surrounded by over 500 Naxalites from all four sides managed to stall their advance for an entire night. The Naxalites ultimately had to abandon their attack and flee the scene. The police, which was waiting a few kilometres away on the periphery of the village, dared approach the village only when the day broke. The suspecting villagers wouldn't even allow the police to approach them. It was only after the SP of Aurangabad identified himself that the force was allowed entry.

Unfortunately, this wouldn't be the last attack on this village. Bandeya would be attacked twice again in a similar fashion, in the dead of night. Each time though, the villagers would be able to contain the Naxalites for the entire night. Ranvijay Singh, the main target of these attacks, went on to contest and win the assembly elections from Goh constituency in 2005. However, he was soon arrested and incarcerated in a murder case.

In an interesting turn of events, the Mianpur carnage by Ranvir Sena prompted Chief Minister Rabri Devi to call the first meeting of the 'coordination committee' of the ruling combine of RJD-Congress. However, it wasn't just the calling of the meeting but its outcome that was more shocking. It was decided at the meeting that to end the cycle of caste massacres, the DMs and SPs of districts would be allowed to select groups of young men and train them in firearms to act as 'protection groups' against armed attacks. The committee also recommended that those among the poor who were willing to own guns should be given licences.[201] The committee didn't even bother to tackle the core issues of land and basic rights, which were leading to these conflicts. The reason was obvious—land redistribution was a difficult nut to crack and was bound to antagonise rich peasants, which also included many from the OBC castes of Yadavs and Kurmis.

The state had basically declared itself incapable of defending the lives of its citizens and wanted each to be on their own. This could have taken a serious turn in caste-ridden Bihar where every individual and community was trying to overpower the other group, often through violent means. This legitimisation of warlords would have only intensified the caste wars, but the proposals never saw the light of day.

Role of the State and Police

The usual state response to instances of massacres revolved around the immediate suspension of police officers in the area—mostly low-ranking and too low in the food chain—along with some money as compensation and additional relief if the standard measures didn't assuage the sentiments. The Laxmanpur Bathe massacre, in which fifty-eight Dalits were killed resulted in the transfer of the home secretary, suspension of the district superintendent of police and the creation of a new post of additional director general of police, to focus on law-and-order problems. However, it barely changed anything on the ground. Nine upper-caste members were killed by the CPI(ML)(Liberation) in a retaliatory attack in Chauram village of the same Jehanabad district within a month. The additional relief such as the promise of a job for a family member of the deceased and pucca houses if the victims were Dalits would seldom be honoured. The promises would often skyrocket to land allotment to Dalits, schools and road connectivity for the village when a chief minister or central minister would visit the massacre site. However, the villagers, attuned to such lofty promises, barely ever expected any of them to fructify.

The state was not just incompetent and insensitive but often complicit too. The visits of politicians to the sites of massacre would often be coloured by their own affiliations. Rabri's refusal to visit Senari because the victim caste, the Bhumihars, opposed her government is just one example. The upper-caste politicians similarly would be quick to visit the sites of massacre in Bhumihar villages but wouldn't show the same alacrity to visit Dalit massacre sites. Chandradeo Verma, who represented Arrah as an MP and had been a union minister of state, made the issue of lifting the ban on the Ranvir Sena the focal point of his campaign in the 1998 parliamentary elections.[202] When the then leader of the opposition Sushil Modi said, 'The RJD cadres are political workers by day and MCC hitmen by night,' he was echoing a common sentiment. Commanders of many private armies used the route of politics to legitimise their positions. Baiju Yadav, the Lorik Sena commander, became an MLA during Lalu's chief ministerial tenure.

The state machinery could rarely ensure that the actual culprits of the massacres be arrested and prosecuted conclusively. The judicial journey of most of the massacres in the 1990s took more than a decade and in certain cases are still sub judice. Sadly, the convicts in most of the cases were acquitted for reasons such as lack of evidence and witnesses turning hostile.

When the chief minister visited the site of the Haibaspur massacre, he promised a compensation of 1,20,000 rupees to the family of each victim, work and food rations for three months and pucca houses for the entire Dalit hamlet. Ten Scheduled Caste members were shot dead after Ranvir Sena had surrounded Haibaspur village on 23 March 1997. The killers also inscribed the name of their organisation on the rim of a well with the blood of one of the victims. A survey by a civil rights team in February 1998, almost a year after the massacre, revealed that only Rs 20,000 had been paid in compensation; no work or food rations had been provided and the pucca houses had only been partially constructed. The little construction that had taken place had further been destroyed lately by police raids in the village.[203] On the conviction front, the situation can be gauged from the fact that the main accused in the Haibaspur massacre, Sardar Lakshman Singh, was arrested only in 2014, seventeen years after the crime.

The Russian and Soviet neurologist Ivan Pavlov had proposed that behaviour is induced by stimulus. Such behaviour on the part of governments, too, is induced by incidental stimuli—just as when a person is killed in a road accident, the public blocks the road not to seek good roads or the conviction of the rash driver but a fat compensation for the family.

If one change could have seriously altered the history of the flaming fields of central Bihar, it would be the role of the police. The massacres had a typical pattern. Villages would be chosen based on the population of targeted castes, the vulnerability of the village such as absence of firearms and police pickets, and lack of road connectivity and electricity. Jehanabad, a district with a population of ten lakh in 1986 and an area of 1,569 sq. kilometres, had an awful thirty kilometres of pucca road to link the area. The attacks would invariably be conducted late in the evening. This ensured that the villagers had no inkling of the approaching attackers and were taken by surprise in their sleep. The darkness would also prevent the victims from escaping the village. However, the biggest advantage of a night-time raid would be the assurance that police wouldn't come for help till sunrise, at least. In several cases, the police, even if willing, couldn't reach the village at night. In Barra, the attackers had felled a huge tree on the only road that led to the village. This gave them ample time to diligently assemble all their victims around the canal and slit their throats. However, in most of the cases, the ill-equipped police wouldn't even dare to venture into such a carnage even if the village had road connectivity. Most police camps were located in the upper-caste inhabited tolas of the village and thus out of reach for Dalits. The police may not have been hostile to Dalits in these cases, but were still inaccessible to call upon.

Even upon reaching, the police would seldom be allowed inside the village boundary by the residents. The scarred villagers would more often than not be unwilling to trust the policemen. Attacks by criminals disguised in police uniforms had been a common modus operandi, taking away the trust earlier placed in the uniform and the establishment. The police's response to these massacres would also often be guided by their own caste identities and loyalties. The police force in central Bihar had traditionally been dominated by the upper castes, mostly Bhumihars and Rajputs.[204] The OBCs had started featuring lately, post the implementation of the Mandal Commission recommendations—even so, it was mostly the Yadavs and Kurmis. These two castes were now also the new landowners in several districts. As a result of which, Dalit massacres began to attract suspicion and even conspiracy theories of an inside job. Some of them were dismissed as the outcome of gang wars between different Naxalite factions.

Union Home Minister Indrajit Gupta commented upon the Bathani Tola massacre in Parliament.

> The failure of the district machinery was the immediate reason for the tragedy. In fact, it has been admitted by the state administration that despite availability of intelligence input about the impending tragedy and even positioning of forces around, the massacre could not be averted either due to connivance or lack of courage on the part of the law enforcement agencies.[205]

The police were not just guilty of dereliction of duty and insensitivity but often complicity, too. In April 1997, in the massacre in Ekwari—the village considered to be the birthplace of the CPI(ML)—the police officers stationed at the village to protect the inhabitants forced open the doors of the houses of villagers. They stood and watched as Ranvir Sena massacred people. The attackers raped two women, a fifteen-year-old and an eight-month-pregnant woman, before killing them. A ten-year-old boy was shot in the head. In the aftermath, as expected, seven police officers were suspended. No policemen were convicted.

According to a People's Union for Democratic Rights (PUDR) report, the judiciary was also often influenced by the social and political background of the people in question.[206] The police were also often accused of harassing villagers, particularly the Dalits, in the guise of raids and of killing them in fake 'encounters'. They arrested many villagers under preventive detention. These charges were bailable; but the detainees, in the absence of property or surety, would often keep languishing in jails. A report published after the visit of a team comprising seven civil liberties organisations to villages of Patna and Jehanabad in February 1998 described the raids conducted by Bihar Police:

> In the course of the raids, the police routinely abuse women in the most vulgar and offensive language. [T]here are no women police at all in the raid. It is the male police [who] enter the houses without consideration for the women's privacy. They abuse the women whose sons/husbands they are looking for. One frequent [accusation] is that the woman has sent her husband away 'so that she may sleep with the extremists'. Women who are going to the fields in the early morning cold are forced to remove the chaddar [blanket] so that the police may see whether they are hiding any arms or ammunition underneath. These 'suspicions' are only meant to insult and humiliate women.[207]

The report added:

> These raids are common in villages where the landless agricultural labourers organised by the various sangathans [meetings] of the CPI(ML) organisations have fought for wage increases and occupation of *gair majarua* [government] land. In some villages the raids are very frequent. Jhunauti [Jehanabad district, Bihar] was subjected to at least twenty raids in the last two months. In Andhrachak, Jehanabad district, Bihar, there

is one raid every week. Sevanan, Jehanabad district, Bihar, is subjected to at least two raids a week.[208]

These raids would often include looting and extortion by policemen. Often under the pretence of *kurki-japti*—attachment of movable property—the police would seize the property of absconding criminals, without following any of the legal procedures for seizure. It is pretty obvious where the seized material would finally land. But the police's role often went far beyond raids, illegal seizure and harassment.

The police, on 15 April 1994, reportedly killed eleven MCC members in an encounter in Gaya district. A similar encounter took place in Kodihara village of Patna district on 27 December 1997. The villagers assembled in the village described how two Naxalites were killed by the police in cold blood after they had surrendered. In August 1995, the police fired at a crowd of 500 people gathered at a CPI(ML)(Liberation) office in Begusarai town. The crowd was peacefully protesting for land reforms. Five people were killed. The police claimed to have fired in self-defence, while the eyewitnesses described the attack as one-sided. Sixty-five people, including twenty-nine women, were arrested on charges of rioting and illegal assembly and severely beaten in custody. Post-mortems were quickly conducted and the bodies cremated to eliminate any possibility of independent autopsies.

However, it would be wrong to single out the police force as being solely responsible for the anarchy. Their operations suffered due to the lack of adequate resources such as weapons, transport and communication technology, a robust intelligence network and proper protection. In a state where sixteen people were being killed, looted or kidnapped every hour, Bihar's ill-equipped police could at best provide a skeleton service.[209] When the then DGP S.K. Saxena said in 1997, 'Given the wretched conditions in which it works, the state police is doing a good job,' he wasn't completely wrong. In 1997, the Bihar Police Association (BPA) estimated the per capita spend on crime control in the state at Rs 16.56; it was the lowest in the country. It said that it needed 35,000 more men and 440 additional police stations to reach the average national police-to-population ratio.[210]

Why the Central Bihar Belt

The late novelist and journalist Shiva Naipaul once forayed into one of the scenes of massacre in Bihar and described the state as the 'end of the world'. However, it must be noted that caste-based violence wasn't spread uniformly across Bihar. In fact, it originated in and peculiarly remained restricted to the districts of the Son River belt of central Bihar. The Naxalite movement originated in Bhojpur and the ensuing caste wars remained restricted to the districts of Gaya, Jehanabad, Aurangabad, Patna, Nawada and Rohtas along with Bhojpur.

Contrary to the common belief that extreme poverty was the reason for the rise of Naxalism in central Bihar, this region is actually more prosperous than either northern or southern Bihar (Jharkhand region). It has benefitted immensely from the country's oldest canal system, on Son river, turning the region into the state's rice bowl. A 1986 report even put the literacy in the region a good 7 per cent higher than the state average of 26 per cent.[211] This is not surprising given that the two oldest universities of the country—Patna University and Magadh University—are located in the region.

What actually led this region to become the epicentre of caste violence lies elsewhere. Land, which is the biggest reason for such conflicts, faces the heaviest pressure in this region.

The region has 25 per cent higher population density than the state's average. Industry is nearly absent and urbanisation less than 10 per cent. While massive migration of landless labourers has helped to ease the pressure on land in north Bihar, the phenomenon remained almost absent in this region. On the other hand, the vicious cycle of debt led to distress sale of land, further swelling the number of landless labourers. In 1986, almost one-third of grown-up males in the region were landless.

Poor implementation of land reforms further added fuel to the fire. In Patna, for example, a bare 0.3 per cent of surplus land had been acquired and distributed by 1984. Imagine this being the state of land reforms and redistribution in the heart of Bihar, three decades after it took the lead in abolishing the zamindari system in the country. Even being an agricultural labourer in the region was not easy, with the minimum wages rarely being paid. Against a minimum wage of Rs 8.50 for unskilled agricultural labour in 1986, the landlords rarely paid more than Rs 3. Where wages were paid in kind, the labourers received no more than 1.25 kilograms against the stipulated 3 kilograms of foodgrains.

Secondly, the largest proportion of the Scheduled Caste population resides in this belt. Of the joint population of Gaya, Jehanabad and Patna, 27 per cent comprises SCs such as Bhuiyas, Musahars and Dusadhs. These castes have traditionally been debarred from holding land. Since they are denied access to the principal means of production, they are forced to work on the fields of others. More than two-thirds of these Scheduled Castes are landless. The worst off among them happen to be the Musahars.

Thirdly, the agricultural labourers and tillers in the area have historically been far more conscious of their rights and have been militant in their approach when compared to their counterparts elsewhere in Bihar. They had received their first boost of social awareness even before Independence when Swami Sahajanand Saraswati launched a 'land to the tiller' movement and set up the first Kisan Sabha. That consciousness combined with immediate issues like dignity and minimum wages inspired these landless classes to rise against the oppressors.

This region also saw the emergence of a section of backward castes such as the Koeris, Kurmis and Yadavs as the main beneficiaries of the land reform efforts and as the new rich. They were even more aggressive than the traditional land-owning forward castes and, in many cases, became the new oppressors. In fact, the massacres of Belchi, Pipra and Dalelchak-Bhagaura were inflicted by the armies of these middle castes. The virtual absence of administration and the ineffectiveness of the police force led the marginalised classes to reach out to the Leftist groups to solve their problems.

The main issue picked up by Naxalite groups, which also saw some success, was the seizing of the surplus and *gair majarua* lands. The gair majarua land is technically common land which is under the control of the government but more often than not has been appropriated or illegally occupied. The MCC, in 1992 claimed to have been responsible for the takeover of 4,500 acres of such land in Gaya alone. In one instance, the land of Naresh Singh, a landowner from Ahiyapur owning almost 800 acres, was acquired by the Naxalites. He retorted by terrorising the villagers. However, after his land was left fallow for an entire season by the labourers, he had no option but to reach a compromise. The impasse was resolved and about 100 landless families of backward castes such as Yadavs, Badhais, Ravidas and Dusadhs began cultivating this land.[212]

End of the Cycle

The deadliest period of caste violence in Bihar can be dated from 1994 to 2000. It is at the end of the decade that it reached its crescendo before dying out, with some flickers time and again but none as major as the ones during this period. So, what led to the sudden end of caste massacres at the turn of the century?

The first amongst these was the emergence of multiple power centres by the year 2000 and the subsequent weakening of the Ranvir Sena. One such power centre was led by Sunil Pandey, an MLA from the Piro constituency of Bhojpur district. These factions often tried to wrest power from each other, often killing their own caste men. Some factions also refused to accept the sena founder Brahmeshwar 'Mukhiya' as their leader and accused him of corruption and nepotism. Ranvir Sena met its gradual demise following the arrest of Brahmeshwar 'Mukhiya' from a building in the busy Exhibition Road in the heart of Patna. The police had received a tip-off from an unknown source, often conjectured to be someone from a warring faction of the sena itself. Mukhiya, wearing a crumpled kurta and dhoti and sporting a two-day-old beard, surrendered without offering any resistance. His arrest was highly uncharacteristic of his larger-than-life image of a dreaded guerrilla commander. Some reports suggested that his arrest may have been an attempt to save himself from the constant life threats from hostile sena factions as well as Maoist organisations.[213] A diary recovered from the sena chief contained the names and telephone numbers of several upper-caste politicians, journalists and police officers.[214]

Brahmeshwar Singh was eventually gunned down by unidentified men on 1 June 2012 while taking a morning stroll in his village in Bhojpur. He had just been acquitted and released from jail by the Patna High Court in the Bathani Tola massacre case. The killing created severe unrest in Bhojpur, Patna and adjoining districts. Supporters of Brahmeshwar Singh went berserk, burning down the recently renovated circuit house, block development officer's office, damaging railway offices in Arrah and paralysing train movement on the Howrah–Delhi route.[215] Some newspapers reported that the police remained a passive spectator since the incumbent JD(U)–BJP government, given the politically sensitive nature of the murder, didn't want to rub the Bhumihars the wrong way.

Brahmeshwar Singh would always quote the mythological character Parashuram:

> I did what Parashuram did. Violent methods are necessary in order to achieve any sort of order in society. Otherwise, injustices will prevail.[216]

Brahmeshwar Singh perhaps fell prey to his own logic.

IN THE NAME OF REVOLUTION

Bihar has a claim to be the ancient heart of India.
These days, it is seen as the armpit.
—*The Economist* (2005)

WHAT BIHAR LOST

Two years after Nitish Kumar took the helm of Bihar in 2005, his government presented a status report on the economic survey of Bihar. It was the first such report by any state in the country.

Among the vast data and analysis the report encapsulated, the most interesting finding was that Bihar was one of the best paymasters in the country. The average annual salary of a state government employee in Bihar was pegged at Rs 1.8 lakh versus Rs 1.21 lakh for a central government employee. Ironic as it may sound, the report highlighted that Bihar lagged behind other states on almost all Human Development Index (HDI) parameters, the HDI for Bihar being 20 per cent lower than the national HDI.[217]

Bihar had never been a leading state since Independence, which was attributable to a number of factors such as population explosion, huge agricultural dependence, lack of industries or even a conducive environment for them, and its landlocked geography. However, 1990–2005 was particularly bad, not only because of policy failures or a faulty economic model but because of the deliberate undermining of the capacity of the state apparatus to deliver basic services to its citizens.[218]

Lalu's first few statements and acts after coming to power resonated with the aspirations of every discriminated or repressed soul in Bihar. His governance initiatives, though novel and aimed at the marginalised, proved to be duds. One such initiative was Charwaha Vidyalaya, which rode a complete cycle of getting attention from international bodies such as the UNICEF before becoming the butt of jokes by the end of the 1990s. A principal reason for the failure of this and other similar initiatives was Lalu's lack of inclination towards creating the necessary administrative structures to support and run them. Lalu deliberately undermined the capacity of the state's administrative apparatus through his rather politically prudent decision-making.[219]

He was sharp enough to understand the repercussions of undermining the state apparatus and its effect on the morale and efficiency of the existing machinery. However, it was a choice he made—a collateral cost for keeping his electorate base satisfied and mobilised. Scholars have often questioned Lalu's capability to administer, beyond merely being a politician. However, it never seemed like a capability issue; rather, it was a deliberately designed era of under-governance.

He would later prove at his stint in the railway ministry during UPA-I that he could administer, too. He took a slew of initiatives, including some in his own inimitable style, such as replacing plastic cups used to serve tea on trains and at stations with kulhads. Under his leadership, the railways turned from a loss-making organisation to generating a cumulative profit of Rs 38,000 crore.[220] Lalu was invited to speak on his management style by global schools such as the Harvard University and Wharton School, and case studies were written on the turnaround. However, in 2009, after his tenure was over, allegations arose that the financial statements were manipulated. This was supported by a report from the Comptroller and Auditor General. The report actually indicated a decline in the railways' performance in the latter years of Lalu's tenure.[221]

It was too late for Lalu to be considered a serious administrator. In Bihar, he had done irreversible damages, which affected every Bihari in their everyday lives.

The effect of the state government undermining its administrative apparatus ran not just as far as the inefficiency of its state programmes but also to the limits of underutilisation of funds, which were available to the state. It is estimated that during the years from 1997 to 2000, Bihar forfeited one-fifth of Central-plan assistance because of underutilisation of funds. In fact, Bihar, during the same period, had the country's lowest utilisation rate for centrally funded programmes.[222] It was the second most populous state of the country, one of the states with the largest number of people living below poverty line, and yet unable to expend the funds available at its disposal.

Santosh Mathew and Mick Moore, in a research paper, explained the major unusual practices that led to such an exceptional underutilisation of public funds and poor performance of the state economy during the 1990s and early 2000s. The four reasons are classified:[223]

> *Centralisation in decision making*: Under Lalu, Bihar had a convoluted process for approval of proposals. It meant that over and above the usual approval by the concerned department and the respective minister, it was sent for screening by a committee of civil servants and then for a final approval by the chief minister in his capacity as planning minister. The limits of approval for the expenses were too small at each level of decision making. The multiple layers of approval made matters worse. Such was the level of centralisation that a court commissioner appointed by the Supreme Court had to comment at a hearing of an Integrated Child Development Scheme (ICDS) Public Interest Litigation (PIL):

'The whole process is time-consuming, resulting in delays in the release of funds ranging from four to six months. Doing away with this rule in itself will expedite financial releases, giving more time to the field staff to use and then claim second instalments.'[224]

Poor record keeping at state, leading to excessive litigation against the state: Governments and bureaucracies swear by documentation. However, in Bihar, the standard of record-keeping deteriorated considerably post 1990.[225] Finding basic records such as those relating to public employment, provident fund contributions and land revenue records became challenging. Same was the case with court orders and their implementation records. In 2005 alone, the state government faced over 5,500 contempt applications in the high court over non-implementation of its orders.[226]

Mismatch between rain, flood and budget cycles: The April–March budget cycle at the centre as well as in states has always been at a mismatch with the rain cycles. In Bihar, this got worse as the full budget wouldn't be approved until June or July. Departments and operating agencies wouldn't know their annual budgets until well into the financial year. Also, the months of August and September, which immediately follow the approval, coincide with Bihar's annual rainfall season, often leading to the suspension of most public engineering works.

Vacancies in state government offices: Lalu had come to power on the rhetoric of breaking the upper-caste hegemony, especially in positions of influence such as the government offices. New appointments were reserved mostly for members of the communities from his electoral coalition. However, these caste groups were historically so deprived that it often became impossible to find suitable candidates with sufficient qualification to be appointed even to the simplest of clerical jobs.[227] In such cases, the posts were rather left vacant. In cases of pre-existing incumbents from upper castes in the public

> sector, the procedures were made so constrained and political oversight so strong that they could barely move their pen to accomplish anything. Lalu's government had a well-designed red tape to deliberately weaken it.

Over a third of important administrative positions such as those of block development officers and circle officers didn't have a full-time incumbent.[228] These are the officers responsible for all development work and land and revenue administration in their respective areas of blocks and circles. In fact, the body responsible for the recruitment of these officers, Bihar Public Service Commission, itself didn't have a chairman for a critically long period.[229] The absence of such important incumbents reflected immediately in the overall public service delivery. Bihar gained the disrepute of having the poorest HDI indicators among all states in India. Throughout the 1990s, the HDI for Bihar consistently remained at least 20 per cent lower than the national average.

The effects of deliberate vacancies extended to education, health and every other sector related to government service delivery.

Health and Education

In the health sector, at its worst, 90 per cent of doctors' posts and 95 per cent of the posts for paramedical staff were vacant.[230] The number of teachers recruited against a sanction of 90,000 posts between 1996 and 2006 was 30,000. The pupil–teacher ratio, which was already a concern for Bihar at 90:1 against the national norm of 40:1, rose to 122:1. The callousness towards the whole personnel issue can be understood by the following episode. The Government of India wanted Bihar to recruit the missing teachers for schools and was willing to pay the cost under its flagship scheme of Sarva Siksha Abhiyan. The state government responded by changing the rules of recruitment in order to be able to recruit teachers from its own electoral base. When the move was struck down by courts, it simply left the positions vacant.[231]

More often than not, even the process of selection for such posts and entire bodies conducting the recruitment were mired in controversies. The average time between the notification for a certain post and a candidate finally joining it would take several years. Colleges were barely able to complete a graduation course for students in the stipulated three years. Postponement of exams, paper leaks and discrepancies in results were so common that it didn't even bother people.

The most blatant and conspicuous misuse of Bihar's education system was demonstrated when Lalu's eldest daughter, Misa Bharti, first secured an MBBS seat at Jamshedpur Medical College on a TISCO quota after failing the entrance test. The TISCO quota was meant for children of Tata employees, which neither Lalu nor Rabri Devi were. Misa Bharti was later transferred to Patna Medical College Hospital (PMCH), citing security reasons, where she topped the MBBS exams with a distinction in gynaecology, while her mother was the serving chief minister of Bihar. Misa, however, didn't practice medicine for even a day in her life. Just a few years later, the family used the same TISCO route to secure a medical college admission for their younger daughter, Rohini.[232]

Infrastructure

The severity of the infrastructural inefficiency can be understood by looking at the vacancies in some of the other important positions and departments in infrastructure during Lalu's regime. The engineering department was one of the biggest sufferers. Positions as critical as that of engineer-in-chief of the two principal engineering departments, the rural engineering department and the road construction department, remained vacant for a long time. So did the 15 positions of chief engineer, and eighty-one out of ninety-one sanctioned positions for superintending engineer in the same two departments.[233]

The condition of road construction was further worsened by the lack of basic protocols such as updation of important documents or schedule of rates. The quality control arm of the road construction department went non-functional for want of personnel, equipment and chemicals.

In 2006, Bihar had a total road length of 81,655 kilometres, of which the national highways accounted for 4.4 per cent and the state highways a meagre 3.9 per cent. This meant that most of the roads were pucca or kutcha village roads, their condition dependent on the mercy of rains.[234] It meant that in the 1990s, one could barely find tarred, unbroken roads even between the most important towns. Muzaffarpur, a town merely seventy-five kilometres from Patna and a business hub of northern Bihar, would take four hours to reach from the state capital, travelling through the barely-existent potholed roads. The village roads or even the district roads were just intermittent patches of concrete on otherwise dusty paths. These would become even worse in the rainy season, when four-wheelers would hardly be able to traverse such paths. A common scene during this time was that of a group of people putting all their strength into pushing out a car wheel stuck in mud and slush.

Mass Migration

On 13 November 2004, a stampede at the New Delhi Railway Station claimed the lives of five women and left at least ten others injured while people were jostling to board the Patna-bound Jan Sadharan Express to be home for the Chhath festival. However, this wasn't the first or last in the series of such stampedes.

Chhath, the festival to pray and to pay reverence to both the setting and the rising sun, is one of the most important festivals for Biharis. Nothing can hold back a Bihari from being home during this festival. This creates an enormous traffic of people on trains, flights, buses and every other mode possible during the week preceding Chhath. The government runs tens of special trains and thousands of extra coaches but it still doesn't suffice for the lakhs who are travelling. At major train stations such as the New Delhi Railway Station, Biharis can be seen swarming the platforms, reaching as early as twelve hours before the scheduled departure. A common sight upon arrival of the trains is that of thousands of people jostling, trying to cram themselves into every possible inch of the coaches, pushing children and luggage inside through emergency windows.

The sight is a clear indication of the mess Bihar has made of itself and its people. Practically every city in India, which has some job to offer, be it any kind, would have some Biharis there. One will be surprised to find numerous Biharis working not just in the fields of Punjab and factories of Mumbai and Delhi but also at highway dhabas in Ladakh, in hardware shops in obscure south Indian towns, in the hotels in Munnar and as autorickshaw drivers in far-east Shillong. They work as security guards, peons, sweepers, construction workers, rickshaw drivers and in every imaginable job sphere. In Nepal, too, there are thousands of Biharis from the bordering northern districts. Even the Nepalese look down upon Biharis. The Indian Consul or the High Commission there doesn't rush to their defence and, in fact, pretends they do not exist. In short, Biharis are seldom welcomed by anybody. Yet they choose to go. The reason is pretty clear: survival. Getting any kind of job, earning minimum wages and being able to save and send a few thousand rupees back home is better than working with five other family members in a half-acre field back home.

Mass migration from Bihar, however, isn't a phenomenon that emerged in the 1990s. The first wave of migration from Bihar happened during the Green Revolution, when labourers from Bihar travelled to the north Indian states of Punjab and Haryana to work in the fields. These labourers who were looked down upon by landowners and often referred to as 'bhaiya'—a general form of salutation in Bihar to anyone who is elderly—provided a cheap option and helped catapult the Green Revolution. It was assumed that Bihari labourers would adjust to the poorest of working conditions; they could be paid much less than the locals and be 'bought and sold' like cattle to farmers by unscrupulous ticket collectors.[235]

The poor governance and the collapse of law and order in the 1990s exacerbated the phenomenon. The rate of migration from Bihar in 2001 was over 200 per cent more than it was in 1991. The average increase in the same period for other states was a mere 21.5 per cent.[236] Also, the poor law and order situation, combined with regular threats of extortion and kidnappings, led to the flight of business men and other professionals and hence, the draining of capital from Bihar. The economic collapse was added to by the annual Kosi floods in northern Bihar. The moving away of business and rising unemployment led to the mass migration of agricultural workers as well as unemployed youth to other parts of the country. Liberalisation had created opportunities at the bottom of the jobs' pyramid, which Bihari migrants were desperate to capture at any cost, no matter what the hardships.

However, the hardships weren't merely economic. Bihari workers and students faced severe xenophobic sentiments across the country. Most notable of these were the violence against Biharis in Maharashtra and the massacre of Bihari workers in Assam. The protests against Biharis in Maharashtra was mainly led by the Shiv Sena and its even more militant faction, the Maharashtra Navnirman Sena. In 2003, the Shiv Sena alleged that 90 per cent of the successful candidates in railway exams were from Bihar, and only 10 of the 500 Maharashtrian candidates could be successful in the same. The Shiv Sena activists ransacked a railway recruitment office in protest against a significant number of non-Maharashtrians being the majority among the 6,50,000 candidates set to compete for a mere 2,200 railway jobs in the state.[237]

A similar spate of anti-Bihari sentiment arose in Assam and some north-eastern states during the early 2000s. Bihari workers were always on the hitlist of the ULFA (United Liberation Front of Assam) militants and locals because they thought the Biharis would dominate and eventually annihilate the local culture and language. In 2000 and 2003, almost 200 Bihari workers were killed in Assam owing to this xenophobia.[238]

In Arun K. Karan's paper on the analysis of this migration, he concludes that there has been a significant shift in the intensity and pattern of migration of Biharis in the last two decades of the previous millennium. The proportion of migration almost doubled while its nature shifted from short- to long-term movement. Almost 90 per cent of the migration in the early 1980s was seasonal, thereby indicating a commitment to travel back home as warranted by the cropping season. By the start of the new millennium, however, the numbers of long-term and seasonal migrants became almost equal.[239]

The migration happened across castes and classes, maybe with varied motivations. Those vulnerable among the upper caste preferred to work elsewhere as the existing caste taboos wouldn't allow them to take up menial or manual wage work in their villages. The lower castes migrated to break free from the clutches of caste discrimination and exploitation in their villages. Karan further says that the nature of migration also changed from rural to rural to rural to urban. While in the 1980s, the destination of migration would generally be the fields of Punjab and Haryana, it changed to urban destinations such as Delhi by the end of the millennium. The occupations in these new destinations required the migrants to stay longer, unlike in the earlier seasonal migration.

The families back home depended heavily on the remittances sent by these migrants. It contributed to almost one-third of the total household income of the migrants' families. Expectedly, the remittances constituted a comparatively larger proportion of the total household income in the case of the landless and lower castes.[240]

Brain Drain

However, it wasn't just menial jobs for which Biharis migrated during this period or still do. Many of them migrated for reasons such as a better quality of life, which often included better educational opportunities.

The education system, specifically higher education, in Bihar had become a joke. It was not just the usual lack of resources and funds that most of the 'BIMARU'[241] states were faced with in the 1990s. The malaise ran much deeper. A 1998 article in *Economic and Political Weekly* mentions that almost 4,000 university teachers who were promoted to professorship joined colleges that did not by any stretch meet the expected educational standards.[242] Many of these teachers were appointed as lecturers through unfair selection processes and later promoted even if they didn't possess the minimum required Master's degree. The colleges themselves were no better than cattle sheds in terms of infrastructure, with libraries and laboratories being a luxury.

These institutions were controlled by Bihar's education mafia, with names such as Ram Lakhan Singh Yadav, a minister in the Narasimha Rao government, and Jagannath Mishra, the former chief minister, pulling the strings. Lalu who had once resolved to take on the education mafia, when he was appointed as chief minister, went on to become the largest patron of such scamsters, his close lieutenant Ranjan Yadav being one of them. Many of these people occupied ministerial positions in Lalu's government, some others were close friends, political brokers or loyal party men.

With the increasing—even if at a snail's pace—literacy and continued poor state of higher education in Bihar, many students started thronging the streets of Delhi and Calcutta for higher education. Delhi became the more preferable option of the two, not just because of language familiarity but a flourishing coaching industry. Delhi also had multiple options such as Delhi University, Jamia Millia Islamia, Jawaharlal Nehru University and a multitude of colleges offering professional degrees. Apart from its dilapidated education and jobs scenario, Bihar had nothing to offer to the youth. The lawlessness and 'rule of might' in the state also instilled in the ambitious and a large population of youth an unwillingness to resign themselves to their fate, a strong pull towards the civil services. Even today, civil servants are treated as gods in almost all rural areas of the state, and the fate of numerous decisions lie—as it did then—solely on their scribbly signatures on thick, soiled files. This enticed a large section of the youth to make whatever sacrifices needed to move to the other side of the table. Delhi being the hot seat of civil services entrance exam preparation attracted a lot of these youth. An oft-repeated expression that states, 'While children elsewhere begin to learn "ABCD", infants in Bihar are taught "UPSC"—the Union Public Service Commission'—highlights the passion in the state for becoming an IAS officer.

However, the difference in motives or the destination of migration didn't provide any solace to Biharis when it came to name-calling and insults. Bihari students would often be marked with their accent and would be derisively called 'Harrys' or 'Harias'. A usual way of pulling someone down would be shouting, '*Oye, Bihari hai kya?*' (Hey, are you a Bihari?). But even this couldn't act as a deterrent to lakhs of Bihari students thronging Delhi's North Campus and Mukherjee Nagar areas every year in search of better prospects.

Bihar Gets Split

The greatest strike on Bihar's economy came in the form of the separation of its mineral-rich southern region to form a new independent state in the year 2000.

Chhotanagpur, which largely defines present-day Jharkhand, was once considered the heart of Bihar. Bihar's first chief minister, Shri Krishna Singh, had envisaged transforming the highly mineral-rich region into India's Sheffield. It was Nehru's vision of heavy industry-based development and Shri Krishna Singh's initiatives that helped the region gain prominent industries such as the Heavy Engineering Corporation in Ranchi, Steel Authority of India Limited (SAIL) plant in Bokaro and fertiliser factory in Sindri. It was with the intention of giving due attention to this region that Chhotanagpur's largest town, Ranchi, was designated as Bihar's winter capital. The whole state cabinet would literally move to Ranchi during the period of October to February every year.

However, this exercise ceased once subsequent governments took charge. This also led to a gradual neglect of the region, or at least the perception of it started growing among the natives of this region. The feeling of alienation gradually strengthened the demand for a separate state. In fact, the demand for a separate state had existed ever since the formation of Bihar, though in a subdued form.

While Bihar was carved out of Bengal in 1911 as a separate state, some sections of the population, especially the tribals, believed themselves to be distinctly different in culture from any of the existing political states surrounding the region. These tribals, mostly inhabiting the southern regions of Bihar and parts of Bengal, Orissa and Madhya Pradesh, had long been demanding a separate Jharkhand state for themselves. However, the first formal impetus was provided by Jharkhand Party, led by Jaipal Singh Munda, the erstwhile captain of the Indian hockey team. In 1955, he submitted a memorandum to the States Reorganisation Committee, which was tasked with examining the demand for new states, advocating for the creation of the state of Jharkhand. It was, however, rejected on grounds that there were several languages and no link language in the region, that the tribals were not in majority and that the separation could have adverse effects on the economy of Bihar.

The demand was renewed with vigour in the 1970s by a political outfit, the Jharkhand Mukti Morcha (JMM), formed at Dhanbad's Golf Maidan at a massive rally in 1973 by Binod Bihari Mahato, Shibu Soren and A.K. Roy. Soren had just entered the scene as a highly energetic adivasi leader who was well-connected with the grassroots and wanted to reform the adivasi society. However, the trio soon split and went separate ways but kept raising their voice for a separate state at different forums. Another split in the JMM in 1986 led to the formation of the All Students Jharkhand Union (ASJU), on the lines of All Assam Students Union, by Nirmal Mahto, an advocate of armed rebellion.

The real impetus to the movement, however, was provided in the mid-1980s when even the BJP and Congress, realising the populism of the demand, started supporting it. This was both to counter the rising strength of the JMM and establish their own base among the area's electorate.

JMM won nineteen seats in the Bihar Assembly elections held in 1990 and became a part of the state government. Lalu, in a bid to save his minority government, promised the adivasi MLAs a separate state. It is from here that a separate state started seeming an inevitable next stop.

A bill for providing autonomy to the Jharkhand Area Autonomous Council (JAAC) in forty subjects, including agriculture, public health and minerals, was passed in 1994 in the Bihar Vidhan Sabha. The council was given power to recommend legislation on these subjects to the assembly through the state government and to frame by-laws and regulations. This could not, however, assuage the aspirations of a separate state. While the state government kept dilly-dallying on the issue of a separate state, the situation escalated dramatically when the central government sent a bill to the Bihar Assembly in 1998, proposing the formation of Jharkhand state. Swords were drawn. Lalu declared that Bihar would be divided over his dead body. But all other major parties in the state, such as the BJP, JMM, AJSU and Congress, united on the issue and launched a movement for the formation of a separate state. Thousands thronged the streets on 21 September 1998, the day the bill for a separate state was introduced in the Bihar Assembly. The slogan 'Pehle maati, phir party' reverberated all around.

The RJD was finally cornered into supporting the bill after it needed the Congress' support to form a government after the 2000 assembly elections. Bihar was divided to form Jharhand on 15 November 2000. Babulal Marandi took oath as the state's first chief minister. The day also happened to be the birth anniversary of Birsa Munda, the tribal leader and folk hero who was one of the earliest to have revolted against the British. Two other smaller states of Uttarakhand and Chhattisgarh, carved out of Uttar Pradesh and Madhya Pradesh, respectively, were also formed on the same day.

The state of Jharkhand didn't just take away almost 45 per cent of the land area of undivided Bihar but essentially changed the entire economic structure of the state. A lion's share of Bihar's mineral deposits and industries went to Jharkhand, thus leaving Bihar solely dependent on agriculture. Industries like coal, steel, petroleum products, motor vehicles went completely into Jharkhand's kitty. What remained with Bihar was food, tobacco, leather and some non-metallic mineral products which were found in Bihar.

Breakdown of Grassroots Democracy

The panchayat elections of 2001 were held in Bihar after a gap of twenty-three years. It was Karpoori Thakur who had last affected panchayat elections in the state in 1978. However, once the tenure of gram panchayats came to an end in 1983, successive governments went on extending the tenure of mukhiyas and pramukhs every six months through ordinances. The state continued with this model of decentralisation through ordinances for around eighteen years. Several mukhiyas grew old and died within this period. Many of them were replaced by new mukhiyas, nominated by the Directorate of Panchayats,

Patna. One of the deputy directors in the department, originally in charge of panchayat elections, was dedicated to the task of nominating new mukhiyas. To top it all, the seats in the State Legislative Council—the upper house of the Bihar Assembly—meant to be filled through indirect elections by the electoral college of elected members of panchayat and municipal body remained vacant.

The 73rd Constitutional Amendment Act passed in 1992 accorded a statutory position to the panchayats and made the elections to panchayats mandatory every five years. While Lalu quickly enacted a State Panchayati Act, as had been made compulsory, he made his intentions clear through the stringent provisions put in the act to perpetuate the government's control over the panchayati raj institutions (PRIs). Lalu wasn't interested in devolution of powers beyond Patna, and despite all superficial political differences, he believed in the plebiscitary politics of Indira Gandhi. This meant that his party was a one-man show and couldn't risk the rise of local-level challengers through a devolution of power. Lalu's party, the Janata Dal first and later the Rashtriya Janata Dal, never really had a ground-level organisation. Lalu would rather allow the new-rich from his favoured castes—mostly creamy OBCs—to manage tenders, get contracts and even siphon off funds in the most ingenious ways. This role was earlier played by people from the upper castes. To Lalu, his organisation merely meant a group of self-seekers and middlemen who exploited the gains of power, and, in return, pledged loyalty to him.

It was this proven model that helped Lalu win the subsequent assembly elections in 1995 and 2000. The party was dependent on his charisma and not the other way round. In the absence of an organised and disciplined party structure, Lalu feared that the panchayat elections may create provincial leaderships and fracture the backward coalition that he had so carefully built. The constituents of Lalu's electorate, particularly the Yadavs and Muslims, may have come in contest with each other at several places, and this would be detrimental to his electoral coalition stability. Offering the possibility of more transparency, the panchayat elections were also antithetical to the vested interests of political brokers, state ministers and civil servants.

Lalu thus did everything he could to forestall the panchayat elections in Bihar. However, the judiciary intervened in April 2000, and the ball for panchayat elections in the state was set rolling. To hold free and fair voting, the Bihar State Election Commission decided to hold the elections in six phases.

As soon as the nominations for the elections began, reports of violence started pouring in. Several merchants and traders were allegedly kidnapped to collect hefty ransom to finance the election expenses of government-favoured candidates. Sushil Modi, the leader of the opposition, reportedly expressed his apprehensions. 'It will be the most dreadful of all the elections held in the state so far.' Kidnapping, murders and violence were not new in the state, but in the absence of an in-depth study, it became difficult to attribute them to the election process. The official numbers put up for poll-related violence accounted for the loss of 129 lives, including that of 50 candidates who were killed in pre-poll violence.[243]

The panchayat elections of 2001 can be termed as a turning point in the empowerment of the lower OBCs.[244] Even with a strength of almost one-third of the total population, and repeated rhetoric by Lalu, they had not benefitted from Lalu's rule as had the upper OBCs—Yadavs, Koeris and Kurmis. The socio-economic status of lower OBCs was not better than Dalits. Combined with the denial of protection that was accorded to Dalits, they felt discriminated against at both ends of the spectrum. However, 35 per cent of their share of the total population consisted of over a hundred castes that were individually insignificant in numbers. There also wasn't any leader like Lalu among their ranks who could forge a lower backward castes unity. This had led to their political marginalisation and being at the receiving end of hollow promises. The 2001 panchayat elections demonstrated that they no longer wanted to remain the electoral fodder for the upper backwards. They tried to forge a lower backward alliance in various places, and although their results were not spectacular, their presence in the power structure at least became noticeable.

A number of Dalit candidates also got elected, mostly from the flaming fields of south Bihar (earlier central Bihar) plain. This was the region where they had had to face the worst caste atrocities, but it was also the area with the highest density of their population, with Gaya, Nawada and Aurangabad ranking among the top three.

THE UNIQUE CRIME INDUSTRIES OF BIHAR

In 2002, Lalu's family courted a fresh controversy during the wedding of his second daughter, Rohini Acharya. Rohini was getting married to the son of Rao Ranvijay Singh, a senior income tax official based in Mumbai. The ostentation and lavishness of the wedding apart, the days leading up to the wedding caused mayhem among the trader community in Patna. Lalu's loyalists prowled the streets of Patna and drove away with as many as fifty new cars from showrooms, apparently to ferry the guests. One of the Maruti showroom owners in the city's Boring Road said that he gave five cars voluntarily. However, ten more new air-conditioned models of Alto and Wagon-R were taken away forcibly. Even petrol for the cars was bought on credit. The police remained a mute spectator to the hooliganism and were hand-in-glove with the miscreants in some cases.

However, the mayhem didn't stop at cars. One of Rabri Devi's brothers allegedly took away one hundred new sofa sets and plush chairs from various outlets to place them in the wedding pandal, which was created as a replica of Mumbai's Taj Mahal Palace Hotel. The only traders who could breathe easy during this time were the florists. The flowers were brought in from

Bangkok, Kolkata, Delhi and other places. The biggest irony—Rohini's father-in-law was an income tax commissioner.

The state government officials were not far behind in their attempts to please Lalu. The nondescript village to which the groom belonged was quickly connected with electricity, telephone lines and a road. The State Electricity Board allegedly suffered transmission losses of over Rs 25 lakh. The entire function was secured by the presence of 300 police personnel, including the Special Task Force (STF) and commandos.[245]

The ostentatious display of wealth and power, not just in this case but even earlier during Lalu's eldest daughter Misa's wedding, was nothing new for the power circles in Bihar. However, the brazenness of Lalu's army of followers right in the heart of the state capital, symbolised the true state of law and order in Bihar.

Some of the other misadventures of Lalu's brothers-in-law were far more brazen and gruesome. One noteworthy episode that sent shockwaves through Patna was the Shilpi–Gautam murder case. Gautam, a young aspiring politician and son of a doctor based in London, was an active member of the youth wing of the RJD. Shilpi, a twenty-three-year-old with the Miss Patna title to her name, was the daughter of a prominent cloth merchant in Patna, Ujjwal Kumar Jain. Gautam and Shilpi were believed to be romantically involved.

On 3 July 1999, the semi-nude bodies of Shilpi and Gautam were recovered from inside a car parked in a garage near 12, Frazer Road, Patna. The quarter belonged to Sadhu Yadav, Lalu's notorious brother-in-law.

Serious questions were raised on the police's role and their investigation, right from the start. Even before the police could secure the crime scene, Sadhu Yadav's supporters reached the scene and created a ruckus. Instead of being properly towed, the vehicle was driven to the police station by a constable, thereby making fingerprint identification impossible. The police's narrative and the potential causes of death were inconsistent. The deaths were initially ruled as suicide and later declared as a case of poisoning. As the investigation proceeded, other inconsistencies kept surfacing. Gautam's body had been quickly cremated without seeking the consent of his family. The police report also revealed that the garage had been locked from the inside, and the key was missing. This indicated that the individual who alerted the police was likely aware of the presence of the bodies.

The mishandled investigation, coupled with the involvement of influential political figures, led to significant political turmoil. The case was eventually transferred to the CBI. Autopsy reports suggested that multiple people had raped Shilpi before her death. The CBI requested a DNA sample from an MLA suspected to be Sadhu Yadav, who declined to provide it. The case was shut four years later, declaring it to be a double suicide.

A few years later, Shilpi's brother Prashant Jain was abducted by unidentified criminals and released twelve days later due to heavy pressure from the police. This was believed to be an attempt to discourage him from pursuing the case further.

While these were individual crimes led by people close to the government or rather a family, the modalities of some other crimes became so standardised and clinical that it took the shape of an industry being run with the connivance of various influential players who also got a share in its proceeds.

At Gunpoint

Early on the morning of 12 December 1994 in Ranchi, two youngsters riding on a scooter reached the house of Radheshyam Rajak, an executive engineer in the Public Health and Engineering

Department of the Government of Bihar. One of the youngsters rose from his seat, pulled out a locally made gun and shot Rajak point-blank. Both subsequently ran away. It was later found that a local contractor had paid the shooters Rs 5,000 to kill Rajak.

This wasn't a stray incident. Murders, and particularly that of engineers, became a common phenomenon in Bihar in the 1990s. Engineers wielded immense power to pass projects and were believed to amass huge wealth. This brought them in contention not just with contractors but others in the corruption chain such as politicians and senior officers.

However, this is not to conclude that extortionists were interested only in high-net-worth individuals. Bihar had an entire spectrum of extortionists for every possible situation and place in the state. Their terror was so pervasive in the lives of every resident of Bihar that even the most powerful and influential didn't want to get on the wrong side. Not just the low ranking but even senior police officials were scared for their and their family's security. The biggest example to validate this was the daylight murder of Gopalganj's district magistrate, G. Krishnaiah, by a mob in 1994. In Lalu's first tenure itself, almost two dozen district and block administrative and police officials were either murdered or abducted and released after much negotiation.[246]

In 1992, a ruling Janata Dal MP, Ramsharan Yadav, and his son Ranveer Yadav barged into Health Secretary T.C.A. Ramanujam's office and thrashed him. The health secretary's mistake was that he had refused to sign a recommendation for wrongful admission of one of Ramsharan Yadav's children to the MGM Medical College in Jamshedpur. Both father and son then casually strolled out of the office. As expected, no action was taken against either of them. This had become a common practice, and it was well understood that thrashing a public official was rarely ever going to attract any action. However, the officials were equally responsible for such treatment. Most of them often benefitted from favours and commissions obtained from criminals and politicians. The obliged officials would hence choose to overlook any criminal acts of people from the ruling dispensation, even going to the extent of helping and protecting them. The kidnappers and killers of one officer would be protected by other officers, and so ran the vicious cycle of crimes and criminals going unpunished.

The most important reason behind the rise in crime in Bihar was persistent unemployment among the youth. The traditional crimes of theft, dacoity and extortion were carried out with higher impunity because administration was clueless and police lethargic. Dacoity and road robberies increased exponentially; numerous new gangs came up in every region and on every highway. In an incident in Dhanbad, a magistrate returning home from Katras after 9:00 p.m. was stopped by a gang and robbed. The robbers weren't even afraid of the fact that the magistrate was travelling in a red beacon car. The Koderma Valley, an important stretch between Patna and Ranchi, became infamous for such robberies. The G.T. Road, running across north Bihar, was another profitable stretch for road robbers because of the high traffic of trucks crossing through it. When road robberies became too competitive and people started to avoid travelling on roads at night-time, some of the gangs turned to robbing trains.

Train robberies increased in number and their nature changed. While earlier robbery was more common on passenger trains, it soon spread to express and mail trains. On 4 March 1997, the Howrah-bound Kalka Mail had just crossed Mughalsarai and entered Bihar. The passengers had nearly fallen asleep post dinner when they heard a commotion. A dozen armed youths had begun looting the passengers. The only resistance came from

Abhay Kumar Singh, a Delhi police inspector who challenged the dacoits with his 9 mm service revolver. While he managed to bring down two dacoits, he ended up losing his own life. The rest of the gang fled with the booty.[247]

This became the most common modus operandi. The robbers would board the train at the previous station and when the train would reach their own locality, they would start robbing the unsuspecting passengers. The passengers would be threatened with knives and guns and made to part with their money, jewellery and other expensive belongings. Migrants returning from bigger cities such as Kolkata and Delhi were sitting ducks. Such incidents also increased during the wedding season when costly jewellery or clothing would be carried by certain passengers. The robbers would then pull the stopping chain and run away, never to be found or caught.

Train robberies became so common in Bihar that the then minister of railways Ram Vilas Paswan threatened to withdraw train services from Bihar unless the law-and-order situation improved. Paswan wasn't overreacting. The first ten days of March 1997 had seen ten train robberies. This included the robbery on Northeast Express in which two army jawans were injured, Bhagalpur–Dadar Express in which four people were killed and women molested and Mahananda Express, in which the plunderers included Government Railway Police (GRP) jawans.

The robberies at gunpoint, knife-point or cases where bikers would just snatch a walking person's watch, chain, purse or other belongings and escape, continued unabated. In fact, these crimes were and are still considered so low in the order of crimes that the police often refuse to file FIRs for such cases, let alone investigate them or catch the culprits. Robberies in buses also continued in the same pattern as trains. Robbers would board a bus as passengers and, upon reaching a secluded place, stop the bus at gunpoint and rob passengers of their belongings.

An interesting experience was recounted by someone who was once travelling through the Koderma Valley. His car was stopped by robbers. On searching, they found only Rs 5,000 on him. The robbers returned the money and requested him not to lodge a complaint at the local police station. Upon asking the reason, the robbers explained that if the policemen came to know of it, they would come to collect their own share of Rs 10,000!

The police stations more often than not would have information of impending robberies. They would conspicuously be absent from such spots. Similarly, even when a high-level drive would be scheduled to catch hold of such robber gangs, they would be informed beforehand by their friends in the police. A large portion of the loot always got shared at different levels within the police force.

The Kidnapping Industry

In 2004, the National Hydroelectric Power Corporation (NHPC) bagged an ambitious rural road construction project worth Rs 19,000 crore under the Pradhan Mantri Gram Sadak Yojana. When asked about the challenging law-and-order situation in Bihar, NHPC's director confidently commented that his company had executed several projects in the worst-hit insurgency areas of the Northeast and in Jammu & Kashmir. Just a month later, two of NHPC's senior employees were abducted while on their way to Bettiah. While one of the employees escaped, the other was released by the captors only after two weeks of drama. The captors had demanded 10 crore to be paid in Mumbai through hawala channels. The NHPC denied having paid any ransom but barely anybody in Bihar trusted their statement.

The kidnapping industry in Bihar is believed to have mushroomed during the 1980s, with West Champaran in north-west Bihar as its epicentre. West Champaran, the place of Gandhi's first and historic satyagraha against forced indigo cultivation, holds a special place on the crime map of Bihar. West Champaran with its riverine and forested land served as the perfect haven for dacoits and hence would often be referred to as the 'Chambal of Bihar'.

However, how the dacoity capital transitioned to a kidnapping capital is an interesting tale in itself. It is largely believed to be the brainchild of an SP in the 1980s who was tasked with checking the rampant dacoities in the area. He met the major dacoity gangs in the area and made them realise that traditional dacoity involved heavy violence, serious risk of capture and harsh punishments. Also, with people increasingly resorting to banking, the loot was dwindling and hence it made sense to shift to a low-risk crime: kidnapping. It would ensure they got good returns as ransom without having to shed blood. The sentencing for such crimes was far less frequent. The proposal found resonance with the dacoits. Soon incidence of dacoities dwindled and cases of kidnapping shot up.

By 1985, the phenomenon had spread to the districts of Rohtas, Bhagalpur and Munger. The 1995 police records confirm that two people were abducted every day in Bettiah, the district headquarters of West Champaran. The commonality between these districts with high incidence of kidnappings was their hilly or riverine terrain and borders with Nepal or neighbouring states such as Uttar Pradesh and Madhya Pradesh.

By the 1990s, these considerations had become immaterial and kidnapper gangs had emerged in hordes in every region of

Bihar. Their terror was so significant that people would often hesitate to buy anything that could draw their eye. Every house without armed bodyguards—or even with them in many cases—was insecure. Venturing out after sunset was considered suicidal and an open invitation to kidnappers. The crime records, though high, didn't actually reflect the true size of the crime industry, as most of the victims never filed an FIR. Filing an FIR would mean a higher ransom the next time they were kidnapped. In many cases, the police wouldn't accept the FIR. The police, caught in the frustration of lawlessness, would often leave it to the perpetrators and victims to settle it between themselves. When pressured in certain high-profile cases, the police would resort to encounter killings and custodial violence of the worst form such crimes. In many cases, the police officers would act as peace brokers and deliver their caste-tainted justice to helpless victims.

Most of the kidnappings were done for ransom. While the targets initially were wealthy farmers, the criminals quickly realised that doctors, engineers, businessmen and contractors would be easier and more lucrative targets. The targeted people would take every possible precaution, right from avoiding any display of wealth to changing their place of stay every week to travelling with guards even when going short distances, but could rarely avoid the inevitability of being kidnapped. The situation became so dire that the North Bihar Chamber of Commerce & Industry had to send a memorandum to the then chief minister, asking to whom they should pay their taxes: the government or the rangdars (extortionists).

Over time, changes in the modus operandi of these criminal gangs led to school-going kids becoming the new and unsuspecting target group for the kidnappers. Kids were soft targets as they were easier to abduct, and parents would do anything to ensure their safe return. The menace elicited this comment from the Bihar High Court in 2005: 'Is it a crime to be born in Bihar? This is not the question of one child. Tell us how children can go to school and pursue studies safely?'[248]

The ransom would vary according to the paying capacity of the abducted and could be anywhere between a few thousands to tens of lakhs. In an amusing case in Bhagalpur, no money was demanded for releasing a school-going boy; the ransom was merely a lavish dinner organised for the kidnappers. The first five months of 1995 recorded close to 700 kidnappings from various parts of the state at an average of around six kidnappings a day.

In many cases, the gangs would sub-contract the kidnapping to a smaller gang at a fixed share of the ransom money. In some cases, the criminals would sell off the victim to inter-state gangs to avoid being at the same location and thus getting caught. Most of these gangs had the patronage of some or the other strongman or politician from their region. This also explained the lack of political will to act against the practice. In the high-profile kidnapping case of a textile merchant, Nand Kishore Lal Tikamani, from Muzaffarpur, the nephew of the mines and geology minister Sitaram Singh was also arrested.[249] Some gangs of the day claimed that they had direct access to the chief minister's residence. People often quote the classic case of a Patna doctor who, after his car was taken away at gunpoint, reached Lalu's residence to find it parked there.

The criminal–politician nexus in kidnappings became apparent in the case of the famous Patna neurosurgeon Dr Ramesh Chandra. Dr Chandra was kidnapped on 17 May 2003 while he was on his way back from a dinner party. A ransom of Rs 50 lakh was demanded from his family. The high-profile case brought the state and the government into disrepute. The police soon rescued Dr Chandra from Chiraura village in Patna district. However, what brought the case more attention was the involvement of Sunil Pandey, the criminal-turned-politician and JD(U) MLA from Piro constituency. Pandey was sentenced to life imprisonment in 2008 for the same. His accomplice in the kidnapping confessed that Pandey had celebrated the successful kidnapping by firing shots in the air at Patna's Maurya Hotel.

Another notorious criminal, Umesh Singh, was wanted in at least twelve kidnapping cases when he was arrested in 2002. The kidnappings included those of a famous businessman, Sajjan Jalan, and the Exide Industries chief Satyabrata Ganguly. However, what was more interesting was the place of arrest of Umesh Singh. He was arrested in Kankarbagh, Patna, from the residence of the son-in-law of a former union minister.[250]

Between 1992 and 2004, a total of 32,085 cases of kidnapping were reported.[251] A number of factors could be said to be responsible for the sudden mushrooming of the kidnapping industry in Bihar in the 1990s. The first would be the widespread unemployment among youth who, in the absence of any significant arrests and conviction, saw this as a low-risk, high-return business. The second was the politician–criminal nexus and in many cases the dual role being played by the same person. This translated into the lack of a political will to tackle the menace. The third reason was police incapacity. The police were and still are hugely burdened given the population that each police station serves. The police would also often be accused of being hand-in-glove with criminal gangs in their areas. The barely existent training and sensitisation of the policemen added to the woes.

The most unique of kidnappings were reported from the Begusarai and Mokama belt where young boys would be kidnapped to be married off at gunpoint, mostly to avoid high dowry costs. Colloquially referred to as pakaruah byah, these forced marriages wouldn't be annulled because of the religious sanctity attached to the ritual of mariage. Additionally, the groom could be charged under dowry laws and would have to fight lengthy legal battles, if he reneged. In the 1990s, numerous cases appeared in newspapers where a certain visiting friend of the groom would be caught hold off and married in the same mandap as his friend. In some cases, even the shahvaala—a minor relative of the groom—wouldn't be spared and be married off alongside the newly anointed bride and groom, cue if he were ten years old! The year 1994 recorded nearly fifty such cases in the Begusarai and Mokama belt.[252] The irony of such kidnappings being that it was and still is considered a saintly act as the girl wouldn't otherwise have found a suitable husband, the biggest reason being dowry.

By the end of the Lalu–Rabri era, the situation had become so bad that the National Democratic Alliance (NDA) government made it a major poll issue in the 2005 assembly elections. Atal Bihari Vajpayee roared in an election rally in Bhagalpur:

> *Kahaan hain mere Kislay aur Deepak? Koi mujhe mere Kislay aur Deepak se mila de ... unhe lauta de ...* [Where are my Kislay and Deepak? Someone please bring back my Kislay and Deepak.]

Kislay and Deepak had recently been kidnapped from Patna and Bhagalpur, respectively. Vajpayee's direct question struck an instant chord not just with the rally audience but the entire state. A huge outrage followed Vajpayee's remark. School children took to the streets to demand Kislay's release and sought the intervention of President A.P.J. Abdul Kalam. The Bihar police was jolted out of their slumber. Deepak was rescued five days after Vajpayee's speech. Kislay was also rescued shortly from Samastipur, his kidnappers killed in an encounter with the police.

Corruption at its Deadliest

Satyendra Dubey, an Indian Engineering Service (IES) officer, was murdered in Gaya on the night of 27 November 2003. He had turned thirty that day.

Satyendra was posted in Koderma as a project director for the National Highways Authority of India (NHAI) and was fighting corruption in the Golden Quadrilateral Project. He had written to the Prime Minister's Office (PMO), too, about this matter.

Born into a family of ten children in the Siwan district of Bihar, Satyendra showed his acumen when he topped the Xth and XIIth state board examinations. He went on to graduate in civil engineering at IIT-Kanpur and subsequently completed his Master's degree from the Institute of Technology, Banaras Hindu University in 1996. Satyendra joined the IES in 2002 and was deputed to NHAI. He was asked to manage a part of the Aurangabad–Barachatti section of National Highway 2 (Grand Trunk Road). The highway was part of the prime minister's ambitious Golden Quadrilateral Project, which aimed to connect several major cities of the country by four-lane limited-access highways. Satyendra Dubey found serious irregularities in the work and finances of the contractor and made him suspend three of his engineers and also rebuild a six-kilometre stretch of poor-quality road.

On the night of 27 November 2003, Satyendra Dubey was returning after attending a wedding in Varanasi. He was shot dead while on his way from the station to his home in Gaya. Satyendra had decided to take a rickshaw since his car was unavailable due to a battery malfunction. The murder created a huge uproar, including in Parliament and the matter was handed over to the CBI.

The twists in the investigation of the case over the next couple of years raised huge doubts if the real culprits would ever be apprehended. The case was initially presented as that of a simple robbery gone wrong. Soon, however, things went awry with the disappearance of rickshaw puller Pradeep Kumar, who was also the prime witness; the deaths of two suspects within twenty-five hours of questioning by the CBI; and the escape of the prime suspect, Mantu Kumar, from the court premises. It was felt that Mantu's escape was engineered by influential people who may have been behind the murder.[253] In 2010, Mantu Kumar and two others were convicted by a Patna court for the murder of Satyendra Dubey.

Satyendra Dubey became the focus of several important documentaries and TV shows. Awards were instituted in his name to honour his fight against corruption. What the whole incident reiterated was the huge power that the business and crime lobbies wielded in Bihar and how dangerous it was to go against them.

Bihar had already earned the infamy of having one of the most corrupt state governments after the fodder scam made the headlines in national news in 1996. The scam shook the political establishment of Bihar. While the public primarily remembers the corruption scene in Bihar during the 1990s through the fodder scam, it was just one among the many scams that took place during the Lalu–Rabri rule. In fact, the other scams rarely came to light, and even if they did, convictions were scarce. The fury of Lalu's supporters at the legal action against him in the fodder scam was not unfounded, as corruption was, and still is, considered an acceptable way of life in the region.

A couple of years before the fodder scam broke out, another major scam was cooking in the corridors of the Road Construction Department of Bihar. The Haldia Oil Refinery in

Kolkata was supposed to supply bitumen for road construction in Chatra district (now in Jharkhand). However, the then road construction minister, Ilyas Hussain, colluded with the engineers and embezzled several metric tonnes of bitumen. Hussain, considered close to Lalu, was jokingly referred to as 'Kuber mantri' in Lalu's cabinet. Hussain, a prominent Muslim face of the Janata Dal in Bihar and later the RJD, represented the Dehri-on-Sone constituency in Rohtas district. He remained the road construction minister from the day Lalu assumed power in 1990 till November 1999, when the CBI arrested him in the bitumen scam case. Hussain's supporters demanded that the former minister's wife be made the new road construction minister, the same way that Rabri was made the chief minister upon Lalu's arrest. The demand was rejected by Lalu.

The matter which came to light in 1997 would take another twenty-two years to reach its conclusion. Hussain would be found guilty and sentenced to four years in prison and slapped with a fine of Rs 2 lakh. Ironically, while barely any roads were constructed during the period, the bitumen required for roads remained a common material for embezzlement and corruption.

A story related to the bitumen scam and Ilyas Hussain became the talk of the town in those days.[254] Hussain was travelling to Delhi to receive some money from the people of the company he had colluded with. Ministers had lenient security checks in those days at the airports. Hussain was able to travel back from the Delhi airport with a bag full of money. However, the news of Hussain's dealings reached Lalu, who reached the Patna airport to receive Hussain. Lalu looked at the briefcase in Hussain's hand and commented:

> '*E ho Ilyas, bada sundar bag liye ho*' (Hey Ilyas, you are carrying a beautiful bag).

A startled Ilyas said, '*Ji, wo Palika me khareede hain*' (Yes, I bought it at Palika).

'*Ketna me khareede?*' (How much did you buy it for?)

'*Ji 2,000 mein*' (I bought it for 2,000).

Lalu smiled and told his PA, '*Ilyas bhai ko 3,000 rupia dijiye, 2,000 briefcase ka aur 1,000 Dilli se dho ke laane ka. Briefcase ghar bhijwa dijiye*' (Give 3,000 rupees to Ilyas Bhai, 2,000 for the briefcase and 1,000 for carrying it from Delhi. Send the briefcase home).

Ilyas knew there was no way out of the trap. However, he remained one of the few to continue with Lalu and his family till he was sentenced in 2019.

In 1994, Lalu appointed Ramashray Prasad Yadav to the chairmanship of Bihar Public Service Commission (BPSC). It was immediately alleged that Lalu was promoting one of his caste men to the important position, and this could hardly be debated. However, as soon as he was appointed to the position, Ramashray Prasad Yadav sold his land in Danapur to Mohd Shameem and Rakesh Ranjan. A few years later, both these buyers gifted their lands to Lalu's children. Shameem and Ranjan became Members of Legislative Council (MLCs) later.

This is not the only case of land transfers that directly involved Lalu and his family members. In fact, Sushil Kumar Modi, in his book *Lalu Leela,* lists several such instances of free land gifts from several people to Lalu and his family members as quid pro quos for awarding contracts or government jobs.

Paper Leak Industry

Another news that brought Bihar on the national scene in 2003 was that of the leaking of CAT papers, the prestigious B-school test held for entrance to the Indian Institutes of Management. The man behind the leak was reported to be Ranjit Kumar Singh, or 'Doctor Don', as he was popularly known in familiar circles of Bihar. Born into a peasant family in Khaddi Lodipur in Nalanda, his story was nothing short of a rags-to-riches folklore. Once Ranjit was caught and the details started surfacing, one realised what a massive racket he was running.

The paper leak industry in Bihar was estimated to be nothing short of 100 crore. The paper leak groups could hand you the exam papers of the most prestigious engineering, medical, banking and a host of other entrance exams in advance, for a fee ranging between 4 to 15 lakh. Among them, Ranjit Don's group was reportedly the best organised. Ranjit's past was chequered and it could be said that he learnt the rules of the game by using them to first build his own career. He matriculated in 1979 first, changed his name and appeared again for the class 10 exams a few years later. Cited as a widely used trick, it is still possible to find this in practice in large parts of Bihar; it is done to reduce one's age officially. In the absence of birth certificates, the class 10 exam passing certificates are the first proof of an individual's age. Ranjit also appeared twice for his higher secondary exams, once as an arts student and later as a science student, because by then he wanted to become a doctor.

By the time Ranjit arrived in Patna in the 1980s, 'setting' was already a buzzword and numerous tricks were being deployed by students to outwit the exam machineries. A popular trick was to apply collectively for any exam, often by sending all applications in the same envelope. This would help the students get consecutive roll numbers and the same exam hall where they would communicate through codes. It worked for many candidates. When the UPSC (Union Public Service Commission) realised it was a trick and stopped allocating running roll numbers to such applications, the candidates started submitting their applications en masse in person at the UPSC headquarters in Delhi. Ranjit was taught the tricks of the trade by his mentor, Dr Irshad Khan, the one whose brainchild was the 'Engine and Bogey' system. This system entailed hiring a meritorious student to sit with the client for exams at a cost of 1.5–2 lakh. The 'engine' would solve the paper and pass the answers to the 'bogey' during exams.

Ranjit studied the nuances of the entire examination process and became the ringmaster. Upon realising how easy it was to trick the MBBS exam system, Ranjit decided to become a doctor. He got admission at Darbhanga Medical College and even secured a degree dubiously six years later in 2000. Ranjit then set up a drug firm, using the newly acquired degree and accumulated 'setting' money. The company's sole purpose purportedly was money laundering.

By this time, Ranjit possessed every trick in the book to crack any exam. He would bribe the staff at printing presses or would collude with the question paper coordination panels. Often, he would track the transport route of question papers to find loopholes. If nothing worked, and he couldn't get the papers in advance, he would simply bribe the exam centre to get his 'engine' and 'bogies' in the same room. However, Ranjit knew well the tightrope he was walking and would keep the entire operation utterly secretive. He would lock the clients in a room the night before the exams and make them mug up the answers. The leaked question papers couldn't be taken out of the room. The clients would be dropped to the exam centres by Ranjit's trusted associates. Ranjit would demand post-dated cheques from his clients before the exam.

Ranjit, however, ran out of luck in 2003 when his key members got arrested in Pune. He had recently married a college student named Deepika in an ostentatious ceremony attended by leading politicians, doctors and bureaucrats.

Years later, Ranjit would confess in an interview about his political ambitions. His followers would claim that he had been falsely implicated in the CAT leak case because he was going to contest the forthcoming Lok Sabha elections from Nalanda against George Fernandes. Ranjit would proclaim that his friendship with Nitish Kumar went sour because Nitish never gave him the ticket he was promised. He would call himself 'a Kurmi fighting a Kurmi'—also Nitish Kumar's caste.[255]

Deepika, his wife, would later fight the 2015 assembly elections from Hilsa, on a Lok Janshakti Party (LJP) ticket.

Courtesy Ranjit, Nalanda University was no longer the unique mention in Nalanda's glorious history as a seat of learning. The district had now earned the reputation of being the hub of paper leak syndicates. One often wonders why Biharis like Ranjit, who could have succeeded anywhere with their intellect choose such paths. Maybe because the state has little use of their intelligence. One doesn't know if it is people like Ranjit Don who make Bihar what it is or if it is the other way round. Bihar has one of the lowest literacy rates in the country, but one of the highest success rates in civil services exams. Such stark dichotomies further perplex the mind, making it impossible to solve the puzzle that has plagued Bihar for decades.

NITISH: THE ENIGMA

One man with courage makes a majority.

—Andrew Jackson

BIHAR MEIN BAHAAR HAI

The assembly elections in February 2005 threw a fractured mandate. The National Democratic Alliance (NDA) of the BJP and JD(U) emerged as the leading coalition with ninety-two seats, while the RJD emerged as the single-largest party with seventy-five seats. However, both camps fell short of the halfway mark of 122.

As soon as the results were declared, both camps started making efforts to woo Ram Vilas Paswan, whose party, the Lok Janshakti Party (LJP), had gained twenty-nine seats and could play the kingmaker. As it became clear that a government couldn't be formed without his support, Paswan was offered every sort of bargain. However, Paswan remained adamant about not supporting either side. His refrain was, 'I will join hands neither with the communal BJP nor with the corrupt and casteist RJD. I will neither take their support nor extend my support to either of them.'[256] Even Sonia Gandhi's attempt to persuade Paswan to back the RJD couldn't move him. Paswan was ready to lead a non-BJP, non-RJD alliance, but to everything else, he preferred President's Rule in the state.

The Congress, which had been reduced from twenty-three seats in 2000 to ten in 2005, was blamed by all parties in the opposition camp for having divided the 'secular' votes and strengthened the NDA position. Given the existing stalemate, the Congress leaders thought that President's Rule wouldn't be a bad idea. They thought it would allow a solution to be worked out, maybe breaking some of Paswan's MLAs and compelling him to cooperate.

With none of the sides being able to form the government, Bihar was put under President's Rule on 6 March 2005. As the state went into President's Rule, MLAs from the LJP started growing restless at Paswan's intransigence. Fed up of Paswan's indecisiveness, seventeen of the twenty-nine MLAs rebelled by pledging support to Nitish Kumar. A majority of these MLAs believed that they had won on the back of an anti-Lalu campaign and must help form a non-RJD government in the state.

The LJP's general secretary, Nagmani, resigned from the post and party. The Bihar LJP chief openly made statements such as, 'Paswan showed disrespect for [the] people's verdict, which was in favour of anti-RJD forces. People will not forgive him for his adamant stand on government formation.'[257] Paswan saw the real danger of a split in his party.

Paswan, who was also a union minister in the UPA government at the Centre, agreed to form a government with the RJD's support, but only with a Muslim chief minister. An uneasy Lalu, taking advantage of the rebellion within the LJP, pressured the UPA to dissolve the house.

One person who played a highly controversial role during this political upheaval was Bihar's governor, Buta Singh. Buta Singh had a colourful stint as the home minister during Rajiv Gandhi's government, during which he had dismissed three constitutionally elected governments, those of Surjeet Singh Barnala in Punjab (1987), the AIADMK government in Tamil Nadu (1988) and S.R. Bommai's government in Karnataka (1989). The last dismissal led to a court battle that brought about a landmark judgment by the Supreme Court in 1994 regarding the use of Article 356. A belligerent Buta Singh once described his own influence over the North Block as: 'Once there was Sardar Patel. Now there is Sardar Buta Singh.'[258]

However, Buta Singh seemed to have learnt little from it. He recommended the dissolution of the assembly on 21 May 2005. The cabinet met at midnight, accepted the report and faxed it to the president's camp office in Moscow, where he was visiting. The president okayed it in the next two hours.

The BJP, which for the first time had had a chance at forming the government in Bihar, couldn't contain its resentment towards the governor, calling him Jhoota [Liar] Singh. Buta Singh seemed to be continuing a long battle with the BJP.[259] However, it wasn't just the BJP that decried the unconstitutionality of the entire process. The Supreme Court, deciding on the case, didn't hide its displeasure. It stated:

> The drastic and extreme action under Article 356 cannot be justified on ... whims and fancies of the governor ... The Council of Ministers should have verified the facts stated in the report of the governor before hurriedly accepting it as gospel truth. Clearly the governor has misled the Council of Ministers.[260]

The opposition used the judgement to demand Buta Singh's resignation. Singh remained defiant, as he had been on similar occasions in the past. However, he had to finally demit office under pressure from an embarrassed Congress leadership. Buta Singh would be rewarded later, however, with the chairmanship of the National Commission for Scheduled Castes (NCSC) in 2007.

The Final Blow

Elections were held again in November 2005. It proved to be a final blow to Lalu's fifteen-year-long hegemony in Bihar. Even before the results had been declared, it had become inevitable that Lalu wouldn't be able to hold his fortress any longer. If there had been any confusion about Lalu's model of social justice, it had been cleared in the minds of people by then. Paswan's breaking away from the alliance also took away the crucial Dusadh votes share from the RJD amidst desertions by several other disillusioned EBCs.

The events following the February 2005 elections, where Nitish Kumar was controversially denied government formation, also resulted in a consolidation of sympathy votes behind the JD(U)–BJP alliance. This led to the NDA, which was scrambling to form the government just a few months ago, returning with an emphatic majority of 143 in the November elections. The two worst losers in the November elections were Lalu's RJD and Paswan's LJP. The former was reduced to a lowest-ever tally of 54 seats in the 243-member assembly. Paswan had to make do with a final tally of ten MLAs.

The Challenge Ahead

When Nitish Kumar became Bihar's new chief minister, his role was far from enviable. Nitish's style and approach was diametrically opposite to that of Lalu's. Both had started their political careers together during the JP movement in the mid-1970s. While Lalu came from the numerically significant caste of Yadavs, Nitish came from the landowning backward caste of Kurmis. Lalu was a prominent face of the movement and a real crowd-puller. He seamlessly metamorphed into a natural politician just a few years later. Nitish, on the other hand, was a more reserved personality who took his own time to season into a significant political figure.

While Nitish was credited with a lot of good work as cabinet minister in the NDA government between 1998 and 2004, fame and recognition would elude him until now. Many insiders from the railway ministry often credit Nitish's initiatives for the railways' turnaround, which Lalu later executed during the UPA regime. Officials often comment that large-scale improvement of railway lines and time-keeping of passenger trains was done during Nitish's regime. Substantial asset replacement during Nitish's stint helped Lalu, as his successor, move more freight on the existing tracks, as per a former railway board member.[261]

While most of these details went unnoticed by the larger public, which hailed Lalu for the turnaround of the railways, Nitish realised during these ministerial stints that development could be good politics. Also, Bihar being at the bottom of all development parameters, he would garner both recognition and votes if even the basics were done right.

However, Nitish had not just inherited a state with the worst economic and human development parameters but also a state apparatus with a corrupt and resigned bureaucracy.

First Things First

Nitish realised that his first task was to create a bureaucratic support system that would help him execute his ideas. Forming such a team had its own challenges. Most of the able bureaucrats, having suffered in the swarm of corruption, misgovernance and political interference, had either moved to Jharkhand during the bifurcation or to central deputations. The unfortunate ones had resigned themselves to the fate of serving in an irredeemable Bihar. The rare bright spots with integrity and the right abilities had been shunted to nondescript postings.

Nitish had clarified his intentions when journalists had asked about his priorities just after his swearing-in. 'Governance, governance, governance,' he had reiterated. Nitish's promise of sushaasan (good governance) faced a lot of daunting and seemingly insurmountable challenges such as low industrialisation and poor infrastructure, including roads and electricity; failed education and health sectors; and a deeply entrenched criminal–politician nexus.

Nitish quickly tried to cobble together a team of officers to execute his immediate priorities. He appointed Ramchandra Prasad Singh his principal secretary. R.C.P. Singh had worked closely with Nitish in his various stints as cabinet minister at the Centre. Though R.C.P. Singh belonged to the UP cadre, Nitish did everything possible to bring him in as a trusted lieutenant. R.C.P. Singh would later go on to join Janata Dal (U) and play extremely important roles in the party and in the government as Nitish's right-hand man.

Nitish also brought in R.K. Singh, a 1975-batch IAS officer who had become famous for stopping Advani's Rath Yatra, as the one to build Bihar's dilapidated roads.

Having assembled a formidable team to execute his ideas of sushaasan on the ground, Nitish now needed to turn towards the legislature. Bihar urgently needed a slew of laws to counter the decrepit socioeconomic structure of the state. Nitish brought in P.K. Shahi as the advocate general of the state to help him with legislation.

Nitish was a thorough socialist, and this reflected in his style of governance, which he spelt out as 'development with justice'.

The panchayat elections were just around the corner when Nitish took over. Nitish took a bold and significant step in reserving 50 per cent of the seats in panchayats for women. In addition, 37 per cent of the seats were reserved for marginalised sections. This included the EBCs (20 per cent), SCs (16 per cent) and STs (1 per cent).[262] Nitish thus tried to give political representation to the two most vulnerable sections of the society, the women and the hitherto unrepresented castes, of course with overlaps. The panchayat polls ended up electing over 54,000 women, including 3,800 mukhiyas and 18 zila parishad presidents. Nitish did this against the opinions of many of his party members, including the Janata Dal (U) president, Sharad Yadav.

Another women-centric scheme that Nitish brought in targeted high-school girls. He helped eight lakh such school-going girls buy cycles. The scheme was later extended to boys as well. This enabled a large crowd of high-school students to attend schools more sincerely and was hailed as a populist as well as effective scheme. True to Nitish's judgement, these initiatives turned out to be politically effective, too, in getting women's votes in the next assembly elections.

Another significant legislative step that Nitish took was repealing the Agricultural Produce Marketing Committees (APMC) Act. The archaic act prevented farmers from selling their produce to the buyer of their choice and served as the fiefdom of intermediaries and vested interests. It had also produced a huge gap in the price paid by end consumers and that received by the farmers. While most states had long been planning to forgo it, Bihar became the first state to repeal it in 2006. This allowed the farmers to sell their produce in the open market at the best price offered and also opened avenues for contract farming.

Nitish's passion for reforms and quick action was also visible in many other areas such as single-window clearance, sugarcane supply and purchase, stamp duty and Value Added Tax (VAT) simplification. While Nitish kept pushing reforms through legislative measures, he also kept a tight grip on administrative issues. Known as a workaholic with a deep understanding of various departments, Nitish expected his ministers and bureaucrats to be on top of things. Cabinet meetings were now a regular affair; Tuesday afternoons were dedicated to them. The bureaucracy, which was used to pushing files over the past fifteen years, was suddenly pushed into the role of problem-solvers. Some bureaucrats would struggle to catch up with Nitish's speed of decision-making and long work hours, undistracted by a family life.

Some of the legislative and policy decisions taken by Nitish showed result after some years, so the people of Bihar didn't instantly see any substantial difference from the old Bihar. Even the push for infrastructure was in its nascent stage and would take time to become visible on the ground. The change needed to be seen outside the chief minister's office and secretariat building. Having taken a slew of legislative measures and put in place bureaucratic and procedural structures, Nitish moved to what he thought was the most crucial task and a litmus test for him. Law and order was the one issue which Nitish hadn't missed to mention in any of his campaign speeches. Now he needed to live up to his promise of a state ruled by law.

Rule of Law

Bihar had never been a poster child of law and order. But in the 1990s it went on to beat itself and become one of India's most lawless states. Bihar had become a hub of criminal activities such as kidnapping, land grabs, contract murders and every conceivable crime. A large house or the purchase of a car was virtually an invitation for kidnapping and ransom. So was venturing out after dark. The roads and markets in business towns like Muzaffarpur, Gaya and Bhagalpur would go desolate after sunset. Encroachment on land and unoccupied property was rampant across the state. The citizens had no recourse in the virtual absence of policing and a fair legal system.

The reasons for such a deterioration in law and order were manifold. At the heart of it was Lalu's belief that to break the upper-caste hegemony, he had to empower the backward castes. The battle for domination soon assumed a casteist character and so did every crime. Everything from the filing of FIRs to investigation and action was dependent upon the caste of the perpetrator, complainant and policemen. People throughout the chain of hierarchy would follow their caste. It is widely believed that to register a case against a Yadav during Lalu's regime, the police had to take a 'clearance'. Even the criminal gangs were mostly based on caste and would try and eliminate other caste gangs.

The other prime reason for such mushrooming of crime was the systematic weakening of police forces in the state. The police were expected to be servile to the government of the day. Initially, the centralised control ran from 1, Anne Marg. Later, this was decentralised and the police would hesitate to contradict what would be asked by any kurta-clad RJD politician anywhere in the state. In fact, when an SP would go to meet goons backed by politicians or in some cases law makers, he had to often take off his shoes before presenting himself. In case of bahubalis like Shahabuddin, a mere phone call from them was the highest order for the police and district administration.

In the absence of any law enforcement structure, bahubalis came in to fill the void. People also, having realised the ineffectiveness of the police department, would resort to asking bahubalis for help. These bahubalis became the providers of justice, and then into perpetrators themselves. Backed by people's support, they slowly reached the chairs of the Bihar Legislative Assembly. By this time, the police had also taken refuge in the bahubalis' gracious durbars.

However, it is important to note that the police departments in the state were severely understaffed and undertrained. The only time in the fifteen years of RJD's rule that police recruitment was done, was marred by controversies. An estimated total of 30,000 vacancies existed in the state police force.

Nitish approached Abhayanand to lead his mission to end the lawlessness and terror that was all-pervasive in Bihar. Abhayanand was then serving as the Additional Director General (ADG) of Bihar Police. A soft-spoken man with an innovative mind, Abhayanand would soon go on to become famous as the co-founder of Super-30. Super-30 first made headlines in the late 2000s when it reported an almost 100 per cent success rate for thirty extremely poor students that it had chosen to coach for cracking the prestigious IIT-JEE exams. Son of a former DGP, Abhayanand was known for his integrity and belief in reformist rather than punitive attitude. Nitish promised him complete backing in terms or resources and legislative support for tougher laws. However, all Abhayanand asked for was a free hand.

Afzal Amanullah was another officer with a stellar reputation who was brought in as the home secretary. He was instrumental in working with the police to establish a 'rule of law'.

It was well known that police stations, over the past two decades, had become the biggest den of crime themselves. Thanas would be crowded with the shoddiest of pan-chewing chhutbhaiya netas with policemen themselves brokering deals. The police would be found to be involved in several crimes, or often have prior knowledge of them. In short, the protector had taken on the role of tormentor, that too with legitimacy.

Nitish's first instruction for improving the criminal justice system was a directive that every FIR had to result in a chargesheet within ninety days. This resulted in 54,000 criminal convictions in the next five years. Within days of Nitish taking over, Sadhu Yadav—Lalu's brother-in-law and Gopalganj MP—was summoned to depose in a flood relief scam case. With his anticipatory bail rejected, Sadhu Yadav was on the run with a nationwide arrest warrant on him. This was the same Sadhu Yadav who was given bail by the police in his drawing room during Lalu's régime after he was charged with threatening a transport commissioner to sign an illegal order at gunpoint. A few months later, the JD(U) strongman Anand Mohan was arrested using force. Another MLA from Nitish's party, Sunil Pandey, went on the run after a case was registered against him.

However, the government's resolve looked even more formidable when it decided to set up fast-track courts to bring the bigger bahubalis to justice. This included Shahabuddin from the RJD, Surajbhan Singh of the LJP and Prabhunath Singh of the JD(U). The inclusion of the JD(U) strongman took the political bias argument out of the equation. Nitish wanted to indicate to everyone that he wasn't going to compromise or do any favours when it came to law and order.

Nitish's trusted man Abhayanand emphasised on convictions to bring people's confidence back in the rule of law. A generally perceived notion of the police's role is to arrest or nab the criminals. However, arrest is only the beginning. The real job of the police is to get a conviction for the criminal. This large gap between arrests and conviction is what had demoralised the public and police alike during the previous regime. Frustrated police officials, having to release criminals under political pressure or not being able to secure convictions, would often turn to extra judicial measures such as encounters.

Convictions, even for smaller crimes, could be a huge disincentive for criminals. The most important being their disqualification from contesting elections and thus stopping the legitimisation of a large number of criminal-turned-politicians. Additionally, a jail term, even if only for a year or two, would generally be a disincentive enough for criminals to not commit crimes in the future. Accompanied by inconvenience to their families, the decimation of networks, rise in competition in their absence and a fall in reputation and perceived strength would generally act as a deterrent for them to resume their career in crime upon release. A general trend in FIRs leading to conviction would also revive the people's confidence in the efficiency of the legal systems. As important as the convictions was the fear of conviction. The psychological battle, if won, would be a job half done.

Abhayanand came up with an interesting way to increase convictions: he asked all SPs to concentrate solely on conviction for illegal possession of firearms. It sounded bizarre initially to concentrate on such a minor offence, when compared to the kind of heinous crimes committed in Bihar. However, Abhayanand had a point.

No major crime could generally be committed without a firearm. It could thus become a common thread of conviction across all musclemen and criminal gangs. Also getting a prosecution in this case was far easier than in the case of other crimes, one major reason being that it didn't require independent witnesses. The raiding officer, along with two other government officers, would be sufficient to testify against the charged person. With a more standardised process of evidence and testimony, the conviction could be secured within a few weeks. While the maximum punishment was relatively lighter, ranging from three years for possessing country-made weapons to six years for regular firearms, the sentence itself had a huge deterrent value. It also made it easier to press other serious charges, if applicable, to the convict while he was incarcerated.

Abhayanand would personally call the SPs between 9:00 p.m. and midnight every day and monitor the progress of these convictions. After some initial pushback, he was able to bring everyone on board when the move started showing results. From twenty-nine convictions under the Arms Act in January 2006, it swelled to almost 25,000 convictions by the end of 2008. The figure looked substantial when compared to the total of 3,781 convictions in the same period under all other IPC cases combined.[263]

Abhayanand also asked the SPs to prioritise cases in a reverse chronological order, as opposed to the general 'first-in, first-out' principle. This helped prevent bottlenecks as older cases are harder to conclude, and this ends up delaying the newer cases, too, creating a vicious circle.

The approach seemed to be working. The police were able to assert themselves and people could suddenly see the law taking the right course. The speedy trials in the Arms Act cases created a ripple effect in other kinds of cases too, in which convictions were more complex. The number of dacoity cases almost halved from 1,191 in 2005 to 640 in 2008. Robbery and road dacoity went down from 2,909 and 287, respectively, in 2004 to 1,536 and 146, respectively, in 2008. Other crimes like bank robberies also went down significantly. The biggest psychological effect of these convictions was seen in the reduction in kidnapping cases from 411 in 2004 to 66 in 2008.[264] However, there were other crimes that didn't see such a decline. Bihar hardly became the poster boy for law and order, but it did experience a general uplift from the abyss it was languishing in earlier.

While the government took immediate cognizance of crimes and took punitive measures, Nitish Kumar also passed the carrot of rehabilitation to criminals. The government offered cash incentives plus benefits like education for children and funds to help build homes for the surrendered criminals. Within the first four months of Nitish's rule, almost 200 notorious criminals surrendered. The government also made the innovation of 'outsourcing' police services to temporary hires. Almost 12,000 posts were filled in the force called the State Auxiliary Police (SAP), specially recruiting young retirees from lower ranks of the armed forces. Well-trained in the use of arms and ammunition and untainted by the prevalent police culture, they proved highly effective in disturbed areas and in controlling violent situations.

Nitish Kumar also demonstrated his seriousness in tackling corruption through a slew of administrative as well as legislative measures. Immediately after his taking over, the chairman of the BPSC (Bihar Public Service Commission), along with several other officials, were arrested in connection with a scam in selection of Bihar administrative services personnel.

However, it wasn't an easy choice or method for Nitish. Nitish understood the role of musclemen, particularly those backed by caste and religious groups, in Bihar's politics. It was in balancing the support of such musclemen while also ensuring they were prosecuted as per the law that Nitish displayed his political acumen. It is interesting to note that despite his repeated criticism of the RJD's attempt to criminalise politics, Nitish's own party didn't lag behind any other in fielding tainted candidates, in election after election. Nitish seemed to have clearly demarcated his electoral compulsions from his administrative processes. He brought candidates with criminal background into his party and fielded tainted candidates if that made sense for him electorally. However, he let the police and law take due course in prosecuting such individuals. He, in fact, would push his administrative machinery for a faster resolution to such cases. This clearly severed the link between a criminal's electoral success and immunity from prosecution.

Nitish's closeness to Anant Singh, the bahubali from Mokama, brought him much criticism. Rumour has it that when Anant Singh first won on a JD(U) ticket in 2005, he brought Nitish to his constituency and weighed him in gold. When questioned by a reporter once on why he had embraced known criminals like Anant Singh, Nitish bluntly retorted, 'There are certain compulsions of politics.'

In 2015, Anant Singh was arrested on murder and kidnapping charges. The move was largely interpreted as a result of Nitish's political realignment with his long-time rival-turned-newfound partner, Lalu Prasad Yadav.

The inclusion of RJD strongman from Kishanganj Mohammad Taslimuddin in the JD(U) just before the 2010 assembly elections is another such example. Taslimuddin's hold on the Muslim-dominated Seemanchal belt was well known to Nitish. To balance the criticism, he ensured that it was his son, rather than Taslimuddin himself, who would fight the elections on a JD(U) ticket.

Push for Infrastructure

If tackling crime was the biggest challenge for Nitish Kumar's administration, infrastructure was not far behind. The condition of roads was worse than imaginable. The average length of roads in 2004 stood at eighty-nine kilometres against a national average of 260 kilometre for every one lakh people.[265] It would take almost an hour to travel on a seven-kilometre stretch between Belaganj, a small market town on NH-33, and Guljana village.

Lalu had a famous reply whenever asked about roads during his administration. He would say, 'It is the rich who own cars, the poor don't need roads.' Sadly, his witty rhetoric couldn't be further from the truth. The poor roads often prevented those severely ill in remote rural areas from reaching hospitals, the police from reaching scenes of massacre and the poor in northern Bihar from escaping the annual floods. Lalu's crafty rhetoric started to look illogical to most who suffered because of the lack of roads. It was then that Lalu famously promised in the 2005 elections that if voted back to power, he would make Bihar's roads as smooth as Hema Malini's cheeks. He didn't return to power.

The condition of roads was a fallout of not just the lack of political will but also the entrenched corruption in the road construction department. Money was to be made for everyone. The allotment of contracts was forged for huge sums; the contractors used sub-standard material to make profits and the inspecting engineers got their cut for overlooking the lapses. Every big and small player in the intermediate chain had their percentages fixed, including the local don who allowed the work to progress in his area, the babus who moved the files between officers and the accounts officer who finally signed the payment cheque.

During the 1990s, a bitumen scam worth Rs 100 crore was unearthed, making bureaucrats extremely cautious and hesitant to take any initiatives, opting to play it safe. Consequently, the ailing road construction department only managed to build a mere 385 kilometres of roads in 2004–05.

R.K. Singh's appointment as the principal secretary for roads was a signal that Nitish had it on top of his agenda. R.K. Singh had a long-standing record of integrity and efficiency. One of the stated objectives of Nitish's administration was to make Patna accessible from any part of the state within six hours.

In his inimitable style, R.K. Singh made surprise visits to ongoing projects in all corners of the state to ensure quality checks himself. Once out to check Bailey Road, a central road in Patna, he found the bitumen content to be lower than the prescribed standard. He immediately filed a case, suspended the engineer and blacklisted the contractor who happened to be a senior JD(U) politician. The firm ways of R.K. Singh found him to be at loggerheads with politicians, contractors and soon his own minister. However, R.K. Singh had the backing of Nitish Kumar. Instead of R.K. Singh, the bureaucrat, being transferred out, the minister was given a new portfolio in the next reshuffle. In the first five years of Nitish's rule, the length of roads increased almost tenfold in Bihar. Against a length of 385 kilometres of road laid out in 2004–05, the year 2009–10 saw 3,474 kilometres of roads being laid out.[266] The road from Belaganj to Guljana is no longer a dusty piece of kuccha road. It now forms a part of a double-lane link road connecting the town of Aurangabad to Patna. The time taken on the same stretch reduced from over an hour to fifteen minutes thanks to the new bridges built over inundated monsoon rivers. The travel time across major towns in the state similarly reduced by over half in most of the cases.

An important role in the same was played by the Bihar Rajya Pul Nirman Nigam (BRPNN). Formed in 1975, with an objective to build bridges in flood-ravaged Bihar, it had failed badly. Having built just 314 bridges in 30 years of its existence, it had also accumulated losses of Rs 17 crore by 2005, and was unable to even pay salaries to its staff.[267] Pratyaya Amrit, a Bihar-cadre IAS officer on deputation in Delhi, was recalled and given the charge of this ailing unit.

Amrit was handed over a significant number of stalled projects, dilapidated bridges and several road and railway projects rendered unusable because the BRPNN had failed to construct the last connecting bridge needed. The BRPNN had become a money-milking-cum-retirement home for engineers who wished to while away their time. However, Amrit turned it around through a series of initiatives. By 2009, he had constructed 518 bridges, against the 314 bridges built in the previous thirty years.[268] The turnover went over twenty times and finally the entity was making a profit of over Rs 90 crore. The BRPNN's contribution of Rs 20 crore towards the Kosi flood relief was the largest contribution to the CM Relief Fund.

Health and Education

The health sector in Bihar was so paralysed by 2005 that it had reached a low-level equilibrium. While there existed a wide network of health centres across the state, most remained locked up since their inauguration, the assigned doctors too busy growing their private practice to ever visit them. Some of the doctors who continued to draw their salaries had left Bihar long ago to settle in metro cities or even abroad. The compounders filled the vacuum with their half-baked knowledge of medicines and would often resort to saline water in malnourished rural Bihar as the last resort. It worked in most of the cases and the compounder would be hailed as an effective medical practitioner, of course deserving of additional fees. However, most remote villages couldn't even avail of these compounders and would turn to quacks and alternative medicine practitioners.

Most of these health centres were also bereft of nurses, medicines or even the basic and ubiquitous Bihari cure for every ailment, saline water. The best health centres had their own buildings and a few corroded iron beds. The worst ones existed just on paper, or just as a foundation stone, the name of the dignitary who had laid it clearly inscribed on it.

The sustained poor supply of health services, coupled with low expectations of service and hence low demand, had plunged the health sector into a low-level equilibrium trap. Nobody asked for the services; nobody provided it. The irony lay in the sheer institutional size of the health department. Close to 10,000 health centres and lakhs of doctors and paramedics merely existed on paper, the functional ones being the exception rather than the norm. Whatever health services were needed was provided by struggling private health centres. More often than not, these centres were run by doctors on government payroll who were supposed to be working at government hospitals. It strangely didn't look like a problem until one delved deeper into it.

In 2004–05, the average number of patients visiting a healthcare facility per month was pegged at thirty-nine. Less than 2 per cent of child births took place in institutions. Total fertility rate and birth rate was the highest in Bihar, leading to a rapid population growth. Infant mortality in 2005 was almost 25 per cent higher than the national average.[269]

The challenge facing Nitish's administration was the low-level equilibrium that Bihar's healthcare had slipped into. The first intervention was to ensure a steady supply of drugs to the health centres. Without the drugs, the medical advice, even if available, would be of little use to poor patients. By July 2006, the average patient footfall at a government health facility had surged to 2,700 from a meagre two-digit figure just a few months earlier. The government also started cash incentivisation for women who used institutional facilities for childbirth. This helped to significantly reduce infant and maternal mortality rates. A call centre was established to continuously monitor the attendance of doctors at primary health centres. Show causes and dismissals were issued in case of absenteeism. Campaigns were run, such as 2010 being declared as the 'Year of the Child' and 2011 as the 'Year of Safe Motherhood'. Immunisation drives were conducted and the percentage of immunised children went up from 17 in 2005 to 66 per cent in December 2010.[270] Bihar was notorious for being one of the last remaining spots on the globe where polio was still prevalent. A dedicated polio campaign helped eradicate the disease. In fact, the commitment to the polio eradication programme was such that, even during a statewide strike of government staff in 2010, the staff on polio duty reported to their camps.

The changes required some out-of-the-box thinking as well. Despite a focused infrastructure ramp-up and a campaign for birthing at health care centres, almost 40 per cent of women were still delivering at home. Most of these deliveries were being conducted by women from one particular caste: Ravidas. This was because women from this community had been assisting in childbirths since centuries, and women felt safe in their hands. In a novel move, the government brought 2,000 Ravidas women into the formal system, trained them, provided them with a kit and decided to pay them Rs 100 per delivery. This initiative significantly lowered both the infant mortality and maternal mortality rates.

The condition of education in Bihar was no better than the other sectors; in fact, it was worse. In the absence of other more necessary needs like roads, electricity, and law and order, education seemed to be a privilege and not an immediate priority. In fact, Bihar had long been one of the worst performing states in the country in terms of literacy. Now fast-forward just a few years into Nitish's rule. A common sight on the roads of

Bihar was a group of teenage girls dressed in neat white and blue salwar-kameezes, cycling their way to or from school.

Nitish's government made efforts to improve the general parameters used to track the state of education. A massive recruitment drive was initiated to hire over 2,00,000 primary school teachers. This resulted in the student–teacher ratio improving from 96 in 2005 to 58 in 2011. Separate toilets for girls were available in just over 8,000 schools in 2005. The number went up to 31,000 schools by 2011. The average annual dropout rate in primary schools fell from 36 per cent to 6 per cent in the same period.[271]

Absenteeism, which had been the bane of the health sector, was as grave an issue in education, too. Pre-2005, a large number of government schools were not open for even 100 days in a year. Others were understaffed, and even the assigned teachers had a high absenteeism rate. The gap was filled in by private schools, which qualitatively were seldom better than government schools but at least were open for 300 days in a year.

Nitish's administration launched initiatives to counter the existing deficiencies in the system, including some novel steps. One such step was providing cash for bicycles and dresses for girl students to tackle the massive drop-out rates prevalent among middle- and high-school girl students. The argument against the fear of leakage in providing cash was that no parents would like to see their daughters attend school without a proper uniform. Similarly, the bicycle would not only create an asset for the family but also raise the girl's status in her family for having brought in a valuable resource. Also with time, the benefits became common knowledge, and the sheer visibility of these benefits created social pressure against any misuse of funds.

According to a report by the Institute for the Study of Labour (IZA), Bihar went from being the worst-performing state in terms of school education in 2005 to converging to the median by 2010.

Similarly, higher education was tackled with a series of initiatives. For example, university vice chancellors were mandated to swiftly fulfil three main obligations: to conduct the admission process on time, conduct examinations on time and declare results on time. A state where it had become the norm for a three-year graduation course to be completed in four years, it was a welcome change. Nitish Kumar must also be credited with bringing a bunch of higher education institutes and medical colleges, including the prestigious All India Institute of Medical Sciences (AIIMS), to the state. The resurrection of the ancient Nalanda University, which originally functioned between the fifth and thirteenth centuries, was another masterstroke.

It's the Economy!

Bihar's economy in the first half of the 2000s decade grew at 3.5 per cent, almost half of the national average of 7 per cent. The state's expenses for 2004–05, viz. interest payments and salary and pension payouts exceeded the state's income.[272] However, during Nitish's first five years, between 2006 and 2011, the state's gross state domestic product (GSDP) growth tripled to cross 12 per cent. This was way above the national average of 8.44 per cent and just marginally behind the country's fastest growing state, Gujarat. In the coming five years, the composition of Bihar's economy also started seeing a shift from agriculture to manufacturing and services. Agriculture came down from a contribution of 29 per cent of the state GSDP to 18 per cent. Critics observed that the shift was seen primarily because of a meteoric growth, averaging 25 per cent in the construction sector.

In 2004, only 0.1 per cent of the total private investment in the country was said to be made in Bihar. Industry accounted for a mere 3.2 per cent of the GSDP in 2005, as against a national average of 20 per cent. A total of 10 of Bihar's 38 districts had no medium- or large-scale industries at all. Of the total value added, 85 per cent came from just three sectors: tobacco, food and beverages, and petroleum products. Traditional industries, such as sugarcane crushing, which once contributed almost a quarter of the country's sugarcane production, had become dysfunctional. The bifurcation of Jharkhand in 2000 had robbed the state of the lion's share of minerals and industries. Another factor that blocked the growth of industry in Bihar was poor infrastructure, including roads, unreliable electricity and underdeveloped communication networks. Transmission and distribution losses amounted to 40 per cent of the total state power output. Added to this were bureaucratic hurdles—lack of working capital, unavailability of land and, the biggest of them, an extremely poor law-and-order situation. Businessmen were the prime target for extortions and kidnappings. The kidnapping of S.M. Sahay, a prominent Patna businessman, in 2004, brought the state into disrepute.

Even centres of heavy industries, such as iron and steel in Jamshedpur, coal in Dhanbad, petroleum refinery in Barauni or cement in Dalmianagar, were either under the control of a few families or, even worse, the mafia, such as in Dhanbad. These industries were not just concentrated regionally but also failed to develop any upstream or downstream linkages with the local market. Thus, the regionally confined heavy industries failed to have any spillover effects in terms of ancillary industries or employment opportunities for the distressed agrarian sector. The only exception to this was the sugar industry, with nearly 40 per cent of the capacity in the cooperative sector.

In the first three decades of the twentieth century, a steady supply of Bihari labour was key to the growth of Indian industry, which was mainly the textile mills in Bombay and Ahmedabad. The established migration patterns didn't provide any incentive to the local landlords to diversify into the industrial segment. Thus, Bihar continued, since the beginning of the century, to serve as a feeder economy for the more flourishing centres of industrial growth.

After Independence, Bihar barely had a large-sized demand market, with the per capita income of its residents falling at the bottom of all the states. Bihar had a large demographic advantage in terms of the pool of labour. However, the force was almost entirely unskilled and easily available elsewhere too, showing no reluctance to migrate. The advantage that the huge deposits of minerals could have given to the state was neutralised by the centre's freight-equalisation policy.

Industrial sickness had become a norm rather than an exception for the land-locked state. By 2001–02, almost 28.3 per cent of the state's registered units were closed. As if this wasn't enough, the financing agencies, viz. the Bihar State Finance Corporation and Bihar State Credit and Investment Corporation themselves became sick from poor recovery of their loans.

The state brought in a slew of reforms to boost investment and create a conducive industrial environment, which started showing some results by the end of Nitish's first term. Bihar has also been lobbying for a larger share of the Centre's resources through a demand for declaration of special category status for the state. Nitish has been strongly vocal about it and is often at loggerheads with the Centre's stance on the same.

When Ratan Tata visited Patna in 2008, he admitted to visiting the capital city after thirty years. Both his visits were in relation to a court case rather than a business visit. Patna had just come in second behind Delhi in a list of Indian cities for 'Ease of Doing Business' published by the World Bank. The proposed investments in 2010 rose to 1.5 per cent of total investments—small compared to Bihar's size but significant if compared to what it attracted just a few years ago.

However, Nitish would soon realise that putting Bihar on the investment and industrialisation map wouldn't be as easy as his other reforms. Ratan Tata, on his 2008 visit, illustrated this through a metaphor that a person with a broken-down car would seek shelter in a house that had electricity, water, telephone and more, not in a ramshackle hut. Bihar, as he meant it, had a long way to go.

Social Engineering

Though development would bring in votes, Nitish knew that the caste factor was as important. A Kurmi by caste, he knew he would need the support of his castemen to remain in power but didn't want to be recognised as the leader of one particular caste.

With Nitish coming to power, the Kurmis saw it as their own turn to rule Bihar in the same manner as the Yadavs had, upon Lalu's ascent. Nitish wanted to tackle this problem even before it raised its head.

In March 2006, just a day before Holi, a Kurmi man shot a roadside Muslim vendor in a minor scuffle over five rupees. The incident took place in Nalanda, a Kurmi stronghold and Nitish's home district. It was a litmus test for the government, which had been swearing by the rule book in matters of crime. The police sprang into action, nabbed the criminal and got him convicted within six months. Another incident which demonstrated the deep-seated caste bias in Bihar occurred in a village called Chandi in the same Nalanda district just a few months later. The newly elected mukhiya happened to belong to the Nai caste, several notches lower than the Kurmis in the caste hierarchy. However, in a meeting of the Gram Shiksha Samiti, or the village education council, he committed the unforgivable offence of sitting on the only chair present at the meeting venue. The Kurmis on the council had to either keep standing or sit on the floor. This enraged them and the mukhiya was shot dead just a few days later. True to its resolve, the government did everything possible to nab the murderers and get them sentenced to life imprisonment within just three months of the crime.

Such cases helped to build Nitish's credibility, and sent out the signal that he wasn't going to be bogged down by caste or religion considerations. Nitish's next task was to break the Muslim–backward vote bank carefully crafted by Lalu.

Striking at the backward caste consolidation, he first constituted a commission to look into the existing caste groups with regard to the allotment of reservation and other benefits. The commission recommended further classification in the SC block for better targeting of government benefits. Nitish accepted the recommendations, which led to the identification of 21 of the existing 22 sub-castes in the SC category as Mahadalits. The Dusadhs, who formed 31 per cent of the SC category, led by Ram Vilas Paswan, were left out. While the legislation noted that the benefits available to Mahadalits would also be available to the landless Dusadhs, it would be denied to the creamy layer of the community. Nitish was thus able to create a divide and earn the support and votes of Mahadalits.

Nitish also ensured that the Muslims perceived him as a secular leader and the alliance with the BJP as just an administrative coalition and not an ideological one. Amanullah's appointment as the home secretary had already sent out a positive message. The reopening of the case and the convictions in the Bhagalpur riots case of 1989 strengthened that perception among the Muslims. This was one of the rare instances in the entire country when a riot case had ended in conviction and sentencing. Most of the convicts in the case were Yadavs, a reason many believed why the case had lingered for so long under Lalu's administration. Nitish also took up the cause of Scheduled Caste status for Dalit Muslims and Dalit Christians in Parliament, a move that won him the trust of the Pasmanda Muslims. Pasmandas are considered to be low-caste Muslims and constitute almost 80 per cent of the Muslim votes in Bihar.

Nitish also tried to create a common identity of Bihari pride in a caste-divided society. Biharis had often been the subject of ridicule in other parts of the country, and so they would often be reluctant to even reveal their identity. This was in sharp contrast to other states, which proudly flaunted their state identities, such as being a Maharashtrian or a Gujarati. In Bihar, the space of primary sub-national identity had long been taken over by caste. Nitish's team started organising Bihar Diwas, or Bihar Day, in 2010, to celebrate and take pride in the Bihari identity.

THE HERO THAT BIHAR DESERVED?

By the time the assembly elections for 2010 were announced in Bihar, one thing had been established: Nitish Kumar knew how to govern. He was hailed as one of the best chief ministers across the country, with numerous awards from reputed media houses and international agencies having been showered upon him. It looked like Bihar finally had the leader it deserved.

Nitish had adeptly handled each issue, social or economic, with the finesse of a statesman. However, it was the last year of his first term that saw Nitish struggling to deal with one of the most controversial and long-standing issues in Bihar, that of land reforms.

Reports were circulating in political circles that Nitish had shown an inclination towards taking on the contentious issue of land reforms in Bihar. The details of the proposed reforms continued to be speculated on heavily across caste- and class-divided Bihar. The actual proposals were based on a report by Debabrata Bandopadhyay, a former bureaucrat credited with successful land reforms in the adjoining West Bengal. The report prescribed a ceiling of fifteen acres for any type of land, agricultural or non-agricultural. It proposed to provide some form of legal rights to bataidaars, or the sharecroppers. It also proposed to free and redistribute 2.2 million acres of land, which were in illegal possession of large landowners through benami transactions or fake donations to trusts and institutions.

What transpired was captured by Bandopadhyay in his conclusive argument for land reforms. 'The countryside of Bihar is apparently peaceful with smouldering embers underneath, which might ignite the bushfire anytime.' The sharecroppers and agricultural labourers constituted almost 40 per cent of the total labour force of the state. Often having suffered injustice at the hands of landowners, they also serve as ready recruits for Left-extremist outfits. Many believed that land reforms would significantly mitigate Naxalism.

The talks of such a reform triggered a huge backlash from affluent castes and even land-owning Kurmis and Yadavs across the state. Nitish's own party seemed to be divided on the issue. So was the opinion of every major party. None of them wanted to risk their political capital by coming out openly to take a position. Nitish had to put a statement in the legislative council that he had no intention of giving effect to the reforms. However, it didn't ease the tensions. His party dissidents thought this could be Nitish's nemesis, which would bring him down. Lalan Singh, an old confidant of Nitish, rebelled. He was joined by Prabhunath Singh, a former party MP from Maharajganj, and Digvijay Singh, the incumbent MP from Banka.

At a rally attended by 1,00,000 farmers, termed the Kisan Mahapanchayat, Lalan Singh warned Nitish of civil strife should the state go ahead with land reforms. He warned Nitish, 'We had made him the party bridegroom and helped him come to power by sending out Lalu. We can do it again should Kumar go against the wishes of the people.'[273]

The arguments of the anti-land reform groups were that the existing system of bataidaari, wherein the landowner could share 50:50 produce with the sharecropper with actual tilling being the latter's responsibility, had worked well in the past. They argued that it benefited the sharecropper to make a living, with the landowner also being able to sustain himself.

While Nitish and all his ministers, including the land reforms minister, Narendra Narayan Yadav, refuted any claims of the bill being brought into the assembly, the discussions outside were enough to raise suspicion in the minds of landowners. Several landowners evicted their bataidaars in the fear that their land could be taken away, should a stronger Nitish come back to power with the ensuing elections.

Nitish kept vehemently denying any plans to implement the reforms while realising simultaneously that every time he made such a statement, he would be forgoing a small portion of the Dalit vote bank he had so carefully gathered.

With the land reform controversy settled eventually, the ensuing elections in November looked more like a formality with the JD(U)–BJP alliance looking more formidable than ever. However, something happened in June that brought the two alliance partners close to a breaking point.

The BJP had scheduled its National Executive Meet in June 2010 in Patna. The meet was expected to kickstart the party's campaign for the upcoming polls in October of the same year. A few days before the meet, posters went up in Patna to welcome Gujarat's chief minister, Narendra Modi, and thanking him for his generous donation of Rs 5 crore for the Kosi flood relief. Nitish, who was certainly uncomfortable with it, was touring parts of north Bihar for the final leg of his Vikas Yatra, the last such tour before the scheduled November elections. He had planned to host a dinner for BJP leaders at his house on the final day of the National Executive Meet. Invitation cards had been printed for each of the BJP's national executive members, and Nitish was said to have taken a personal interest in the food arrangements. However, as the morning newspapers landed in Nitish's hands the next day, he went livid with anger. Full-page ads had appeared in the two leading dailies *Dainik Jagran* and *Hindustan*, thanking Narendra Modi for his contribution to Bihar flood relief, with a picture of him and Nitish holding and raising their hands in unison. The picture had been taken at a Ludhiana rally of the NDA and had always made Nitish uncomfortable. He didn't want to be seen so close to Modi, given the latter's chequered past.

Nitish thought the full-page ads were not just distasteful but also made a mockery of his kind hospitality. Nitish immediately got in touch with Sanjay Jha—a BJP legislator who would later join the JD(U) in 2012—and told him that the dinner won't happen. The staff was instructed to pull down the shamiana erected at his residence and to put out the kitchen fire. Sushil Modi tried unsuccessfully to reason with Nitish. *'Galat message chala jaayega chunav ke pehle'* [274] (This will send out the wrong message before elections).

Nitish could be extremely stubborn on some matters, though. His reply was curt and definitive. '*Galat message chala gaya hai. Aap logon ne bheja hai. Meri jaankari ke bina yeh sab chhapa kaise?*'[275] (The wrong message has already been delivered. You people have done it. How could this be printed without my knowledge?).

The next few days were tense with Narendra Modi further hurting Nitish's ego with his statement in the National Executive Meet. He put out a Gujarat–Bihar comparison. 'Come to Gujarat and see what a prosperous place we have created there.' There was no mention of Nitish, but he sure was being put down.

Nitish soon declared that he had returned the five-crore cheque from Gujarat. Many, including senior BJP leaders, believed Nitish had gone too far. An upset Nitin Gadkari told

Sharad Yadav, the JD(U) president, in a meeting in Delhi, 'It wasn't a personal cheque for Nitish; it was meant for the people of Bihar. Nitish is insulting us.'[276]

It took a lot of political manoeuvring to settle the issue and for the BJP and JD(U) to face the elections as a united coalition. The results of the 2010 assembly elections started looking obvious as the polls came closer. Development on the ground was visible. Roads between major cities were being built at a pace never seen before. Hundreds of villages that had never seen electricity had been electrified. The average hours of downtime had also gone down significantly. Law and order, while still facing challenges, was several notches better than just five years ago. The kidnapping and extortion industry was definitely having a bad day. Biharis felt optimistic for the first time.

Nitish, wherever he went for campaigning, would be greeted with an enthusiastic crowd ready to hear him speak. With a half smile, Nitish would just say, '*Agar kaam kiye hain to hamare kaam ka mazoori de dijiye* (If you think I have delivered, pay me my due).' Lalu projected himself as the chief ministerial candidate for RJD–LJP, turning the election into an almost presidential contest. However, this made it easier for the voters to compare and contrast the rules of two chief ministerial candidates.

The NDA won by a landslide, winning 206 out of the 243 seats. The RJD could bag only 22 seats, its worst performance ever. Ram Vilas Paswan's LJP, which had fought alongside Lalu, could barely scrape up three seats. Rabri Devi, Lalu's wife and former chief minister, lost in the family stronghold of Raghopur. She couldn't even win Sonepur, the other seat she had picked as a back-up. The elections also dealt a blow to the Congress' plans of revival in Bihar. The Congress fared its worst ever, securing just four seats from all of the 243 seats it had contested.

The results not only demonstrated the faith of Biharis in the new government but also in the leadership of Nitish, who was no more a first-time chief minister. A down-to-earth man with simple tastes, Nitish had raised the expectations of his people. He had delivered on most of the promises he had made during his last campaign, and Bihar was ready to give him another chance. 'This is Bihar's *nayi kahani* [new story]. Voters had to choose between politics and antiquated politics. They have chosen to surge ahead,' Nitish said, upon his landslide win, echoing the cliché that hope had won over fear.

Nitish had created a higher benchmark for himself. He would soon face interviews, where he would be asked about his inclination for the top job in Delhi. He would, however, shrug it off by saying that he is a grassroots politician with his feet firmly on the ground. '*Bihar ki seva, desh ki seva hai*' (Serving Bihar is serving the nation) would be his retort.[277]

Nitish's Political Acumen

Nitish's political challenges seemed no less than his administrative challenges. In a state where every regional party associated itself with a particular caste, such as the RJD with Yadavs, the LJP with Paswans, and the JMM with adivasis, he took all possible measures not to be perceived as a Kurmi-centric party. Even later, the new party entrants in Bihar politics such as the RLSP (Rashtriya Lok Samta Party), the VIP (Vikassheel Insaan Party) and the HAM (Hindustani Awam Morcha) would identify themselves with the specific castes of Kushwaha, Mallah and Musahar respectively.

Nitish also slowly reined in the influence of strong personalities within the party, thus reducing the scope for multiple power centres. Unlike its predecessors, the JD(U) never suffered a split and was hardly affected when even significant names such as its Samata Party-founding partner George Fernandes or JD(U)-founding leader Sharad Yadav were shunted out. Nitish became both the president of the party as well as the leader of house legislators. Ironically, in this case, he followed all other regional parties in making the JD(U) an individual-centric party. He also made sure that the individual was him. Nitish would often be accused of dictatorial ways by his partymen and ministers alike. Does this mean that when it came to concentrating power in one's own hands, Nitish fell to the general political tendency? Maybe or maybe not. Nitish had seen up close the effect of multiple power centres within a party—ending in splits such as in the Janata Dal—and understood the dangers it posed to his government. One such instance was when his long-time confidant Lalan Singh parted ways from him just before the 2010 assembly elections. Nitish also didn't let Upendra Kushwaha, a powerful Koeri leader, affect the JD(U)'s fortunes in spite of Kushwaha's constant love-hate relationship with Nitish and repeated mergers and splits of his faction with and from JD(U). Nitish strongly believed in the political dictum that you have to be in power first to be able to do anything good. It may be the inclination to this principle that led him to concentrate power in himself and thus avoid any dangers to his party and government.

However, it wasn't just his own party but a coalition that had been heading the government in Bihar ever since the fall of the RJD. Coalitions have rarely had such longevity as has been seen in Bihar. Coalitions are delicately balanced partnerships and depend on a number of factors, such as the relative strengths of parties, overlap and contrast in messaging and vote banks, the electoral advantages of going alone versus as a coalition, and personal equations between senior leaders of the coalition.

Samata Party and subsequently the JD(U) remained a loyal constituent of the NDA ever since their coalition in 1996. George Fernandes, its founder, even served as the NDA's convenor during Vajpayee's tenure.

End of a Long Friendship

Nitish, by 2013, had been in alliance with BJP for over seventeen years. The alliance had worked beautifully, first in uprooting Lalu's rule in Bihar and then in delivering on electoral promises. By the end of his first term, Nitish had catapulted from being a silent performer to an adored leader. His growing stature within the coalition was also sure to draw irritants from the BJP, which had a better strike rate on the overall seats that it contested in the 2010 elections. However, apart from minor hiccups, the stability of the JD(U)–BJP alliance never faced a serious threat until 2013.

Narendra Modi had started emerging as a potential prime-ministerial candidate by the start of the decade of 2010. In 2011, Modi undertook the Sadbhavana Yatra, a roadshow throughout Gujarat. While the stated purpose of the yatra was to promote social harmony, Modi's ambitions for prime-ministership first became public during this yatra. When Modi won the Gujarat elections for the third consecutive time in 2012, leaders of all the NDA constituents were called to his oath-taking ceremony. While all other prominent NDA allies were present during this ceremony, the JD(U) remained conspicuously absent.

On 9 July 2013, Modi was declared the campaign committee chief for the upcoming 2014 parliamentary elections. The JD(U) declared a week later that it was pulling out of the seventeen-year-old alliance as it would not conform to Modi's leadership. Eleven BJP ministers were expelled from Nitish's cabinet.

The BJP and a section of the electorate criticised Nitish for his dictatorial stance. He would often be asked why he was associated so long with the BJP if he had such problems with Modi, who had been Gujarat's chief minister from the same party for fourteen long years.

Nitish decided to go it alone in the 2014 Lok Sabha elections. The opposition hailed him as the saviour of secularism and rumours arose of him harbouring national ambitions as the leader of a probable third front. However, the results were a huge shocker for Nitish. His party could bag just two seats, down from the twenty it had secured in 2009, while its erstwhile partner, the BJP, bagged 31 out of the 40 seats. He chose to resign, taking responsibility for the debacle.

However, even in relinquishing his position, Nitish played a political masterstroke. He sprang a surprise by choosing hitherto unknown Jitan Ram Manjhi as his successor. Manjhi belonged to the Musahar caste, one of the lowest in the caste hierarchy. Manjhi belonged to the same caste and district (Gaya) as the late Dasrath Manjhi, the legendary Mountain Man who had carved a path through Gehlaur Hills with a hammer and chisel.

Manjhi had been a legislator and minister since the 1980s and had been by turns a member of all major parties in Bihar, moving from the Congress to the Janata Dal, the RJD and finally settling in the JD(U). However, that would change soon. Despite a long career, he wasn't a natural successor to Nitish, and when Nitish appointed a Mahadalit as the chief minister, it was hailed as a huge step towards demolishing historic caste injustices. His critics called it a political ploy to fuel casteist sentiments by choosing Manjhi as a puppet that he could control. Neither were completely wrong.

Interestingly, back in 2005, Manjhi had been sacked by Nitish, just after the day of swearing-in, for his alleged involvement in a fake B.Ed-degree racket. Manjhi's chief ministerial term was marked by instability with some JD(U) MLAs deserting him, and the Congress and RJD coming forward to provide outside support.

Not long thereafter, in February 2015, the party asked Manjhi to resign. Having tasted chief-ministership, Manjhi turned renegade and refused to resign. Subsequently, he was expelled from the party and he had to resign from his chief-ministerial position. Manjhi's tenure was short-lived and nothing spectacular, but the way he was evicted from office had suddenly made Manjhi emerge as a tall Mahadalit leader. He would go on, in May 2015, to form his own party—the Hindustani Awam Morcha.

Rumours were rife by then that Nitish might ally with his old foe Lalu for the upcoming assembly elections. After a number of backroom discussions and burying of hatchets, the duo came together with the Congress clambering aboard. Lalu conceded the chief-ministerial position to Nitish.

The common plank spelt out during the joint conference, was as expected—saving secularism. However, the two leaders and their parties also showed a surprising bonhomie, right from the announcement of the alliance through the entire campaign. Both knew that they were fighting against a formidable BJP led by their master strategist Amit Shah and popular leader Modi. Unlike the NDA, the Mahagathbandhan also declared their list of candidates together. Both Nitish and Lalu sacrificed some important seats to keep the coalition together. Nitish surprised everyone by declaring that he wouldn't contest and would rather focus on campaigning. It seemed like both were fighting for their lives and differences, however grave, could be resolved later. Both ensured that the vote transfer between the numerically significant Yadavs (Lalu's caste) and Kurmis (Nitish's caste) happened seamlessly.

The BJP that raised the issue of the return of jungle raj if Lalu came back to power seemed to be on the backfoot when it came down to caste arithmetic. The Mahagathbandhan came to power with a formidable 173 out of the 243 seats. The NDA and BJP fared badly, with the latter winning just 53 seats. Nitish was sworn in as the chief minister in a star-studded rally that included Rahul Gandhi, Mamata Banerjee, Arvind Kejriwal and Deve Gowda, among others. Tejashwi Yadav, Lalu's younger son, was sworn in as the deputy chief minister. Lalu's elder son, Tej Pratap, who fumbled twice during his swearing-in was given charge of three important ministries, including health.

While all looked hunky-dory on stage and during the campaign, the Nitish–Lalu bonhomie was, as always, hanging by a thread. Nitish had been Lalu's staunchest critic for twenty years, while Lalu had always considered Nitish to be his junior. Even during the electioneering, Nitish was upset by a demeaning statement Lalu had apparently made in Bhagalpur. Lalu had reportedly said about the formation of the alliance, '*Nitish mere gor mein gir gaye toh kya hum unhe uthakar phenk dete*?' (Nitish fell at my feet. Should I have thrown him out?).[278]

He later clarified that he had said 'god' meaning lap and not 'gor' meaning feet. Nitish wasn't convinced and had communicated his displeasure through JD(U) president Sharad Yadav. While Lalu himself thereafter avoided making such controversial statements, his colleagues continued to attack Nitish in some way or the other. It wasn't hard to guess at whose behest they were doing so.

Some RJD leaders were reportedly unhappy at Nitish holding the top job despite being the junior partner in the alliance. The JD(U) had won 71 while the RJD had grabbed 80 seats in the elections. In January 2016, Raghuvansh Prasad Singh, an old

Lalu confidant, lashed out at Nitish for the deteriorating law-and-order situation in the state.

A few months later, in September 2016, Shahabuddin came out of jail and didn't waste any time in attacking Nitish. He declared, '*Hamare neta Lalu hain, Nitish ji to paristhitiyon ke mukhyamantri hain*' (My leader is Lalu. Nitish's chief-ministership is the result of circumstances).[279]

Nitish expected a word of support from Lalu or for him to at least caution his partymen from making such statements. But nothing of that sort happened. In fact, Lalu would often cursorily comment that Nitish and him were oldies and should retire, and the baton be passed to the youth. It was evident who he meant by youth—his younger son Tejashwi.

Reports also reached Nitish that Lalu had been directly talking to senior officials in Bihar and passing them instructions. Lalu was also reported to have invited and held meetings with senior officials at his residence. Nitish objected to such interference in governance. However, he knew Lalu far too long to know that such objections wouldn't deter him.

With a discomfort that made it difficult to run the government, Nitish slowly started to move towards the opposite camp. He broke ranks to publicly laud Modi for demonetisation as well as the Uri surgical strike in 2016. Modi also thanked Nitish for his support. The general conviviality between the chief minister and the prime minister was visible when they shared the dias in January 2017 at a function to mark the 350th anniversary of Guru Gobind Singh in Patna. They didn't stop from showering lavish praise on each other. The final signs of discord were confirmed when Nitish broke ranks with the opposition to support NDA's candidate Ram Nath Kovind in the presidential elections.

All this while the attacks from the RJD on Nitish continued, who kept registering his discontent with the Congress top brass. Nitish was evidently uncomfortable, but he didn't want to be seen as flip-flopping by going back into the NDA fold, which he had so vehemently opposed just a couple years ago. He found the perfect opportunity when corruption charges were slapped against his deputy, Tejashwi Yadav. He asked him to put in his papers or make a rebuttal of the charges against him. Nitish saw it as a move that would salvage his image of being uncompromising on the issue of corruption. However, Lalu didn't accept either of the two options.

After a few days of warnings and counter-objections, Nitish finally resigned on 26 July 2017 as the chief minister of Bihar. He said about his resignation:

> Ever since the corruption charges were levelled against RJD leaders, we have been asking them to at least explain those charges. We also met Tejashwi and told him that the image that is being created, he should clarify all that. But this did not happen. The situation got so bad that it became difficult for me to work. We had followed the Gathbandhan Dharma and tried to protect it. But now my conscience does not allow me to continue.[280]

Prime Minister Modi was quick to congratulate Nitish on his decision. The BJP quickly followed to offer Nitish the support of its legislators. Nitish took oath as Bihar's twenty-second chief minister the next day. The only difference now was that his allies and opposition had changed places in the vidhan sabha.

Paltu Ram

Nitish's going back to the NDA fold after snapping ties with the RJD earned him the monikers of Palturam (somebody who's too quick to change his stance) and Kursi Kumar (someone ready to do anything to hold on to a position). Lalu shot back at Nitish saying, 'Nitish is a snake, just like a snake sheds its skin, Nitish sheds his skin and wears a new skin every two years. Does anyone doubt that?'[281]

It felt like Nitish had made an honest mistake switching over to its bête noire, the RJD, and was back into his natural alliance, the NDA. However, the enigma that Nitish is, he surprised everyone again in August 2022, when he switched sides again from the NDA back to the RJD. In less than eight years, Nitish had switched thrice, from BJP to RJD to BJP and back to RJD.

Nitish alleged that BJP had made regular attempts to weaken his party. The JD(U) president Lalan Singh said that the BJP had humiliated their leader, Nitish Kumar, on multiple occasions and they could not have accepted it anymore.

However, Nitish avoided talking about the switch as strongly as he had the last time, switching from RJD to BJP. He sounded less convincing, the internet memes of him more unforgiving. Even Nitish's closest aides avoided answering questions on such frequent switches to completely opposite poles.

Nitish had sounded tired and easily irritated during the 2020 assembly elections. When he asked for one last chance to serve as the chief minister, it felt like he wanted to retire gracefully after having served the state to the best of his ability. However, with the 2022 switch, Nitish looked lost, trying to hold on to something that was quickly slipping from his hands to the next generation. It felt like Nitish wanted to do too many things before retiring. He wanted to secure the JD(U)'s future beyond his own term, and he wanted to challenge Modi for the top job as well as keep holding on to his influence in Bihar.

Looking Ahead

In over seventeen years that Nitish has led Bihar, he has undoubtedly established himself as a good administrator and politician. He used every trick in the political rule book to ensure that he was able to lead Bihar without compromising on some of his core principles. What those core principles are have been a matter of speculation for everyone. When Nitish joined hands with the BJP to first come to power, he said he would be uncompromising on corruption. That he asked his minister Jitan Ram Manjhi to resign within hours of his swearing-in for his name had come up in a fake B.Ed scam demonstrated his commitment. However, Nitish not just compromised but formed an alliance with Lalu's RJD ahead of the 2015 polls, a party he had dubbed as an epitome of corruption his entire life. He also remained silent in 2022, when questioned on his realignment with the RJD and its heir Tejashwi Yadav, an association he had earlier broken because of corruption charges against Tejashwi.

When Nitish left the NDA's fold after the nomination of Narendra Modi as its prime-ministerial candidate, he declared he wouldn't compromise his secular credentials. However, he had been a part of the same coalition for seventeen years while Modi had held important positions such as that of the chief minister of Gujarat and other important party positions. Coming together with his long-term foe, Lalu was seen by people as a shrewd political move rather than any adherence to principles. The release of Shahabuddin during the Mahagathbandhan's term also marred Nitish's image of not going soft on criminals. Shahabuddin, in a show of power, drove from Bhagalpur to his hometown Siwan in a cavalcade of 600 cars upon his release from jail.

Nitish is an enigma, even to people close to him. He is known to be a hard taskmaster and someone who appreciates hardworking, talented people. However, Nitish doesn't become overly dependent on anyone. This was well reflected when Nitish removed Abhayanand from his key position in maintaining Bihar's law and order because of his inability to reconcile differences with the then DGP. The same could be said about the way Nitish, in January 2020, shunned election strategist Prashant Kishor, when it looked like Kishor had overstepped his role in the party. Kishor had crossed swords and expressed openly his displeasure on several party matters, including the ways of the party general secretary R.C.P. Singh. The fact that Nitish was quite fond of Kishor and had inducted him directly as vice president into the party hardly mattered. It seemed like Nitish chose his trusted lieutenant R.C.P. Singh over Kishor. R.C.P. Singh belonged to the same caste and district as Nitish and had become a de facto number two in the JD(U). However, even this long friendship would come to an end in 2022 when Nitish would grow suspicious of Singh's equations with the BJP leadership.

That Nitish ushered in a new era in Bihar's politics is indisputable. What is debatable, though, is whether Nitish has been able to accomplish what he set out to do or what people expected him to do, especially after a stellar first term.

Not just political but some of Nitish's administrative decisions too have been subjected to extensive public scrutiny and criticism. The total ban on the sale and consumption of alcohol in Bihar since 2016 is one such decision. While the government claims that it has led to a reduction in crimes and cases of domestic violence, economists argue that it has had a negative effect on the state economy which was already in doldrums before the imposition of the ban. They have also questioned the implementability of this ban.

Bihar is often rocked by incidents and controversies that are unimaginable in any developed society. In 2018, a horrific case of sexual abuse, rape and torture of girls at a shelter home in Muzaffarpur came to light. Sexual abuse of 34 out of 42 of the girls living at the shelter was confirmed in a medical examination.[282] There were allegations of negligence and corruption involving local officials. Nitish Kumar's government faced criticism for not acting promptly against those involved and for failing to protect vulnerable children.

In June 2019, Muzaffarpur witnessed a health emergency in the form of acute encephalitis syndrome (AES), resulting in the deaths of more than 150 children. Nitish's government was severely criticised for the poor handling of this emergency. During the peak of the Covid pandemic, the sight of countless migrant labourers walking hundreds of kilometres from different corners of the nation to return to their homes in Bihar underscored the prominent problems of migration and unemployment prevailing in the state.

Bihar still features at the lowest among the bigger states in human development index parameters. Images and videos of mass cheating from Bihar keep flashing in social media feeds, raising concerns about the quality of education and the very integrity of the examination process. Annual floods keep ravaging a large part of north Bihar. And allegations of corruption tainting the relief efforts make the headlines alongside. The state frequently witnesses conflicts rooted in caste divisions, resulting in violence. The regional parties and their leaders strategically align themselves in these matters to cater to the interests of their respective caste-based constituents.

Bihar's narrative is marred by recurring crises and uncertainty. It remains far removed from the progress and harmony that would be vital to the country's second most populous state. Every once in a while, a new leader, marked by their assertive voice, emerges to ignite the hopes and ambitions of the people of Bihar. Bihar consistently presents itself as a fertile ground for such leaders to flourish, often to the detriment of its own well-being. Amidst sporadic flickers of hope, one is often left pondering, with a sense of apprehension, if Bihar will regress into the same abyss, the very jungle raj it once grappled with.

AFTERWORD

As I write the Afterword, Nitish Kumar has switched sides again. After weeks of negotiations, backdoor meetings and speculation, Nitish decided to switch to BJP from RJD and take oath as the chief minister of Bihar for the ninth time. People are surprised and yet not. However, the switch isn't the only incident to have marked the continuing tumult in Bihar. Nitish has long been twisting and tossing to find a comfortable footing in Bihar and national politics.

On 10 April 2023, the Bihar government made a seemingly small change to the Prison Manual, 2012. The amendment allowed for the early release of convicts found guilty of killing a government servant on duty. It was evident that this modification was aimed at facilitating the release of Rajput strongman Anand Mohan, charged with the lynching of Gopalganj DM G. Krishnaiah in 1994. Mohan, who had by then already spent more than fifteen years behind bars, was on parole for his son's engagement when he received the news.

Nitish Kumar, known for his claims of 'sushasan', or good governance, found himself under scrutiny as this decision contradicted his rhetoric. It was during his first term in 2007 that Anand Mohan was convicted and awarded capital punishment, which was later commuted to life imprisonment by the Patna high court. The dichotomy couldn't be more apparent. Many called it Nitish's last-ditch attempt to salvage his diminishing support base. Nitish's formidable electoral base of EBCs combined with Kurmis–Koeries has lately been eroding. In March 2023, the BJP appointed Samrat Choudhary, son of Shakuni Choudhary and a Koeri leader, as the new state president and then as Bihar's deputy chief minister. This was clearly meant to woo the kindred castes of Kurmis-Koeries away from Nitish's fold. Freeing Anand Mohan was a desperate attempt by Nitish to win the support of Rajputs, traditionally BJP supporters.

Before the switch, Nitish was the chief architect of an attempt to create a national coalition to challenge the BJP in the 2024 Lok Sabha elections. By early 2023, Nitish seemed determined to unite opposition parties and met with Congress president Mallikarjun Kharge and Rahul Gandhi on 12 April 2023. Gandhi hailed it as a historic step towards opposition unity, providing the Congress' support to Nitish's efforts. Nitish then criss-crossed the country, meeting key opposition leaders, including Arvind Kejriwal, Mamata Banerjee, Hemant Soren, Sharad Pawar and Uddhav Thackeray. It looked like Nitish was moving forward with purpose and conviction. Some even compared this to V.P. Singh's attempt at creating a coalition for the 1989 general elections. Despite Nitish's denial of any prime ministerial ambitions, speculations were rife that he aimed to be the opposition's candidate, passing the Bihar chief ministership to his deputy Tejashwi Yadav.

The efforts started to pay off when the first meeting of sixteen opposition parties was held in Patna on 23 June 2023, chaired by Nitish. The alliance, named the Indian National Developmental Inclusive Alliance (I.N.D.I.A.), expanded in a subsequent meeting in Bengaluru, where ten more parties joined. However, Nitish Kumar, along with Lalu Prasad Yadav and Tejashwi Yadav, returned to Patna by chartered plane without attending the joint press conference. This sparked off rumours that Nitish was angry at not being made the convener of the group. Nitish's hopes were further dashed when, in a subsequent meeting, Mallikarjun Kharge's name was propped up as the prime ministerial candidate for the I.N.D.I.A. Bloc. In the next meeting, Nitish Kumar snapped at Dravida Munnetra Kazhagam (DMK) leader T.R. Baalu when the latter asked for a translation of Nitish's speech, which was delivered in Hindi. Uncharacteristic of Nitish Kumar, it was seen as an outcome of frustration over his diminishing role in the alliance.

With the approaching 2024 Lok Sabha polls, the Bihar government released the results of a caste-based survey on 2 October 2023. This survey was the first such exercise since the 1931 decennial census. The proposal for a caste-based survey had had swords drawn since the floating of the idea. Opponents of the idea contended that the census fell under the Union List of subjects and that the state government didn't have the legal authority to conduct it. The Bihar government, however, contended that the survey would give detailed information on the socio-economic conditions of various caste groups and was necessary to create better-targeted government policies for them.

Amidst the debates, the data for the survey was released on Gandhi Jayanti; the coincidence was barely missable. The survey revealed the total strength of OBC and EBC communities at a combined 63 per cent of the population, sparking debates on their inadequate representation. The Yadavs formed the largest sub-group at 14 per cent, while Nitish Kumar's caste, the Kurmis, came in at a distant 2.87 per cent. The combined strength of the general category turned out to be just above 15 per cent.

News channels across the country ran debates on caste, representation and reservation. Several caste groups, especially the upper castes, contended that they were deliberately underrepresented in the survey. The biggest caste group, the Yadavs, started talking about their natural right to the leadership of Bihar. Some called the data release premature and politically motivated, as it only enumerated caste strengths without giving any details on their socio-economic conditions. Some even questioned the veracity of the data collected. Since no proof or document for income claims was sought, it was said that people had understated their incomes in a bid to qualify for new government schemes.

Nitish Kumar, in an astute political move, called an all-party meeting on the very next day to discuss the findings of the caste-based survey. The government shortly brought in a bill to increase the reservation in Bihar to 75 per cent (including the EWS quota of 10 per cent), well past the 50 per cent ceiling set by the Supreme Court. Nitish said that he was ready to go beyond 75 per cent if needed. The bill was passed by a unanimous vote.

It looked like a revisit of 'Mandal versus Kamandal', with the BJP banking on its Hindutva consolidation against the backdrop of the Ram Mandir inauguration in January 2024, and the JD (U)–RJD combine bringing caste right back into the political fray. Opposition parties, including the Congress, the Samajwadi Party, and others, made calls for a nationwide caste census. It seemed like a potent tool to counter Hindu vote consolidation, especially in the Hindi heartland. The Congress even made it a major point in its manifesto for the state elections in Rajasthan, Madhya Pradesh, Chhattisgarh and Telangana, which were held in November 2023. However, the state election results which the BJP swept, suggested that the caste census didn't have too many takers among the electorate.

Nitish Kumar has been facing challenges not only in deciding his coalition partner but on other fronts as well. He has been caught in multiple faux-pas lately. In September 2023, a petitioner appearing in Nitish's Janata Darbar brought up an issue concerning the home ministry. Nitish directed one of the officials to dial the home minister, forgetting that he himself held the portfolio. Just two months later in the assembly, Nitish launched a tirade against the Dalit leader and former chief minister Jitan Ram Manjhi, expressing regret over his decision to have made him the chief minister. The JD (U) legislators kept trying to calm a livid Nitish. However, his indiscreet comments on female impregnation, almost in graphic detail, just a week later in the same assembly, are what brought him most into disrepute. His controversial remarks drew widespread criticism, leading to a public apology.

Amidst attacks from all quarters, speculations went rife in December 2023 that his close lieutenant and JD (U) president Lalan Singh was conspiring with the RJD to dislodge Nitish and make Tejashwi Yadav the chief minister. With a battle for significance at the national level and a battle for survival in his own state, Nitish did what he does best. He threw signals that he may be shifting sides again. In a national executive meeting of the JD (U) held shortly thereafter on 30 December 2023, Nitish took over the presidency of the party from Lalan Singh. Among several theories, Lalan Singh's failure to project Nitish as the I.N.D.I.A. Bloc's architect and his growing proximity to the RJD were considered to be the prime reasons. Nitish Kumar's moves unsettled his alliance partners, who, in a bid to keep him happy, offered him the post of convener of the I.N.D.I.A. Bloc. They realised that if he crossed over to the BJP, opposition unity would fizzle out.

They weren't wrong. Nitish switched. Mamata Banerjee and Bhagwant Mann, already sensing the eventual demise of the coalition, declared that TMC and AAP would fight the elections alone in their home states of West Bengal and Punjab.

Nitish's switch seems to be a death knell for an opposition unity which he himself had started.

The clear winner in all of this has been the BJP.

Bihar has been the only state in the Hindi heartland where the BJP hasn't ever been able to secure a majority on its own. While in Uttar Pradesh, which at many levels seems similar to Bihar, the BJP has been able to secure decisive mandates in successive elections. The Hindu consolidation that seems to work well in Uttar Pradesh seems to bow down to caste considerations in Bihar. The current uncertainty surrounding Nitish's future leaves Bihar at a crucial political crossroads. The upcoming 2024 general elections and 2025 state elections will unveil the political landscape of Bihar, a region that has never succumbed to political complacency.

NOTES

1. Sadhana cut or the fringe haircut was made famous by veteran Bollywood actress Sadhana Shivdasani, in the 1960s and 1970s.
2 Santosh Singh, *Ruled or Misruled: Story and Destiny of Bihar* (Bloomsbury, 2015).
3 Sankarshan Thakur, *The Brothers Bihari* (HarperCollins, 2015).
4. Backward castes are also known as middle castes, intermediate castes or Other Backward Castes (OBCs). They are considered to be historically disadvantaged vis-à-vis the upper castes and hence are accorded certain constitutional provisions. The OBC has another sub-section known as Extremely Backward Castes (EBCs), which is the group of more disadvantaged castes among the OBCs.
5. Uttam Sen Gupta, 'Congress(I) Culture of Imposing a Leader Wouldn't Have Worked: Laloo Prasad Yadav', *India Today*, March 1990, https://www.indiatoday.in/magazine/nation/story/19900331-congressi-culture-of-imposing-a-leader-wouldnt-have-worked-laloo-prasad-yadav-813793-1990-03-31.
6. Sankarshan Thakur, *The Brothers Bihari* (HarperCollins, 2015).
7. Sankarshan Thakur, *The Brothers Bihari*.
8. Santosh Singh, *Ruled or Misruled: Story and Destiny of Bihar* (Bloomsbury, 2015).
9. Indu Bharti, 'Bihar New Government, New Hope', *Economic & Political Weekly*, 25(26), June 1990.
10. Indu Bharti, 'Bihar New Government, New Hope'.

11. Indu Bharti, 'Bihar New Government, New Hope'.
12. Joy Sengupta, 'Lalu's Dream School in Ruins: Once Conceptualised as Charwaha Vidyalaya, the Centre Now Is Just a Grazing Ground for Cattle', *The Telegraph Online*, 26 October 2010, https://www.telegraphindia.com/bihar/lalu-s-dream-school-in-ruins-once-conceptualised-as-charwaha-vidyalaya-the-centre-now-is-just-a-grazing-ground-for-cattle/cid/470509.
13. Singh, S. (2015). *Ruled or Misruled*. Bloomsbury Publishing. Loc 1041 of 5843.
14. Santosh Singh, *Ruled or Misruled: Story and Destiny of Bihar* (Bloomsbury, 2015).
15. A. Ramaiah, 'Identifying Other Backward Classes', *Economic & Political Weekly*, 27(23), 6 June 1992, pp. 1203–07.
16. A. Ramaiah, 'Identifying Other Backward Classes'.
17. Ramachandra Guha, *India after Gandhi: The History of the World's Largest Democracy* (Picador, 2012), p. 607.
18. Indu Bharti, 'The Bihar Formula', *Economic & Political Weekly*, 25(44), 3 November 1990.
19. Ramachandra Guha, *India after Gandhi*, p. 609.
20. Ramachandra Guha, *India after Gandhi*, p. 609.
21. The Indian Express, 'Mandal Commission Report, 25 Years Later', *The Indian Express*, 1 September 2015, https://indianexpress.com/article/india/india-others/sunday-story-mandal-commission-report-25-years-later/.
22. Sanjay Kumar, *Post-Mandal Politics in Bihar: Changing Electoral Patterns* (SAGE Publications, 2018), p. 62.
23. Arun Sinha, *Nitish Kumar and the Rise of Bihar* (Penguin India, 2011).
24. Indu Bharti, 'Bihar: Survival Against Heavy Odd', *Economic & Political Weekly*, 26(3), January 1991, https://www.epw.in/system/files/pdf/1991_26/3/survival_against_heavy_odds.pdf.
25. Inderjit Badhwar and Farzand Ahmed, 'V.P. Singh's Main Survival Tactic Is to Create Caste Division within His Own

and Other Parties', *India Today*, 31 October 1990 (updated 30 September 2013), https://www.indiatoday.in/magazine/special-report/story/19901115-violent-anti-mandal-protests-threaten-to-escalate-into-no-holds-barred-war-in-bihar-813241-1990-11-15.

26. Pankaj Pachauri, 'Decision to Implement Mandal Commission Report Threatens to Pit Indian against Indian', *India Today*, 15 September 1990, https://www.indiatoday.in/magazine/cover-story/story/19900915-decision-to-implement-mandal-commission-report-threatens-to-pit-indian-against-indian-812989-1990-09-15.
27. Saba Naqvi Bhaumik, 'Decision to Implement Mandal Commission Report Stirs Up Protests across India', *India Today*, 30 September 1990, https://www.indiatoday.in/magazine/special-report/story/19900930-decision-to-implement-mandal-commission-report-stirs-up-protests-across-india-813545-1990-09-30.
28. Pankaj Pachauri, 'Decision to Implement Mandal Commission Report Threatens to Pit Indian against Indian', *India Today*, 15 September 1990, https://www.indiatoday.in/magazine/cover-story/story/19900915-decision-to-implement-mandal-commission-report-threatens-to-pit-indian-against-indian-812989-1990-09-15.
29. S.P. Udayakumar, 'Historicizing Myth and Mytholocizing History: The "Ram Temple" Drama', *Social Scientist*, 25(7–8), July–August 1997, https://www.jstor.org/stable/3517601.
30. India Today, '1990: L.K. Advani's Rrath Yatra—Chariots of Fire', *India Today*, 25 December 2009, https://www.indiatoday.in/magazine/cover-story/story/20091228-1990-l.k.-advanis-rath-yatra-chariot-of-fire-741621-2009-12-24.
31. K.N. Panikkar, 'Religious Symbols and Political Mobilization: The Agitation for a Mandir in Ayodhya', *Social Scientist*, 21(7–8), July–August 1993, pp. 73–8, https://www.jstor.org/stable/3520346?seq=1.

32. Ramachandra Guha, *India after Gandhi: The History of the World's Largest Democracy* (Picador, 2012), pp. 582–8.
33. Inderjit Badhwar and Farzand Ahmed, 'V.P. Singh's Main Survival Tactic Is to Create Caste Division within His Own and Other Parties', *India Today*, 31 October 1990 (updated 30 September 2013), https://www.indiatoday.in/magazine/cover-story/story/19901031-v-p-singh-main-survival-tactic-is-to-create-caste-divisions-within-his-own-and-other-parties-813179-1990-10-31.
34. Inderjit Badhwar and Farzand Ahmed, 'V.P. Singh's Main Survival Tactic Is to Create Caste Division within His Own and Other Parties', *India Today*, 31 October 1990 (updated 30 September 2013), https://www.indiatoday.in/magazine/cover-story/story/19901031-v-p-singh-main-survival-tactic-is-to-create-caste-divisions-within-his-own-and-other-parties-813179-1990-10-31.
35. Lalu Prasad Yadav and Nalin Verma, *Gopalganj to Raisina: My Political Journey* (Rupa Publications, 2019), p. 88.
36. Interestingly, R.K. Singh would later be picked by Advani to serve in his Home Ministry in the National Democratic Alliance (NDA) government from 1999 to 2004. Singh would also joined the BJP in 2013 and serve as a minister in successive Modi governments.
37. Lalu Prasad Yadav and Nalin Verma, *Gopalganj to Raisina: My Political Journey* (Rupa Publications, 2019), p. 88.
38. Pankaj Pachauri, '10-month-old BJP-Janata Dal Alliance Had Not Been a Harmonious One', 15 November 1990 (updated 27 September 2013), https://www.indiatoday.in/magazine/cover-story/story/19901115-10-month-old-bjp-janata-dal-alliance-had-not-been-a-harmonious-one-813217-1990-11-15.
39. N.K. Singh, 'BJP Leader Advani Describes Nine-month Rule of V.P. Singh Government as Dismal', 15 October 1990 (updated 30 September 2013), https://www.indiatoday.in/magazine/cover-story/story/19901015-bjp-leader-advani-

describes-nine-month-rule-of-v.p.-singh-government-as-dismal-813114-1990-10-15.

40. Harinder Baweja and Prabhu Chawla, 'Chandra Shekhar Gets Congress(I) Support to Head a Lame Duck Govt with 60 MPs', *India Today*, 30 November 1990 (updated 27 September 2013), https://www.indiatoday.in/magazine/cover-story/story/19901130-chandra-shekhar-gets-congressi-support-to-head-a-lame-duck-govt-with-60-mps-813310-1990-11-29.
41. Indu Bharti, 'Bihar: Survival Against Heavy Odd', *Economic & Political Weekly*, 26(3), January 1991, https://www.epw.in/system/files/pdf/1991_26/3/survival_against_heavy_odds.pdf.
42. Arnab Mukherji and Anjan Mukherji, 'Bihar: What Went Wrong? And What Changed?' Working Paper No. 2012-107, National Institute of Public Finance and Policy, New Delhi, September 2012, https://www.nipfp.org.in/media/medialibrary/2013/04/WP_2012_107.pdf, p. 16.
43. S. Ravi, EACPM-WP20-State-Finances, July 2023, https://eacpm.gov.in/wp-content/uploads/2023/06/EACPM-WP20-State-Finances.pdf, last accessed 24 October 2023.
44. *The Times of India*, 'Bihar's Growth Story: All Sides Have Let the State Down', *The Times of India*, 16 October 2020, https://timesofindia.indiatimes.com/blogs/toi-editorials/bihars-growth-story-all-sides-have-let-the-state-down/.
45. Rajni Kothari, *Caste in Indian Politics* (Orient Longman, 1991), pp. 216–17.
46. Anugrah Narayan Sinha, *Mere Sansmaran (My Reminiscences)* (Kusum Prakashan, 1961), p. 1.
47. Rajni Kothari, *Caste in Indian Politics* (Orient Longman, 1991), p. 230.
48. Rajni Kothari, *Caste in Indian Politics*, p. 240.
49. Universal Adult Franchise was introduced by the Constitution of India in 1950. It essentially means that all Indian citizens, irrespective of caste, creed, gender, race or ethnicity, have the right to cast their vote. When first introduced, the minimum age

to exercise one's right to vote was twenty-one years. However, in 1989, the Sixty-First Amendment Act lowered the voting age from twenty-one to eighteen years.

50. Subrata Mitra and Harihar Bhattacharya, *Politics and Governance in Indian States: Bihar, West Bengal and Tripura* (World Scientific Publishing, 2013), p. 157.
51. Sanjay Kumar, *Post-Mandal Politics in Bihar: Changing Electoral Patterns* (SAGE Publications, 2018), p. 15.
52. Census of India 1931: Bihar and Orissa, Vol. VII, Part I, p. 267.
53. Hiral Dave, 'In Fact: In New Hardik Platform, Echoes of a Famous Earlier Navnirman', *The Indian Express*, 5 October 2015, https://indianexpress.com/article/explained/in-fact-in-new-hardik-platform-echoes-of-a-famous-earlier-navnirman/.
54. Ghanshyam Shah, 'The Upsurge in Gujarat', *Economic & Political Weekly*, 9(32/34), 10 August 1974, pp. 1429–54.
55. Agricultural Production, https://www.indiabudget.gov.in/budget_archive/es1969-70/2, last accessed 24 October 2023.
56. Lalan Tiwari, *Democracy and Dissent* (Mittal Publications, 1987), p. 28.
57. Katherine Frank, *Indira: The Life of Indira Nehru Gandhi* (HarperCollins, 2002).
58. S.S. Ray was a Congress politician from West Bengal. He also wore the hats of a lawyer and diplomat and held several offices. This included being a cabinet minister in Indira Gandhi's government during 1971-72, chief minister of West Bengal during 1972–77 and later the governor of Punjab in the 1980s and the Indian Ambassador to the United States of America in the 1990s. Ray was considered a close confidant of Indira Gandhi and a troubleshooter for the party.
59. D.K. Barooah was a Congress politician from Assam, who served as the Congress president during Emergency from 1975 to 1978. He also served as the Governor of Bihar during 1971–73 and a union cabinet minister for petroleum and natural gas in the Indira Gandhi ministry during 1973-74.

60. P.N. Dhar, *Indira Gandhi, the 'Emergency', and Indian Democracy* (Oxford University Press, 2000).
61. Coomi Kapoor, 'The Emergency: Jayaprakash Narayan Recited Dinkar Evocative Poem, "Singhasan Khaali Karo, Ke Janta Aati Hai", Harvard-returned Subramanian Swamy and Member of Rajya Sabha Presciently Speculated "What if Mrs. Gandhi Introduced Marital Law"', *Satyaagrah*, 1 June 2022, https://satyaagrah.com/reading/coomi-kapoor/1653-gandhi-introduced-martial-law.
62. https://u.demog.berkeley.edu/~jrw/Biblio/Eprints/PRB/files/61.3IndiasPopulationReality_Eng.pdf, Page 14
63. Devang Pathak, & Devang Pathak. (2017, March 14). The untold story of "The Turkman Gate massacre" during India's emergency. Homegrown. https://homegrown.co.in/homegrown-voices/the-untold-story-of-the-turkman-gate-massacre-during-indias-emergency
64. Coomi Kapoor, 'George Fernandes: Rebel without a Pause', *Mint*, 20 June 2015, https://www.livemint.com/Sundayapp/dxWMisYxo5tz1XfTtA0QdI/George-Fernandes-Rebel-without-a-pause.html.
65. Coomi Kapoor, `George Fernandes: Rebel without a Pause', Mint, 20 June 2015, https://www.livemint.com/Sundayapp/dxWMisYxo5tz1XfTtA0QdI/George-Fernandes-Rebel-without-a-pause.html.
66. Sushil Kumar Modi, *Beech Samar Mein* (Prabhat Prakashan, 2015).
67. The Indian National Congress (Organisation), also known as Congress (O), Syndicate, or Old Congress, was a political organisation that emerged in India after Indira Gandhi was expelled from the Congress party for indiscipline. Indira Gandhi set up another party with the name, Indian National Congress (Requisitionists) or Congress (R). The INC (O) was led by K. Kamaraj and later Morarji Desai. The split is also seen as a division of ideology. While Indira wanted to tread the path of

populist policies to regain support for the party, the INC (O) wanted a more right-wing agenda and distrusted Soviet Union's support. In the 1977 general elections, the INC (O) fought under the banner of Janata Party.

68. Sanjay Kumar, *Post-Mandal Politics in Bihar: Changing Electoral Patterns* (SAGE Publications, 2018), p. 29.
69. Sanjay Kumar, *Post-Mandal Politics in Bihar*, p. 36.
70. Farzard Ahmed, 'Bihar CM Bindeshwari Dubey Fights Jagannath Mishra, Mafia Gangs in Battle for Dhanbad', *India Today*, 30 June 1986 (updated 5 February 2014), https://www.indiatoday.in/magazine/indiascope/story/19860630-bihar-cm-bindeshwari-dubey-fights-jagannath-mishra-mafia-gangs-in-battle-for-dhanbad-801002-1986-06-30.
71. Devesh Vijay, *Writing Politics: Left Discourses in Contemporary India* (Popular Prakashan, 2004), p. 126.
72. Praveen Patil, 'Bhagalpur: The Etymology of a Forgotten Riot', *Swarajya*, 11 February 2016, https://swarajyamag.com/politics/bhagalpur-the-etymology-of-a-forgotten-riot.
73. Prabhu Chawla, 'Finance to Defence: PM Rajiv Gandhi Removes V.P. Singh from the Limelight', *India Today*, 15 February 1987 (last accessed 24 October 2023), https://www.indiatoday.in/magazine/cover-story/story/19870215-finance-to-defence-pm-rajiv-gandhi-removes-vp-singh-from-the-limelight-798500-1987-02-14. https://en.wikipedia.org/wiki/Vishwanath_Pratap_Singh - cite_ref-11
74. Barbara Crossette, 'Indian Government Lodges First Charges in Weapons Scandal', *The New York Times*, 23 January 1990, https://www.nytimes.com/1990/01/23/world/indian-government-lodges-first-charges-in-weapons-scandal.html?scp=57&sq=%22v%20p%20singh%22&st=cse.
75. Barbara Crossette, 'Indian Government Lodges First Charges in Weapons Scandal'.
76. Barbara Crossette, 'Indian Government Lodges First Charges in Weapons Scandal'.

77. Steven R. Weisman, 'Turmoil and a Scandal Rake a Toil on Gandhi', *The New York Times*, 24 August 1987, https://www.nytimes.com/1987/08/24/world/turmoil-and-a-scandal-take-a-toll-on-gandhi.html?scp=199&sq=%22v%20p%20singh%22&st=cse.
78. K. Srinivasan, 'Rise and Fall of V.P. Singh: General Election 1989—Emergence of Caste Politics in Large Caste', *PrimePoint*, http://www.primepoint.in/2013/10/rise-and-fall-of-v-p-singh-genral.html.
79. Sankarshan Thakur, *The Brothers Bihari* (HarperCollins, 2015).
80. Jeffrey Witsoe, 'Corruption as Power: Caste and the Political Imagination of the Postcolonial State', *American Ethnologist*, 38(1), 2011, pp. 73–85.
81. HT News Desk, 'Bihar Caste Census Survey: 112 EBC Castes under Reserved Category. See Full List', *Hindustan Times*, 2 October 2023, https://www.hindustantimes.com/cities/patna-news/bihar-caste-census-survey-112-ebc-castes-under-reserved-category-see-full-list-101696243258377.html.
82. Jeffrey Witsoe, 'Social Justice and Stalled Development', Center for the Advanced Study of India, 2006, p. 15.
83. Santosh Mathew and Mick Moore, 'State Incapacity by Design: Understanding the Bihar Story', Working Paper 366, Institute of Development Studies, University of Sussex, 2011.
84. Santosh Mathew and Mick Moore, 'State Incapacity by Design: Understanding the Bihar Story', p. 21.
85. Saxena cited in Jeffrey Witsoe, 'Social Justice and Stalled Development', 2006, p. 26.
86. Jeffery Witsoe, 'Rethinking Postcolonial Democracy: An Examination of the Politics of Lower-caste Empowerment in North India', *American Anthropologist*, 113(4), 2011, pp. 619–31.
87. Lalu Prasad Yadav and Nalin Verma, *Gopalganj to Raisina: My Political Journey* (Rupa Publications, 2019), p. 106.

88. Manish K. Jha and Pushpendra, 'Governing Caste and Managing Conflicts: Bihar, 1990–2011', in Ranabir Samaddar (ed.), *Government of Peace: Social Governance, Security and the Problematic of Peace* (Routledge, 2015), p. 9.
89. Prasanna Kumar Chaudhary and Srikant, *Swarg par Dhawa: Bihar Mein Dalit Andolan (1912–2000)* (Vani Prakshan, 2005), p. 379.
90. Vijay Nambisan, *Bihar Is in the Eye of the Beholder* (Penguin, 2001), p. 114.
91. Ramachandra Guha, *India After Gandhi* (MacMillan, 2007), pp. 582–98.
92. K. Jaishankar and Debarati Haldar, 'Religious Identity of the Perpetrators and Victims of Communal Violence in Post-Independence India', https://web.archive.org/web/20110710195454/ http://www.erces.com/journal/articles/archives/v02/v_02_04.htm.
93. Farzand Ahmed, 'Bihar CM Laloo Prasad Yadav Reveals a Political Sharpness, Acumen No-one Suspected', *India Today*, 15 February 1993 (updated 16 August 2013), https://www.indiatoday.in/magazine/special-report/story/19930215-bihar-cm-laloo-prasad-yadav-reveals-a-political-sharpness-acumen-no-one-suspected-810665-1993-02-15.
94. Times of India, 'I Dream of the Old Glory Days of Bihar', *Times of India*, 1 January 2012, https://timesofindia.indiatimes.com/home/sunday-times/deep-focus/I-dream-of-the-old-glory-days-of-Bihar/articleshow/11323112.cms?.
95. Sankarshan Thakur, *The Brothers Bihari* (HarperCollins, 2015).
96. Shrikant (ed.), *Bihar: Chitthiyon ki Rajneeti* (Vani Prakashan, 2012), pp. 137–52.
97. S.N. Chaudhary, *Power-Dependence Relations: Struggle for Hegemony in Rural Bihar* (Har-Anand, 1999), p. 242.
98. Christophe Jaffrelot, 'The Rise of the Other Backward Classes in the Hindi Belt', *The Journal of Asian Studies*, 59(1), 2000, pp. 86–108.

99. Sankarshan Thakur, *The Brothers Bihari* (HarperCollins, 2015).
100. A disastrous flood, caused by the breakage of the Kosi embankment near the Indo-Nepal border in 2008, forced nearly 30 lakh people out of their homes. The adjacent Seemanchal region has recently been politically in the news as it has become the hotbed of Muslim politics in Bihar and India. The sub-division with a Muslim population of almost 46 per cent saw Asaduddin Owaisi's party, AIMIM, virtually insignificant in Bihar, win five assembly seats in a major electoral shocker in the 2020 assembly elections.
101. Tarique Anwar, 'The Gangs of Purnea: The Journey of Gangsters from Intimidation to Elections', *Firstpost*, 12 October 2015, https://www.firstpost.com/politics/the-gangs-of-purnea-the-journey-of-gangsters-from-intimidation-to-election-2465124.html.
102. Peter Pophan, 'Up in Arms: The Bizarre Case of the British Gun-runner, the Indian Rebels and the Missing Dane', *Independent*, 6 March 2011, https://www.independent.co.uk/news/uk/crime/arms-bizarre-case-british-gun-runner-indian-rebels-and-missing-dane-2230475.html.
103. This would help Pappu Yadav defeat the heavyweight politician Sharad Yadav from Madhepura in 2014, even after a long absence from the active political scene. Ranjan herself would contest and win from Supaul constituency in the same election on a Congress ticket.
104. कुमारी पल्लवी, 'आपराधिक छवि से लव स्टोरी तक, किसी फिल्मी स्टोरी से कम नहीं है बिहार के बाहुबली नेZता पप्पू यादव की कहानी', Lokmat News (Hindi), 31 May 2019 (last accessed 22 October 2023), https://www.lokmatnews.in/crime/pappu-yadav-history-read-inside-story-normal-man-turned-to-politician-love-story-ranjeet-ranjan/.
105. 'Just People'. Retrieved 22 October 2023, from http://blogs.hindustantimes.com/just-people/2009/03/24/just-people/.
106. Giridhar Jha, (2014, April 26). 'Mohammad Shahabuddin, Anand Mohan among Bahubali MPs Who Still Hold Sway in

Bihar', *India Today*, 26 April 2014 (last accessed 22 October 2023), https://www.indiatoday.in/elections/bihar/story/anand-mohan-mohammad-shahabuddin-rjd-pappu-yadav-lalu-prasad-190490-2014-04-26.

107. https://web.archive.org/web/20150610131126/http://archive.tehelka.com/story_main34.asp?filename=Ne201007LAW.asp (last accessed 22 October 2023).
108. Farzand Ahmed, 'Samata Party's Anand Mohan Singh Doesn't Conceal His "Commitment" to the Gun', *India Today*, 15 July 1996 (last accessed 22 October 2023), https://www.indiatoday.in/magazine/cover-story/story/19960715-samata-party-anand-mohan-singh-plans-to-highlight-laloo-jungle-raj-835042-1996-07-15.
109. Anant St Das, 'Law's Arm: 13 Years Long', *Tehelka*, https://web.archive.org/web/20150610131126/http://archive.tehelka.com/story_main34.asp?filename=Ne201007LAW.asp (last accessed 22 October 2023).
110. Anant St Das, 'Law's Arm: 13 Years Long'.
111. Ritu Chaturvedi, *Bihar Through the Ages* (Sarup & Sons, 2007), p. 265.
112. Farzand Ahmed, 'Vaishali Assembly By-election Brings Touch of Glamour', *India Today*, 31 May 1994 (last accessed 22 October 2023), https://www.indiatoday.in/magazine/indiascope/story/19940531-vaishali-assembly-by-election-brings-touch-of-glamour-809179-1994-05-31.
113. Farzand Ahmed, 'Inspiring Success Story of Gopalganj District Magistrate G. Krishnaiah', *India Today*, 31 December 1994 (last accessed 22 October 2023), https://www.indiatoday.in/magazine/states/story/19941231-inspiring-success-story-of-gopalganj-district-magistrate-g.-krishnaiah-810103-1994-12-31.
114. Smita Gupta, 'Pinned Lynch', *Outlook*, 5 February 2022 (last accessed 22 October 2023), https://magazine.outlookindia.com/story/pinned-lynch/235751.

115. No title. Retrieved 22 October 2023, from https://praharlive.com/underworld-story-3/
116. Santosh Singh, 'G Krishnaiah: How Anand Mohan and His Men Killed the Gopalganj DM', *The Indian Express*, 27 April 2023, https://indianexpress.com/article/cities/patna/a-murder-most-foul-a-family-criminal-enterprise-and-the-rifle-bullet-combination-revisiting-the-murder-of-gopalganj-district-magistrate-g-krishnaiah-8578017/.
117. Santosh Singh, 'G Krishnaiah: How Anand Mohan and His Men Killed the Gopalganj DM'.
118. Sanjay Singh, '6 Bihar Politicos Convicted for Killing IAS Officer', *DNA*, 2 October 2007 (last accessed 22 October 2023), https://www.dnaindia.com/india/report-6-bihar-politicos-convicted-for-killing-ias-officer-1124806.
119. Financial Express Online, 'Nitish Kumar Refers to Don-Turned-Politician Anand Mohan as "Old Friend", Says Making Efforts for His Release', *The Financial Express*, 21 January 2020, https://www.financialexpress.com/india-news/nitish-kumar-refers-to-don-turned-politician-anand-mohan-as-old-friend-says-making-efforts-for-his-release/1830138/.
120. तिवारी माधव, 'बिहार का बाहुबली: मुन्ना शुक्ला, जो जेल में करवाता था नाच', Zee News, 21 October 2020 (last accessed 22 October 2023), https://zeenews.india.com/hindi/zee-hindustan/elections/bahubali-of-bihar-who-is-munna-shukla-know-here/770459.
121. कुमार रचित, 'दिलीप सिंह: जिस मंत्री के लिए की बूथ कैप्चरिंग, उसे ही हराकर बने थे विधायक', Aajtak, 26 September 2020 (last accessed 22 October 2023), https://www.aajtak.in/elections/bihar-assembly-elections/story/dilip-singh-brother-of-anant-singh-political-career-bihar-vidhan-sabha-chunav-2020-tstb-1135537-2020-09-26.
122. कुमार रचित, 'सूरजभान सिंह: वो बाहुबली, जिसके अपराध की तपिश से सिहर उठा था बिहार', Aaj Tak, 16 September 2020 (last accessed 22 October 2023), https://www.aajtak.in/elections/bihar-assembly-elections/ story/profile-of-surajbhan-singh-murder-cases-bihar-assembly-elections-2020-1130618-2020-09-16.

123. कुमार रचित, 'दिलीप सिंह: जिस मंत्री के लिए की बूथ कैप्चरिंग, उसे ही हराकर बने थे विधायक', Aaj Tak, 26 September 2020 (last accessed 22 October 2023), https://www.aajtak.in/elections/bihar-assembly-elections/story/dilip-singh-brother-of-anant-singh-political-career-bihar-vidhan-sabha-chunav-2020-tstb-1135537-2020-09-26.
124. AnantKumarSingh(RJD):Constituency-MOKAMA(PATNA), Affidavit Information of Candidate, 22 October 2023, https://myneta.info/Bihar2020/candidate.php?candidate_id=9683.
125. Krishna Kant, 'The Gun That Killed JNU's Chandra Shekhar 20 Years Ago Was "Secular"', *The Wire*, 1 April 2017 (last accessed 22 October 2023), https://thewire.in/politics/gun-killed-jnus-chandra Shekhar-secular.
126. Krishna Kant, 'The Gun That Killed JNU's Chandra Shekhar 20 Years Ago Was "Secular"'.
127. The Hindu, 'Three Sentenced to Life in Chandrasekhar Murder Case', 25 March 2012 (last accessed 22 October 2023), https://web.archive.org/web/20200402111424/https://www.thehindu.com/news/national/other-states/three-sentenced-to-life-in-chandrasekhar-murder-case/article3220897.ece.
128. Outlook, 'From the Barrel of a Gun', *Outlook*, 5 February 2022 (last accessed 22 October 2023), https://www.outlookindia.com/magazine/story/from-the-barrel-of-a-gun/211253.
129. News18, 'SC Fires at MP for His Gun Craze', News18, 8 January 2007, https://www.news18.com/news/india/sc-fires-at-mp-for-his-gun-craze-255657.html.
130. Feb 2005 Election. Retrieved 22 October 2023, from https://web.archive.org/web/20210219224459/https://m.rediff.com/election/2005/feb/03spec.htm
131. HT Correspondent, 'Nitish's Record Gets Beating', *The Hindustan Times*, 23 May 2006, https://www.hindustantimes.com/india/nitish-s-record-gets-beating/story-AdqNMkOeMQZib970lxtiiI.html.
132. J.P. Yadav, 'On Way to Court, Bihar Cops Parade Gangster with Garland of Slippers', *The Indian Express*, 16 August 2006

(last accessed 22 October 2023), http://archive.indianexpress.com/news/on-way-to-court-bihar-cops-parade-gangster-with-garland-of-slippers/10698/.

133. N.K. Singh and Nicholas Stern, *The New Bihar: Rekindling Governance and Development* (HarperCollins, 2013), p. 43.
134. Times of India, 'Bihar's Growth Story: All Sides Have Let the State Down', *The Times of India*, 16 October 2020 (last accessed 25 October 2023), https://timesofindia.indiatimes.com/blogs/toi-editorials/bihars-growth-story-all-sides-have-let-the-state-down/.
135. N.K. Singh and Nicholas Stern, *The New Bihar*, p. 38.
136. N.K. Singh and Nicholas Stern, *The New Bihar*, p. 86.
137. Brahmdev Singh Sharma, *Bihar ki Badhali*.
138. Walter Hauser, 'From Peasant Soldiering to Peasant Activism: Reflections on the Transition of a Martial Tradition in the Flaming Field of Bihar', *Journal of Economic and Social History of the Orient*, 47(3), 2004, p. 426.
139. Subrata K. Mitra, *The Puzzle of India's Governance: Culture, Context and Comparative Theory* (Routledge, 2006), p. 103.
140. Sushil Kumar Modi, '1990s Were the Most Violent Years in Bihar's Electoral History, that Gloomy Picture Has Changed', *The Indian Express*, 8 May 2019, https://indianexpress.com/article/opinion/columns/bihar-elections-violence-politics-lok-sabha-elections-evm-5715811/.
141. Farzand Ahmed, 'CEC Postpones Elections in Bihar for Fourth Time, Laloo Asked to Head Caretaker Government', 31 March 1995 (update 1 July 2013; last accessed 25 October 2023), *India Today*, https://www.indiatoday.in/magazine/cover-story/story/19950331-cec-postpones-elections-in-bihar-for-fourth-time-laloo-asked-to-head-caretaker-government-807124-1995-03-30.
142. Sankarshan Thakur, *The Brothers Bihari* (HarperCollins, 2015).
143. Arvind Sinha and Indu Sinha, 'Bihar: Setback to Political Arrogance', *Economic & Political Weekly*, 31(26), 29 June 1996.

144. Firstpost, 'Lalu Prasad Yadav Convicted in Fodder Scam: How a One Line Fax Unearthed Corruption Scandal, Unseated Ex-Bihar CM', *Firstpost*, 8 January 2018, https://www.firstpost.com/india/lalu-prasad-yadav-convicted-in-fodder-scam-how-a-one-line-fax-unearthed-corruption-scandal-unseated-ex-bihar-cm-4293169.html.
145. Rediff on the Net, 'Anatomy of a Scam', *Rediff*, http://www.rediff.com/news/jun/18bihar2.htm (last accessed 25 October 2023).
146. Firstpost, 'Lalu Prasad Yadav Convicted in Fodder Scam: How a One Line Fax Unearthed Corruption Scandal, Unseated Ex-Bihar CM', *Firstpost*, 8 January 2018, https://www.firstpost.com/india/lalu-prasad-yadav-convicted-in-fodder-scam-how-a-one-line-fax-unearthed-corruption-scandal-unseated-ex-bihar-cm-4293169.html.
147. Rediff on the Net, 'Anatomy of a Scam'.
148. Rediff on the Net, 'Anatomy of a Scam'.
149. Rediff on the Net, 'Gujral Caught in JD-RJD Crossfire', http://www.rediff.com/news/dec/19guj.htm (last accessed 25 October 2023).
150. 'Inder Kumar Gujral', Wikipedia, https://en.wikipedia.org/w/index.php?title=Inder_Kumar_Gujral&oldid=1180822160 (last accessed 19 October 2023).
151. Tara Shankar Sahay, 'Gujral Caught in JD-RJD Crossfire', Rediff, http://m.rediff.com/news/dec/19guj.htm.
152. 'Fodder Scam', Wikipedia, https://en.wikipedia.org/w/index.php?title=Fodder_Scam&oldid=1124099487 (last accessed 27 November 2022).
153. The Indian Express, 'PM Gowda Wept, Fainted When I Confronted Him Over Fodder Case: Lalu', *The Indian Express*, 4 August 2008 (last accessed 22 October 2023), http://archive.indianexpress.com/news/PM-Gowda-wept-fainted-when-I-confronted-him-over-fodder-case-Lalu/344375.

154. Tribune, 'Gujral Told Me to Go Slow on Laloo: Ex-CBI Chief', *Tribune*, 26 April 2005 (last accessed 22 October 2023), from https://www.tribuneindia.com/2005/20050427/nation.htm.
155. TNN, Fodder scam cost me dear: Lalu - Times Of India. (2012, October 22). Web.archive.org. https://web.archive.org/web/20121022035317/http://articles.timesofindia.indiatimes.com/2006-12-20/patna/27814446_1_fodder-scam-lalu-rabri-lalu-prasad>
156. TNN, 'Fodder Scam Cost Me Dear: Lalu', *Times of India*, 20 December 2006 (last accessed 22 October 2023), https://timesofindia.indiatimes.com/city/patna/Fodder-scam-cost-me-dear-Lalu/articleshow/856729.cms?referral=PM.
157. Retrieved 22 October 2023, from https://web.archive.org/web/20171224215207/ http://www.dnaindia.com/web/20171224215207oe_/http://www.dnaindia.com/india/report-lalu-paid-off-a-debt-to-his-wife-handsomely-1093659
158. Swapan Dasgupta and Farzand Ahmed, 'Dragged from the Kitchen to Bihar Assembly, Rabri Devi Learns Politics Fast', *India Today,* 11 August 1997, https://www.indiatoday.in/magazine/cover-story/story/19970811-dragged-from-the-kitchen-to-bihar-assembly-rabri-devi-learns-politics-fast-831912-1997-08-11.
159. Farzand Ahmed, 'Rabri Devi: Bihar's New Queen is an Unknown Quantity', *India Today*, 4 August 1997 (last accessed 22 October 2023), https://www.indiatoday.in/magazine/cover-story/story/19970804-rabri-devi-bihars-new-queen-is-an-unknown-quantity-831840-1997-08-04.
160. Prakash Louis, *People Power: The Naxalite Movement in Central Bihar* (Wordsmiths, 2002), pp 242–6.
161. Krishna Chaitanya, 'Bihar: Bara Massacre and After', *Economic & Political Weekly*, 27(15–16), 11 April 1992.
162. Manish Kumar and Subrat Nanda, 'With Rs 4,000 Crore Assets, This Rajya Sabha Candidate May Be the Richest', NDTV, 14

March 2018 (last accessed 22 October 2023), https://www.ndtv.com/india-news/with-rs-4-000-crore-assets-this-rajya-sabha-candidate-may-be-the-richest-1823548.

163. Krishna Chaitanya, 'Bihar: Bara Massacre and After'.
164. Krishna Chaitanya, 'Bihar: Bara Massacre and After'.
165. André Béteille, *Studies in Agrarian Social Structure* (Oxford University Press, 1974), p. 157), cited in Sumit Saurabh Srivastava, 'State, Senas and Sites of Violence: Bearing on A.R. Desai's Works on the Understanding of Rural Bihar', *The Eastern Anthropologist*, 65(1), 2012, pp. 33–52.
166. Sumit Saurabh Srivastava, 'State, Senas and Sites of Violence'.
167. F.T. Jannuzi, *Agrarian Crisis in India: The Case of Bihar* (Orient Longman, 1974), p. 100, cited in Sumit Saurabh Srivastava, 'State, Senas and Sites of Violence'.
168. See Bharti (1988: 2519). Also see Oommen (1984: xviii). For a detailed account of the reasons of its failure in Bihar, see F.T. Jannuzi, *Agrarian Crisis in India*, pp. 97–104.
169. Francine R. Frankel, 'Caste, Land and Dominance in Bihar: Breakdown of the Brahmanical Social Order', in Francine R. Frankel and M.S.A. Rao (eds.), *Dominance and State Power in Modern India: Decline of a Social Order* (Oxford University Press, 1989), pp. 46–132, cited in Sumit Saurabh Srivastava, 'State, Senas and Sites of Violence'.
170. Bela Bhatia, 'The Naxalite Movement in Central Bihar', *Economic & Political Weekly*, 40(15), 9–15 April 2005, p. 1.
171. During the fourth state assembly elections that year, Jagdish Mahato, an educated youth from the Koeri caste, was severely beaten by the henchmen of the landlords for attempting to prevent them from rigging votes. Meanwhile, news of the Naxalbari uprising, which took place the same year, had spread far and wide. Naxalite slogans calling for armed revolution had also started appearing on the walls of some towns of Bhojpur. The Naxalite message caught the imagination of Jagdish Mahato,

who started looking for like-minded friends. In this endeavour, he was joined by Rameshwar Ahir, a Yadav dacoit turned rebel who had returned to Ekwari after serving a twelve-year sentence for murdering a constable. The *izzat ki ladai* had begun.

At this stage, Jagdish Mahato is reported to have travelled to West Bengal in order to forge links with Naxalite leaders there. The Naxalites who subsequently came to Bhojpur later developed into the present CPI(ML)(Liberation). Initially, the focus was on annihilation of oppressive landlords and their henchmen, and a fight against the state. The struggle against the landlords was not only about land but also against their samanti (feudal) attitudes and behaviour. Jagdish Mahato is said to have described this hangover from the past in the following words: 'The landlord's moustache has got burnt but the twirl still remains.' Jagdish Mahato and Rameshwar Ahir were killed in 1972 and 1975, respectively. Sometimes fondly called Marx and Engels, these two founders of the Naxalite movement in Bhojpur had no prior Communist background. See Bela Bhatia, 'The Naxalite Movement in Central Bihar'.

172. Gaurang Sahay, '"Freedom from Fear" vs. "Freedom from Want": Understanding Human Security in the Context of Rural Violence in Bihar', preliminary draft, https://www.academia.edu/8464367/Freedom_from_Fear_vs_Freedom_from_Want_Understanding_Human_Security_in_the_context_of_rural_violence_in_Bihar (last accessed 24 January 2021).
173. Prakash Louis, *People Power*.
174. Details of Indira Gandhi's trip are available at https://www.theweek.in/theweek/cover/2021/08/12/life-hasnt-changed-much-for-residents-of-village-where-indira-arrived-on-elephant.html.
175. Prakash Louis, *People Power*, pp. 242–46.
176. Ram Shakal Singh and Champa Singh, *Indian Communism: Its Role towards Indian Polity*, First edition, (Mittal Publications, 1991), p. 128.

177. Jose Nedumpara, *Political Economy and Class Contradictions* (Bihar: Anmol Publications, 2004).
178. People's Union for Democratic Rights, 1997, p. 12.
179. ADRI report cited in Nicolas Jaoul, 'Naxalism in Bihar: From Bullet to Ballot', in Laurent Gayer and Christophe Jaffrelot (eds), *Armed Militias of South Asia: Fundamentalists, Maoists and Separatists* (Columbia University Press, 2009), p. 34..
180. Vijay Nambisan, *Bihar Is in the Eye of the Beholder* (Penguin Books India, 2003), p. 81.
181. Shashi Bhushan Kumar and Umesh Kumar, *Naxalism and Caste Militancy in Bihar* (Saad Publications, 2017), p. 80.
182. Jose J. Nedumpara, *Political Economy and Class Contradictions* (Anmol Publishers, 2004).
183. Shashi Bhushan Kumar and Umesh Kumar, *Naxalism and Caste Militancy in Bihar*, p. 76.
184. Srivastava, S. S. (2012). 2012. "State, senas and sites of violence: Bearing of A.R. Desai's works on the understanding of Rural Bihar", The Eastern Anthropologist, 65(1): 33-52. www.academia.edu. https://www.academia.edu/7413258/2012_State_senas_and_sites_of_violence_Bearing_of_A_R_Desai_s_works_on_the_understanding_of_Rural_Bihar_The_Eastern_Anthropologist_65_1_33_52
185. Sanjay K. Jha and Farzand Ahmed, 'Maoist Communist Centre Avenges Death Sentence of Eight Activists by Killing Five Policemen', *India Today*, 15 February 1996, https://www.indiatoday.in/magazine/indiascope/story/19960215-maoist-communist-centre-avenges-death-sentence-of-eight-activists-by-killing-five-policemen-834334-1996-02-15.
186. Prakash Louis, *People Power*.
187. People's Union for Democratic Rights. (1997). Agrarian Conflict in Bihar and the Ranbir Sena. 33, p. 24.
188. People's Union for Democratic Rights. (1997). Agrarian Conflict in Bihar and the Ranbir Sena. 33, p. 24.

189. Shashi Bhushan Kumar and Umesh Kumar, *Naxalism and Caste Militancy in Bihar*, p. 98.
190. Shashi Bhushan Kumar and Umesh Kumar, *Naxalism and Caste Militancy in Bihar*, p. 98.
191. Shoumojit Banerjee, 'All Accused in 1996 Bihar Dalit Carnage Acquitted', *The Hindu*, 17 April 2012 (last accessed 6 October 2020), https://web.archive.org/web/20191222060533/https://www.thehindu.com/news/national/all-accused-in-1996-bihar-dalit-carnage-acquitted/article3321368.ece.
192. Shoumojit Banerjee, 'All Accused in 1996 Bihar Dalit Carnage Acquitted'.
193. Ashwani Kumar, *Community Warriors: State, Peasants and Caste Armies in Bihar* (Anthem Press, 2007), p. 133.
194. Prakash Louis, *People Power*.
195. Sanjay Kumar Jha and Bharat Desai, 'Land Disputes in Bihar Drive Landlords, Peasants into an Endless Spiral of Violence', *India Today*, 15 December 1997 (last accessed 7 October 2020), https://www.indiatoday.in/magazine/states/story/19971215-land-disputes-in-bihar-drive-landlords-peasants-into-an-endless-spiral-of-violence-831078-1997-12-15.
196. Shashi Bhushan Kumar and Umesh Kumar, *Naxalism and Caste Militancy in Bihar*, p. 102.
197. Alok Pandey, 'In 1999 Massacre of Dalits in Bihar, All Acquitted, Questions Raised', NDTV, 16 January 2015 (last accessed 7 October 2020), https://www.ndtv.com/india-news/in-1999-massacre-of-dalits-in-bihar-all-acquitted-questions-raised-727990.
198. Bihar Times, 'The Senari Carnage: The Last Mass Killing of Bhumihars in Bihar', *Bihar Times*, 16 November 2016 (last accessed 7 October 2020), http://www.bihartimes.in/Newsbihar/2016/Nov/newsbihar16Nov10.html.
199. The Guardian, 'War of Vengeance Leaves Ghost Villages in Its Wake', *The Guardian*, 29 March 1999, https://www.theguardian.com/world/1999/mar/29/1.

200. The Tribune, 'Ranvir Sena Massacres 35 in Bihar', *The Tribune*, 18 June 2000 (last accessed 7 October 2020), https://www.tribuneindia.com/2000/20000618/main1.htm.
201. V. Krishna Ananth, 'Legitimising Gun Culture in Bihar', *The Hindu*, 23 June 2000 (last accessed 6 October 2020), https://www.thehindu.com/todays-paper/tp-miscellaneous/tp-others/legitimising-gun-culture-in-bihar/article28028663.ece.
202. Nira Yuval-Davis, Kalpana Kannabiran and Ulrike Vieten (eds), *The Situated Politics of Belonging* (SAGE Publications, 2006), p. 135.
203. Smita Narula, B*roken People: Caste Violence Against India's 'Untouchables',* Human Rights Watch, 1999 (last accessed 8 October 2020), https://web.archive.org/web/20190514140618/https:// www.hrw.org/report/1999/03/01/broken-people/caste-violence-against-indias-untouchables.
204. Smita Narula, *Broken People*.
205. Government of India, XI Lok Sabha Debates, Session II, Budget, 1996.
206. Smita Narula, *Broken People*.
207. Smita Narula, *Broken People*.
208. Smita Narula, *Broken People*.
209. Farzand Ahmed, 'Poorly Armed, Cash-strapped Bihar Police Fails to Control Lawlessness, Faces Criticism', India Today, 15 May 1997, https://www.indiatoday.in/magazine/states/story/19970515-poorly-armed-cash-strapped-bihar-police-fails-to-control-lawlessness-faces-criticism-831365-1997-05-15.
210. Farzand Ahmed, 'Poorly Armed, Cash-strapped Bihar Police Fails to Control Lawlessness, Faces Criticism'.
211. Farzand Ahmed and Ajay Kumar, 'Root Cause of Almost All Rural Conflicts in Bihar Attributed to Land', *India Today*, 31 December 1986 (last accessed 6 October 2020), https://www.indiatoday.in/magazine/special-report/story/19861231-root-cause-of-almost-all-rural-conflicts-in-bihar-attributed-to-land-801564-1986-12-31.

212. People's Union for Democratic Rights (PUDR), *Bitter Harvest: The Roots of Massacres in Central Bihar*, Secretary, PUDR, 1992, p. 15.
213. Ashwani Kumar, *Community Warriors*, p. 159.
214. Ashwani Kumar, *Community Warriors*, p. 159.
215. Pranava K. Chaudhary and Rajiv Nayan Agrawal, 'Brahmeshwar Singh's Murder: Bihar Braces for Retaliatory Killings', *The Times of India*, 2 June 2012.
216. Shashi Bhushan Kumar and Umesh Kumar, *Naxalism and Caste Militancy in Bihar*, p. 124.
217. The Times of India, 'Bihar's "First" Economic Survey Report Tabled', *The Times of India*, 7 March 2007, https://timesofindia.indiatimes.com/city/patna/Bihars-first-Economic-Survey-Report-tabled/articleshow/1729260.cms.
218. http://re.indiaenvironmentportal.org.in/files/file/Wp366.pdf (last accessed 22 October 2023).
219. http://re.indiaenvironmentportal.org.in/files/file/Wp366.pdf (last accessed 22 October 2023).
220. Nandini Vaish, 'Lalu Prasad Yadav Brings Profits for Indian Railways', *India Today*, 12 March 2007, https://www.indiatoday.in/magazine/cover-story/story/20070312-lalu-yadavs-budget-of-railway-748941-2007-03-11.
221. Mahendra Kumar Singh, 'Lalu's Railways Turnaround Tale Was a Cosmetic Exercise', *The Times of India*, 6 August 2011, https://web.archive.org/web/20131005011819/http://articles.timesofindia.indiatimes.com/2011-08-06/india/29858215_1_zonal-railways-traffic-earnings-lalu.
222. http://re.indiaenvironmentportal.org.in/files/file/Wp366.pdf (last accessed 22 October 2023).
223. Santosh Mathew and Mick Moore, 'State Incapacity by Design: Understanding the Bihar Story', Working Paper 366, Institute of Development Studies, University of Sussex, 2011.
224. Naresh Saxena and Nandini Nayak, 'Implementation in Bihar and Jharkhand', ICDS, https://www.academia.

edu/11325943/Nayak_N._and_Saxena_N._C._2006_._ICDS_Implementation_in_Bihar_and_Jharkhand_Economic_and_Political_Weekly.

225. http://re.indiaenvironmentportal.org.in/files/file/Wp366.pdf (last accessed 22 October 2023).
226. http://re.indiaenvironmentportal.org.in/files/file/Wp366.pdf (last accessed 22 October 2023).
227. Santosh Mathew and Mick Moore, 'State Incapacity by Design: Understanding the Bihar Story', Working Paper 366, Institute of Development Studies, University of Sussex, 2011.
228. Santosh Mathew and Mick Moore, 'State Incapacity by Design'.
229. Santosh Mathew and Mick Moore, 'State Incapacity by Design'.
230. Santosh Mathew and Mick Moore, 'State Incapacity by Design'.
231. Santosh Mathew and Mick Moore, 'State Incapacity by Design'.
232. India Today, 'Now, Laloo Yadav Secures MBBS Seat for His Second Daughter through Backdoor', *India Today*, 27 April 1998, https://web.archive.org/web/20180703221400/https://www.indiatoday.in/magazine/indiascope/story/19980427-now-laloo-yadav-secures-mbbs-seat-for-his-second-daughter-through-backdoor-826271-1998-04-27.
233. Santosh Mathew and Mick Moore, 'State Incapacity by Design'.
234. http://finance.bih.nic.in/Reports/ESR-2006-07-EN.pdf, p. VII.
235. Arvind N. Das, 'India in the Image of Bihar', *Economic & Political Weekly*, 33(49), 5 December 1998.
236. Asian Development Research Institute (ADRI), *Current Agrarian Situation in Bihar* (ADRI, 2008).
237. BBC News, 'Threats Hit India Rail Job Drive', BBC News, 21 November 2003, https://web.archive.org/web/20040515201355/http://news.bbc.co.uk/1/hi/world/south_asia/3227782.stm.
238. Patna Daily, '40 Bihari Workers Killed by ULFA Activists in Assam', *Patna Daily*, 6 January 2007, https://web.archive.

org/web/20090211042318/http://www.patnadaily.com/news2007/jan/010507/biharis_killed_in_assam.html.

239. Asian Development Research Institute, *Current Agrarian Situation in Bihar*.
240. Anup K. Karan, 'Changing Pattern of Migration from Rural Bihar', http://www.bihartimes.in/articles/general/anup_karan.html.
241. BIMARU is an acronym coined by demographer Ashish Bose in the mid-1980s and has been used to refer to Bihar, Madhya Pradesh, Rajasthan and Uttar Pradesh, to imply they have lagged in terms of economic growth, healthcare and education.
242. Arvind N. Das, 'India in the Image of Bihar'.
243. Girish Kumar, 'Bihar Panchayat Elections: Overcoming State's Resistance', *Economic & Political Weekly*, 36(20), 19 May 2001.
244. Shaibal Gupta, 'Subaltern Resurgence: A Reconnaissance of Panchayat Election in Bihar', Crisis States Programme Development Research Centre, http://eprints.lse.ac.uk/28305/1/WP8_SG.pdf (last accessed 24 October 2020).
245. Farzand Ahmed, 'Laloo Prasad Yadav's Army of Riders Ensures His Daughter's Wedding Is Not Forgotten Easily', *India Today*, 10 June 2002, https://www.indiatoday.in/magazine/states/story/20020610-laloo-prasad-yadav-army-of-raiders-ensures-his-daughter-wedding-is-not-forgotten-easily-795122-2002-06-10/.
246. Sharma, *Bihar ki Badhali*, p. 108.
247. Farzand Ahmed, 'Train Robberies: Violent Crimes, Looting of Passengers on Bihar Routes Cause Jitters', *India Today*, 31 March 1997, https://www.indiatoday.in/magazine/crime/story/19970331-train-robberies-violent-crimes-looting-of-passengers-on-bihar-routes-cause-jitters-830221-1997-03-31.
248. Farzand Ahmed, 'Bihar Schoolchild Kidnapping Snowballs into Major Poll Issue, Court Takes Police to Task', *India Today*, 17 October 2005, https://www.indiatoday.in/magazine/states/story/20051017-bihar-schoolchild-kidnapping-

snowballs-into-major-poll-issue-court-takes-police-to-task-786767-2005-10-17.

249. Navin Kumar, 'News of a Kidnapping', *Outlook India*, updated 6 February 2022, https://www.outlookindia.com/magazine/story/news-of-a-kidnapping/205548.
250. TNN, 'Exide Chief's Abductor Held in Bihar', *The Times of India*, 23 December 2002, https://timesofindia.indiatimes.com/city/kolkata/exide-chiefs-abductor-held-in-bihar/articleshow/32104871.cms.
251. Abhay Mohan Jha, 'Kidnapping: It's Now a Rich Industry in India', *The Times of India*, 27 January 2005, https://timesofindia.indiatimes.com/india/Kidnapping-Its-now-a-rich-industry-in-India/articleshow/1001952.cms.
252. Outlook, 'Flourishing Lawlessness', *Outlook*, 8 November 1995 (updated 6 February 2022), https://magazine.outlookindia.com/story/flourishing-lawlessness/200139.
253. Satyendra Dubey's Wikipedia profile, https://en.wikipedia.org/wiki/Satyendra_Dubey.
254. Anuranjan Jha, *Gandhi Maidan: Bluff of Social Justice* (Hind Yugm, 2020), p. 74.
255. ET Bureau, 'Stories of Bihar: The Don Finally Finds His Domain', *The Economic Times*, 22 October 2022, https://economictimes.indiatimes.com/news/politics-and-nation/stories-of-bihar-the-don-finally-finds-his-domain/articleshow/49487949.cms?from=mdr.
256. Farzana Ahmed and Bhavdeep Kang, 'Bihar Elections: Power Struggle in Patna as Paswan Refuses to Join Hands with Lalu Yadav', *India Today*, 14 March 2005 (updated 23 March 2012), https://www.indiatoday.in/magazine/states/story/20050314-bihar-elections-ram-vilas-paswan-refuses-to-join-hands-with-lalu-yadav-788111-2005-03-14.
257. "Cracks Appear in Paswan's LJP." The Times of India, 21 May 2005, timesofindia.indiatimes.com/cracks-appear-in-paswans-ljp/articleshow/1117522.cms. Accessed 22 Dec. 2023.

258. Priya Sahgal, 'Bihar Assembly Dissolution: Governor Buta Singh Carried Forward an Old Tradition?' *India Today*, 6 June 2005 (updated 5 April 2012), https://www.indiatoday.in/magazine/cover-story/story/20050606-bihar-assembly-dissolution-governor-buta-singh-carried-forward-an-old-tradition-788658-2005-06-06.
259. Buta Singh was the communications minister in the Vajpayee government in 1998, after having left the Congress. However, within a month he was chargesheeted in the JMM bribery case and was asked to resign by Vajpayee. Singh strongly resisted and had to be sacked by Vajpayee.
260. Priya Sahgal, 'Bihar Assembly Dissolution: SC Indicts Buta Singh, Setback for Congress, UPA', *India Today*, 6 February 2007 (last accessed 25 October 2023), https://www.indiatoday.in/magazine/nation/story/20060206-bihar-assembly-dissolution-sc-indicts-buta-singh-setback-for-congress-upa-783683-2006-02-05.
261. Forbes, 'A Person of the Year: Nitish Kumar', *Forbes*, 3 January 2011, https://www.forbes.com/2011/01/03/forbes-india-person-of-the-year-nitish-kumar.html#49c229bb997c.
262. TNN, 'Nod to Quota for EBCs in Local Bodies', *The Times of India*, 13 January 2006, https://timesofindia.indiatimes.com/city/patna/nod-to-quota-for-ebcs-in-local-bodies/articleshow/1370289.cms.
263. Rajesh Chakrabarti, *Bihar Breakthrough: The Turnaround of a Beleaguered State* (Rupa Publications, 2013), p. 59.
264. Rajesh Chakrabarti, *Bihar Breakthrough: The Turnaround of a Beleaguered State* (Rupa Publications, 2013), p. 60.
265. Rajesh Chakrabarti, *Bihar Breakthrough*, p. 86.
266. Sinha, A. (2020). *Battle for Bihar*. Penguin Enterprise. p 302.
267. Rajesh Chakrabarti, *Bihar Breakthrough*, p. 99.
268. Chakrabarti, R. (2013). Bihar Breakthrough. Rupa Publications India.

269. Asian Development Research Institute (ADRI), *Economic Survey 2006-07*, Finance Secretary, Government of Bihar, 2007.
270. ADRI, *Economic Survey 2006-07*, p. 122.
271. Chakrabarti, R. (2013). Bihar Breakthrough. Rupa Publications India.
272. ADRI, *Economic Survey 2006-07*.
273. Mammen Matthew, 'Troubled Land of Bihar', *Hindustan Times*, 10 May 2010, https://www.hindustantimes.com/patna/troubled-land-of-bihar/story-2SNWzqkAP5yA1G5MwwqzMJ.html.
274. Sankarshan Thakur, *The Brothers Bihari* (HarperCollins, 2015).
275. Sankarshan Thakur, *The Brothers Bihari* (HarperCollins, 2015).
276. Sankarshan Thakur, *The Brothers Bihari* (HarperCollins, 2015).
277. Times of India, 'I Dream of the Old Glory Days of Bihar', *The Times of India*, 1 January 2012, https://timesofindia.indiatimes.com/home/sunday-times/deep-focus/i-dream-of-the-old-glory-days-of-bihar/articleshow/11323112.cms.
278. Prabhash K. Dutta, 'Why Nitish Kumar Junked Lalu Prasad Yadav to Join Hands with Narendra Modi', *India Today*, 27 July 2017 (last accessed 25 October 2023), https://www.indiatoday.in/india/story/lalu-prasad-yadav-nitish-kumar-narendra-modi-nda-1026557-2017-07-27.
279. ABP News Bureau, 'Nitish CM because of Circumstances, My Leader Is Lalu: Shahabuddin', ABP Live, 11 September 2016, https://news.abplive.com/news/india/nitish-cm-because-of-circumstances-my-leader-is-lalu-shahabuddin-413713.
280. Indian Express, 'Nitish Kumar Takes Oath as Bihar Chief Minister', *Indian Express*, 27 July 2017, https://indianexpress.com/article/india/nitish-kumar-resigns-as-bihar-chief-minister-tejashwi-yadav-lalu-yadav-grand-alliance-jdu-meeting-governor-4768045/.
281. https://twitter.com/laluprasadrjd/status/893114246019465216?ref_src=twsrc%5Etfw%7Ctwcamp%5Etweetembed%

7Ctwterm%5E893114246019465216%7Ctwgr%5Ed40cda14bf02382420adfef5dad434df2d3797ce%7Ctwcon%5Es1_&ref_url=https%3A%2F%2Fpublish.

282. Soutik Biswas, 'The Horror Story Inside an Indian Children's Home', BBC News, 10 August 2018, https://www.bbc.com/news/world-asia-india-45124802.

ACKNOWLEDGEMENTS

A book is never an author's work alone but the outcome of the support of several people who contribute to its creation and success. I extend my heartfelt gratitude to those who played pivotal roles in bringing this book to fruition.

Firstly, I express my sincere thanks to Minakshi Thakur and Karthika V.K. at Westland Books, and Dipti Patel, my literary agent, for their unwavering support and dedication in bringing the essence of this book to life.

In 2021, during the challenging times of the Covid-19 pandemic, I found myself gasping for breath in the ICU at Medanta, Ranchi, for an agonising fifty-five days. I am grateful to have lived to see this book fructify. My gratitude extends to the medical team led by Dr Tapas Sahoo and all those who played a crucial role in helping me overcome the seemingly insurmountable odds. It was the same time that Covid took away Nilankan, one of my closest friends for two decades. I miss him dearly.

This book wouldn't have been possible without a lot of people who were directly or indirectly involved with it. I am grateful to my family members, including my wife, Aishwarya Sharan. The joyful arrival of our newborn daughter in our lives has added greatly to the happiness at the completion of this book. I am grateful to my sister Sulochana Sharma, my brother-in-law Sandeep Kumar and my lovely nephew Agastya, for being a constant pillar of strength and support. I am grateful to my extended family, especially the younger ones—Nitin Sharma, Minakshi, Barun Shahi, Rishav, Srishty, Gopal, Satyam, Prince, Sakshi, Saksham and Pihu—for bringing cheer to our lives.

I have been blessed with some very close friends throughout my life. Some of them blur the boundaries between family and friendship. I am grateful to such childhood friends who have stayed with me since my formative years in Rajrappa, a small CCL township in Ramgarh, Jharkhand.

The institutions and organisations I have been a part of have significantly shaped my journey, allowing me to pursue my passions, including writing this book. I extend my gratitude to my alma maters DPS Bokaro, BIT Mesra and XLRI Jamshedpur. I am thankful to my colleagues and friends from my stint at Asian Paints.

I am thankful to Dr Raman Singh, former chief minister of Chhattisgarh, Shri Rajat Kumar, IAS, Shri Arun Bisen and extremely supportive friends at the Chief Minister's fellowship in Chhattisgarh, where I first learnt the nuances of bureaucracy and politics.

I express my gratitude to Shri Dharampal Singh, my political mentor, for guiding me through the uncertainties of venturing into politics. I have been blessed to have continued guidance from the current political leadership of Shri Babulal Marandi and Shri Karmveer Singh.

Special thanks to my start-up co-founder, Santosh Kumar, for consistently serving as a sounding board for both personal and professional matters. My appreciation extends to all the members of our start-up, Biofie, for their collective efforts in helping build such a remarkable organisation.

Kartavyapath, a social initiative where we teach mathematics to underprivileged kids, holds a special place in my heart. I express my gratitude to the friends and volunteers who have been part of this meaningful endeavour.

My sincere thanks go out to those who read and provided suggestions for this project, including Tuhin Sinha, Vandana Gahlawat, Nikhil Mishra, Sebati Iyengar and Abhineet Mishra. I am equally thankful to those who supported me in navigating life's challenges while I was engrossed in writing, editing and getting the book published. Among them are Shri O.P. Choudhary, Shri Vikash Preetam, Ravi Ranjan and my childhood friend Santosh Kumar. From my BIT days, Kundan Kumar, Jeevitesh Singh, Sumit Jha, Mrigendra Kumar, Setu Saurabh, Biswapriya Mazumder, Rajat Saxena and Prakash Kumar. Also, my friends from XLRI, Krishna Chaitanya, Aaditya Udupa, Smriti Khanna and Ram Krishna Shukla.

Lastly, this book owes much to the extensive study and referencing of earlier works on Bihar. I specifically mention the influence of senior journalists Sankarshan Thakur and Santosh Singh, whose books served as invaluable sources of information and inspiration.